Rachel Miller writes as a conservative
under its authority. She calls us to ex
not to remove ourselves from its authority in our lives, and gives us diagnostic tools from the Word to renovate our understanding of men and women in the church, in the home, and in society at large.

Rachel teaches the history of views on sex and gender in secular cultures and then shows us the ways that some evangelical teaching on the sexes is built more on secular philosophy than on biblical truth. In the end, while historical context sheds great light on the Scriptures, Rachel wins us with Scripture itself. She offers us a well-researched survey of Scripture on biological sex and gender that will inspire and aid readers to gain a biblical vision of men and women working in unity and interdependence in God's kingdom.

—**Wendy Alsup**, Author, *Is the Bible Good for Women? Seeking Clarity
and Confidence Through a Jesus-Centered Understanding of Scripture*

Most of the Christians I know want to be the men and women of God. But what does that mean, exactly? Who's in charge? Who gets the final say? What does it mean to be *masculine* or *feminine?* Enter Rachel G. Miller and her new book, *Beyond Authority and Submission.* In these pages, you'll find a compelling vision for how men and women can work together unfettered by social and historical expectations. Tracing the broader themes of Scripture, with careful attention to theology and the text, Miller calls men and women alike to live in the fullness of all that God has made us to be.

—**Hannah Anderson**, Author, *Made for More: An Invitation to Live in
God's Image*

Rachel Miller has written an excellent book on men and women that honors the Bible's position while avoiding extremes. Highly recommended!

—**Todd S. Bordow**, Pastor, Cornerstone Orthodox Presbyterian
Church, Houston; Author, *What Did Jesus Really Say about Divorce?*

Rachel Miller has done an excellent job of bringing clarity and discernment to a discussion that is often emotionally charged and contentious. Biblically reasoned, confessionally informed, and drawing from the resources of church history, Miller's work cuts through rhetoric and assumptions to show us that sometimes ideas that are labeled "biblical" can in fact be loaded with cultural notions. While much of the contemporary discussion about "gender roles" focuses primarily on authority and submission—who is allowed to do what?—Miller shows that there is a need for us to go beyond this narrow focus and instead promote unity, interdependence, and service. She invites readers not to ignore or dismiss Scripture but to go deeper in their understanding of its meaning and implications. In *Beyond Authority and Submission,* many Apolloses have the opportunity to listen and learn from a wise Priscilla.

—**Jacob Denhollander**, PhD Student, The Southern Baptist
    Theological Seminary

Rachel challenges popular yet extrabiblical and unbiblical beliefs about women and men and what roles are considered appropriate for them in marriage, the church, and society. However, she doesn't simply offer a critique. She also sets forth a compelling, gospel-centered vision of biblical manhood and womanhood that centers on unity, interdependence, and service. The gospel is to be paramount in all things, which includes issues of manhood and womanhood. Rachel makes this crystal clear. Men and women are co-image-bearers, co-heirs in Christ, and co-laborers for the gospel. We are different from each other, and yet we need each other. I heartily recommend this book!

—**John Fonville**, Pastor (Anglican Church in North America),
    Paramount Church, Jacksonville, Florida

Beyond Authority and Submission is a fascinating and eye-opening look at womanhood and the extent to which historical tradition, rather than the Bible, has defined what Christians believe about womanhood. This book will encourage readers to be Bereans—to turn to Scripture as their sole authority. May Rachel's book serve to bring more unity in marriages and the church as we seek to co-labor with one another for the good of the gospel and the building up of Christ's church.

—**Christina Fox**, Speaker; Author, *Sufficient Hope: Gospel Meditations and Prayers for Moms*; Content Editor, *enCourage*

Rachel Miller writes with her characteristic verve and wisdom as she addresses the vexed subject of women and men—a subject on which there is often more heat than light. If we are to follow the Bible when it says we should be slow to speak and quick to listen, then this is one such occasion on which we would be wise to listen well. She has made a valuable contribution to the discussion of how we negotiate between the extremes of patriarchy and feminism in the church today. Her arguments deserve to be taken seriously and weighed well as we seek to be faithful to Scripture in our generation.

—**Liam Goligher**, Senior Minister, Tenth Presbyterian Church, Philadelphia

When James reminds us of God's requirement to live unstained by the world, he is giving us a near impossible task. The Christian religion carries thousands of years of cultural baggage that has accumulated as an inevitable consequence of our human frailty. In taking on our theology of men and women, Rachel Miller leads us back to our roots—to our salvation and freedom in Jesus Christ.

—**Valerie Hobbs**, Senior Lecturer in Applied Linguistics, University of Sheffield, Sheffield, UK

In this extremely practical and helpful book, Rachel Green Miller peels back layer after layer of what she describes as "unbiblical and extrabiblical beliefs" that have created a competitive and antagonistic environment between men and women in the church. She then casts a vision for what life could be when men and women work together toward unity, interdependence, and service, all while inhabiting the God-ordained roles that Scripture lays out for the family of God. I, too, long for a church that is full of grace, forgiveness, and mercy, and this book has given me many things to think about as I carry out my role as director of spiritual formation. I highly recommend this book to anyone who desires to see our churches filled with co-laborers for the kingdom of God.

—**Abby Ross Hutto**, Author, *God for Us: Discovering the Heart of the Father through the Life of the Son*

The debate that rages about men and women is full of history, rhetoric, and labels. Rachel Miller takes us on a remarkable journey that navigates us away from the hyperbole and man-made traditions and sets our feet solidly on the Scriptures. This book desperately needed to be written, and Rachel has done so brilliantly—with insight, clarity, sobriety, and love.

—**Sam Powell**, Pastor, First Reformed Church, Yuba City, California

Rachel Miller sets out to peel back some of the layers of extrabiblical and cultural assumptions about the nature of men and women in the home, church, and society. She succeeds at engaging her sources critically, with an incisive yet reader-friendly style. This book will help to tease out some of your own lingering doubts about the usefulness of rigid gender stereotypes. Expect to learn from history, to have your assumptions questioned, and to become better equipped to engage more thoughtfully with this important topic, regardless of whether you call yourself egalitarian, complementarian, or anything else!

—**Eowyn Stoddard**, Missionary, Mission to the World

There is a very real danger, in our current cultural moment, that the polarization that characterizes the political landscape might well come to exert an unfortunate influence on both the rhetoric and the content of discussions among Christians on a number of controversial topics. The temptation to respond to one extreme error by adopting its mirror image is strong but rarely—if ever—correct. And there are few topics in the public square that are more divisive than the relationship between the sexes. It is therefore a pleasure to commend this book by Rachel Miller, which eschews the cheap extremism and bombastic rhetoric that characterize conservative Christian responses to feminism and instead plots not a middle way but a biblical way through the subjects of authority, submission, masculinity, and the like. She is not interested in making the Bible fit 1950s ideals of what men and women should be; rather, she wants to help the reader to think about what the Bible actually means in the present. This is a refreshingly sane read.

—**Carl Trueman**, Professor of Biblical and Religious Studies, Grove City College, Grove City, Pennsylvania

BEYOND AUTHORITY AND SUBMISSION

WOMEN AND MEN IN MARRIAGE, CHURCH, AND SOCIETY

RACHEL GREEN MILLER

P&R PUBLISHING
P.O. BOX 817 • PHILLIPSBURG • NEW JERSEY 08865-0817

Unless otherwise noted, Scripture quotations are from the New American Standard Bible® (NASB), Copyright © 1960, 1962, 1968, 1971, 1972, 1973, 1975, 1977, 1995 by The Lockman Foundation. Used by permission.

Scripture quotations marked (ESV) are from the ESV ® Bible (The Holy Bible, English Standard Version®), copyright © 2001 by Crossway, a publishing ministry of Good News Publishers. Used by permission. All rights reserved.

Scripture quotations marked (NIV) are from the HOLY BIBLE, NEW INTERNATIONAL VERSION®. NIV®. Copyright © 1973, 1978, 1984, by International Bible Society. Used by permission of Zondervan Publishing House. All rights reserved.

Scripture quotation marked (KJV) is from the King James Version of the Bible.

Italics within Scripture quotations indicate emphasis added.

Printed in the United States of America

Library of Congress Cataloging-in-Publication Data

Names: Miller, Rachel Green, author.
Title: Beyond authority and submission : women and men in marriage, church, and society / Rachel Green Miller.
Description: Phillipsburg : P&R Publishing, 2019.
Identifiers: LCCN 2019005645| ISBN 9781629956114 (pbk.) | ISBN 9781629956121 (epub) | ISBN 9781629956138 (mobi)
Subjects: LCSH: Sex role--Religious aspects--Christianity.
Classification: LCC BT708 .M565 2019 | DDC 261.8/357--dc23
LC record available at https://lccn.loc.gov/2019005645

For Matt, my strongest encouragement—
yesterday, today, and forever.

"My beloved is mine, and I am his." (Song 2:16)

And for Jonathan, Gabriel, and Nathanael—
God has given me the desires of my heart.

"He gives the barren woman a home,
making her the joyous mother of children."
(Ps. 113:9 ESV)

CONTENTS

FOREWORD

Rachel Miller is the perfect person to write this timely book that challenges the lens that many in the church use to view the nature of men and women and their so-called roles in the church, home, and society. In the last thirty years, the church has been flooded with resources on biblical manhood and womanhood. I remember reading many of these resources when I first married, wanting to be a godly wife and to properly respond to the sexual revolution that is pervading our culture. I learned about some new movements in the church, such as complementarianism and egalitarianism, that worked to build a framework for what the Bible teaches regarding masculinity, femininity, and the contributions of men and women. These movements became polarizing for those who joined their councils, coalitions, and alliances, as their positions were taught as gospel truths. I found myself in an evangelical subculture that built a framework of authority and submission to describe the nature of men and women. Is this really what the Bible teaches? While looking for some fellow critical thinkers, I discovered Rachel's blog, *A Daughter of the Reformation*. Her writing is a breath of fresh air.

Rachel is a laywoman. Maybe you are wondering what qualifies her to write such a book, when there are so many distinguished pastors and scholars who have written on the topic of biblical manhood and womanhood. There are several reasons why an informed laywoman like Rachel has much to contribute to this discussion.

7

First of all, Rachel has firm convictions about upholding the ordination of qualified men in the church and about husbands being servant leaders in their homes. While not aligning with a movement, Rachel does want to contribute as a complementary, reciprocal voice in response to the many we have read and heard. So she is what we would consider a reforming voice within her own camp. If complementarianism truly is complementary, it should value this kind of engagement. Published resources for the church are meant to be thoughtfully engaged. Most authors do not presume to be the final voice on matters such as these; rather, they aim to offer their interpretation of pertinent scriptural principles in hopes to move forward in a biblical understanding of the sexes. Rachel's book is a sharpening response from the pew.

Second, Rachel has nothing to personally gain. She is not aligned with any organization that will boost her status or career in exchange for her offering a biblical way to view men and women beyond authority and submission. In fact, her speaking against the grain of many of her peers is a brave endeavor. One reason why it is so difficult to have these discussions is because most of the authors are aligned to organizations that make their livelihood dependent on not budging from the organization's framework. Since Rachel is an ordinary laywoman, a faithful Christian who upholds the confessions of her church, and is not on the payroll of a parachurch organization, she has more freedom to write from the conclusions of her historical research and biblical convictions. Perhaps instead I should say that she has nothing to lose. But, just like the subject she is writing on, it's a little more complicated than that. Writing against the accepted grain in your own circles comes with a price. Rachel has counted the cost and cares enough about the way men and women co-labor together to write this book.

And third, Rachel has already proven to be a discerning and helpful voice on men and women in the church. Before the infamous Trinity debate that kicked off in 2016,[1] Rachel Miller was writing articles on her blog, challenging the orthodoxy of the prevalent teaching on the eternal

---

1. See "Highlights on the Trinity Debate," The Alliance of Confessing Evangelicals, accessed May 20, 2019, http://www.alliancenet.org/trinity-debate.

subordination of the Son and its sister teaching, the eternal subordination of women. Rachel has followed the doctrine on authority and submission in the Godhead and between the sexes, and has challenged its biblical grounds, before many of the scholars or pastors in her camp would speak out. Thankfully, we are now seeing a renewal of focus and resources being published on an orthodox teaching of the Trinity.

I am thankful for Rachel's further contributions in this book, as she examines whether some of the ideas about the nature of men and women and our relationships in the home, church, and society are biblical traditions that have been faithfully handed down or are ones that the church has picked up from the Greeks, Romans, and Victorians. Are our assumptions biblical or cultural? What if, in its attempt to be a Christian voice in response to the sexual revolution of the culture, the church has inadvertently been arguing from a different secular position? Should our framework for men and women be authority and submission, or can we return these categories to their proper place while recovering a lens of unity, interdependence, and service for both men and women?

Maybe Rachel didn't foresee just how fitting it would be when she named her blog *A Daughter of the Reformation*. She lives according to the Reformation confessions that she upholds. One of those cries is *Semper Reformanda*—the church is always reforming. We continually need to align our teachings with the authority of the Scriptures. This is something all readers should be able to agree with. I commend this book to you as a valuable contribution to the continuing discussion on the nature, relationships, and value of men and women, with the expectation that it will be a catalyst for fruitful, biblical reform.

Aimee Byrd

ACKNOWLEDGMENTS

Since I was a little girl, I've dreamed of writing a book. It's a blessing to see my dream become a reality, and I'm thankful for all those who have had a part in making this book possible.

In particular, I'd like to thank my husband, Matt, for being a constant source of encouragement and prayer and for being my calm in the storm. I love you more each day. I'd also like to thank my boys, Jonathan, Gabriel, and Nathanael, for their support and love. They have celebrated each milestone in the book process with me.

My parents, Jon and Carolyn, have always been supportive and encouraging. They taught me to love the Lord and to cherish the Word. They also faithfully modelled the beauty of companionship in marriage. I am so thankful for you both.

Every writer needs friends who are willing to listen and give honest feedback. Aimee Byrd and Valerie Hobbs are my "kindred spirits." Thank you for being my friends and for your support. It means the world to me.

I'd like to thank the team at P&R Publishing for giving me this opportunity. Thank you, Amanda and Kristi, for your work in polishing my words and making this book what it is. I appreciate your help and kindness.

Thank you to my friends both online and in the real world. Your support and encouragement have brightened my day and given me the push to continue.

Lastly, I want to thank the writers, pastors, elders, leaders, and ordinary church members who stand up for the truth of the gospel and are willing to contend for the faith. You give me hope for the future of the church. May God make us all faithful co-laborers in Christ.

Soli Deo Gloria

INTRODUCTION

*Our theological views about creation, gender, and the household
context affect the way we think about women's status, roles,
and contributions to the church, home, and society.*

AIMEE BYRD[1]

Over the years, my parents have renovated several homes. One house had pink flamingo wallpaper. Another had worn shag carpeting that unnerved our dog. But my favorite was a house that had a horrible old carpet throughout the living room. Imagine our surprise and joy when we found beautiful hardwood floors underneath it.

Whenever a house has something beautiful hidden like that, I invariably ask, "Why would anyone cover this up?!" The truth is that things like hardwood can take work to maintain, so sometimes they're covered up because carpet seems easier to handle. Other times, things like plastic couch covers are added to a house to protect the wood or furniture. But most of the time, the layers inside a house reflect changing styles. What's fashionable today is outdated tomorrow. Once you peel back the layers of dated wallpaper, ancient carpet, dirt and grime, and chipped paint, you begin to see the timeless beauty of a house.

---

1. Aimee Byrd, *No Little Women: Equipping All Women in the Household of God* (Phillipsburg, NJ: P&R Publishing, 2016), 13.

13

A CONCERNING SITUATION

In a similar way, our theology runs the risk of being trendy. This is particularly true of our beliefs about women and men. Sometimes we add a layer or two to our theology because we think our man-made rules are easier to keep. Other times we add hedges to it as a reaction to what's going on in our culture and as a protection for what we believe. Over time, we end up with layers and layers of extrabiblical and even unbiblical ideas that cover up what the Bible teaches.

That's why I wrote this book. I've become increasingly aware of what's being taught in conservative circles about the nature of women and men and what's considered appropriate in marriage, the church, and society. It's troubling, and much of it isn't biblical. In addition, I see that authority and submission have become *the* lens through which all of women's and men's interactions are viewed—even to the point that some people try to figure out if it's okay for a woman to write a book that a man may learn from. Does a woman's authorship create a "direct, authoritative confrontation" that could be compromising?[2]

Maybe you've noticed these kinds of discussions too. Maybe you can't put your finger on what's bothering you. You may be concerned or confused—or both—by what you're hearing. You may wonder where these ideas come from. If so, this book is for you.

Why? Because as theologically conservative Christians, we must acknowledge where extrabiblical and unbiblical ideas about women and men have permeated, weakened, and confused our teachings. We need to move beyond a focus on authority and submission in order to incorporate equally important biblical themes into our discussions, such as unity, interdependence, and service. As we do, we will strengthen our vital relationship as co-laborers in Christ.

---

2. John Piper, "Do You Use Bible Commentaries Written by Women?" Desiring God, March 27, 2013, http://www.desiringgod.org/interviews/do-you-use-bible-commentaries -written-by-women. Piper concludes that this is acceptable. "'She is not looking at me and confronting me and authoritatively directing me as a woman.' There is this interposition of the phenomenon called *book* and *writing* that puts the woman as author out of the reader's sight and, in a sense, takes away the dimension of her female personhood."

WHO BELIEVES WHAT?

In discussions about men, women, and gender, various labels describe the different beliefs that Christians hold. The most common ones are *feminism, egalitarianism, complementarianism,* and *patriarchy.* At this point, you may be curious about where I fit in.

If you considered the four positions on a continuum, feminism would be on one end of the spectrum and patriarchy on the other. These two views of men and women are fundamentally opposed and have very little or no overlap. We will go into greater detail about the evolution of the feminist movement, but for the purposes of this discussion, feminism promotes the equality of women, believes that men and women are virtually interchangeable, and may prefer feminine pronouns and names for God. On the other extreme, patriarchal beliefs emphasize the differences between women and men and show a strong preference for male authority in all aspects of life.

That leaves us with the two middle-ground positions. Egalitarians believe that men and women are fundamentally equal but not interchangeable, and that they should "share authority equally in service and leadership in the home, church, and world."[3] Complementarians believe that women and men are "equal before God as persons and distinct in their manhood and womanhood" and that "distinctions in masculine and feminine roles are ordained by God as part of the created order."[4]

So which am I? I believe that

- God made humans, male and female, in His own image (see Gen. 1:26–27)
- in Christ, men and women are equal before God (see Gal. 3:28)
- women and men are interdependent and should serve each other (see 1 Cor. 11:11–12)

3. "CBE's Mission and Values," Christians for Biblical Equality International, accessed November 21, 2018, https://www.cbeinternational.org/content/cbes-mission.

4. "Danvers Statement," The Council on Biblical Manhood and Womanhood, accessed November 21, 2018, https://cbmw.org/about/danvers-statement.

- marriage was designed to be between one man and one woman—ideally for life (see Gen. 2:24)
- husbands are called to sacrificial, servant leadership of their wives and to love them as Christ loves the church (see Eph. 5:25–33)
- wives are called to yield voluntarily to their husbands—to submit to them as the church submits to Christ (see Eph. 5:22–24)
- only qualified men should be ordained leaders in the church (see 1 Tim. 3:1–13)

If you notice what I believe about marriage and ordination, you'll see that I'm not a feminist or an egalitarian. And I'm not patriarchal. So am I complementarian? I used to think so. After all, I believe that husbands are the leaders of their families. I believe that wives should submit to the leadership of their husbands. I believe that ordained church leaders should be qualified men. Isn't that what complementarians believe?

Yes, but that's not all that complementarians are expected to believe. The complementarian movement has done good things: affirming the complementarity and equality of men and women, affirming that husbands are to lead their wives sacrificially and that wives are to submit to the leadership of their husbands, and affirming the ordination of qualified men. But extrabiblical and unbiblical ideas have been incorporated into the movement's teaching as well. These ideas have more in common with Greek, Roman, and Victorian beliefs than with the Bible.

Not all who call themselves complementarians share these beliefs. However, because complementarianism as a movement has embraced these ideas, I'm not comfortable with calling myself a complementarian. If you are concerned as well, know that you're not alone.

THE PURPOSE OF THIS BOOK

The topics of sex and gender are everywhere. Conservative Christian books, articles, and conferences focus on answering questions about roles in marriage, biblical manhood and womanhood, biblical sexuality, purity before marriage, pornography and its effect on families, and responses to same-sex marriage, transgenderism, and a sexually saturated culture.

But not just conservative Christians are attempting to answer these questions. All around us, people debate what gender and sexuality mean. Bruce Jenner transitioned into Caitlyn. Fallon Fox, who was born a man, boxed against Tamikka Brents, who was born a woman, in a women's division match. Colleges ask which pronouns students prefer: *he*? *she*? *zhe*? Gender seems to mean everything and nothing.

As Christians, we need to speak out about what the Bible teaches about women and men, the definition of marriage, and the purposes and boundaries of sexuality. But we need to be very careful about what we say. Our society needs clear teaching from the Bible. That means that we need to study the Bible and allow the Scriptures to peel back any layers of unbiblical and extrabiblical beliefs we have added. Are we making things too hard and twisting ourselves up in knots? Is there a better way? I think there is.

What the Bible teaches about men, women, and gender is both simpler and more difficult than we are often told. The Bible doesn't give us detailed lists with bullet points to answer all our questions. Thankfully, it *does* give us guidelines and boundaries to help us know where to begin and how to address these topics.

We will first look at biblical themes that will help us in our discussions about women and men. Then we will look at how various historical cultures and developments have influenced our beliefs. In the second half of the book we will look at prevalent teachings about the nature of women and men and how these views affect our interactions in marriage, church, and society. We will also consider what the Bible teaches on these topics and how we can apply its truths to our lives.

I wrote this book because I care deeply about what the Bible teaches about women and men. My desire is for women and men to be co-laborers in all of life so that our families and churches will be strengthened and encouraged. Working together, we can then be a blessing to our society, which so desperately needs the truth of the gospel.

PART 1

A LENS FOR OUR RELATIONSHIPS

1

"MUTUALITY OF RESPECT AND LOVE"

WHAT ARE AUTHORITY AND SUBMISSION?

The sorrow of the whole human story is not that we have authority,
it is the way we have misused and neglected authority.

ANDY CROUCH[1]

Paul's concept of "submission" contained notions of mutuality of
respect and love and thus clearly transcended the secular notion.

PHILIP TOWNER[2]

Imagine you are in World War II Germany. Nazi soldiers are banging on doors. The government is making people disappear. Friends and relatives have been sent away or are in hiding. You don't know if you might be next. You live in fear of what could happen if you step out of line, even unintentionally. The terror is palpable.

1. Andy Crouch, *Strong and Weak: Embracing a Life of Love, Risk, and True Flourishing* (Downers Grove, IL: InterVarsity Press, 2016), 39.
2. Philip H. Towner, *1–2 Timothy & Titus*, The IVP New Testament Commentary Series (Downers Grove, IL: InterVarsity Press, 1994), 238.

Is that what authority is—raw power exercised without restraint or care for others? Consider the dystopian books and movies that are so popular in our culture: *The Hunger Games, The Handmaid's Tale, The Man in the High Castle, 1984,* and *Fahrenheit 451.* We're afraid of unbridled authority. After all, we live in a world that pursues freedom and independence. We've fought wars to protect and defend ourselves and others from tyranny and oppression. We're rugged individualists. No one tells us what to do, right?

But many conversations among Christians raise questions about authority and submission—especially when it comes to how women and men should interact. Why would wives submit to their husbands? Don't they have minds of their own? Are husbands supposed to have the last word when it comes to making decisions? If only men should be ordained in the church, does that mean that women have no say? We wonder about the meaning and purpose of authority and submission.

If we don't have a clear picture of how Scripture defines authority and submission, then we can't help but be confused. In this chapter, we will look at what the Bible teaches us about the nature of authority and submission and what authority and submission should look like in our lives.

THE NATURE OF AUTHORITY AND SUBMISSION

Authority and submission aren't bad things in themselves. What bothers us, rightly, are the ways they have been abused. It's crucial that we separate out misuses of authority and submission from the biblical picture of godly authority and appropriate submission.

How do we do that? To start, we need to consider the nature of authority and submission. Where do authority and submission come from?

God: The Source of All Authority and Submission

The foundation of a biblical understanding of authority and submission is the fact that we are humans, male and female, made in the image of God. In the beginning, God made us and gave us authority—the right to command and lead—over the rest of creation. He commanded us to rule over "every living thing that moves on the earth" (Gen. 1:28). This authority is part of the very nature of humanity, and it is good when used appropriately.[3] God-honoring authority protects, cares for, provides for, and promotes the well-being of others.[4] In our fallen world, godly authority also restrains evil and punishes sin and wickedness (see Rom. 13:4). Life without authority is anarchy and chaos.

However, because we are created beings, our authority must be limited.[5] Only God has unlimited authority. He is God and our Creator. We are created and are not God (see Rom. 1:18–25). This contrast lies at the heart of submission and is essential for us to grasp. Submission—voluntarily yielding to the authority of another—isn't feminine or masculine; it's characteristic of our human nature.

Each of us has authority in some relationships and owes submission in others. Common sense tells us that we should recognize the situational authority of others. For example, when a doctor tells us that we have an illness and need treatment, it is wise for us to recognize his or her authority and to submit to the treatment. Similarly, we know we should follow the instructions of teachers, counselors, police officers, coaches, and even traffic signs. Additionally, the Bible gives us both general guidance and specific direction regarding authority and submission in particular relationships, as we will discuss.

Jesus Christ: Our Example for God-Honoring Authority

In addition to submitting to God as our Creator, Christians are called to submit to Jesus Christ, because He is our Savior and head of the church (see Eph. 5:23–24). The apostle Paul writes that Jesus "is also head of the body, the church; and He is the beginning, the firstborn from the dead, so that He Himself will come to have first place in everything" (Col. 1:18).

All other authority in our lives is delegated, limited, and qualified. This is a necessary limitation, both because we aren't God and because of our sinfulness.[6] But the submission of believers to Christ is ultimate.

3. See Crouch, *Strong and Weak*, 37–38.
4. See Crouch, 111–12.
5. See Crouch, 36.
6. See Steven R. Tracy, "What Does 'Submit in Everything' Really Mean? The Nature and Scope of Marital Submission," *Trinity Journal* 29 (2008): 287.

There is no higher authority. Jesus Christ is God, and so He truly is our authority in every aspect of our lives.

Left to our own sinful natures, we tend to abuse power—but Jesus will never abuse His authority or sin against us. Godly authority is different from worldly authority. As Jesus taught His disciples, we are to lead by serving.

> The rulers of the Gentiles lord it over them, and their great men exercise authority over them. It is not this way among you, but whoever wishes to become great among you shall be your servant, and whoever wishes to be first among you shall be your slave; just as the Son of Man did not come to be served, but to serve, and to give His life a ransom for many. (Matt. 20:25–28)

While this kind of authority is often referred to as "servant leadership," it's a misunderstanding to think this means that leadership should be softened by servanthood. A servant leader isn't so much a leader who learns to serve but a servant who learns to lead through service.[7] New Testament professor Michelle Lee-Barnewall writes, "Christ indicates that servanthood is a prerequisite for being a leader. Thus, rather than considering how servanthood modifies a type of leadership, it may be better to ask how servanthood forms a necessary basis for leadership, even authority."[8]

What should servant leadership look like? Jesus. His life is the picture of humble service. He washed His disciples' feet (see John 13:1–17). He served to the point of laying down His own life to pay for our sins.

Jesus Christ: Our Example for God-Honoring Submission

In addition to being our model for God-honoring authority, Jesus Christ is the model of submission for all of us—male and female. He said, "I have come down from heaven, not to do My own will, but the will of

---

7. Michelle Lee-Barnewall, *Neither Complementarian nor Egalitarian: A Kingdom Corrective to the Evangelical Gender Debate* (Grand Rapids: Baker Academic, 2016), p. 138, NOOK.

8. Lee-Barnewall, 140.

Him who sent Me" (John 6:38), and the Bible gives us many examples of Jesus's submission to the Father.

You may be wondering, since Jesus *is* God, how can He submit *to* God? Jesus is both God and human. As God, Jesus is equal in power, glory, and majesty with the Father. As a human, He has a human nature and a human will to submit in obedience to God the Father. When the Bible talks about Jesus's submission or obedience, it refers to His human nature and will and His role as Mediator between God and humanity.

Before elaborating on specific relationships, Paul explains that we should be "submitting to one another out of reverence for Christ" (Eph. 5:21 ESV). We do this, in part, by showing honor toward others, deferring to others, and considering the needs of others before our own (see Phil. 2:3–4). When we do these things, we follow Christ's example. Christ submitted to God in His life, death, and resurrection and put the needs of His people before Himself. "He humbled Himself by becoming obedient to the point of death, even death on a cross" (Phil. 2:8).

Whether we lead or follow, we are called to be like Christ. Is Christ's authority an example exclusively for men? And is His example of submission just for women? No—both His God-honoring leadership and self-sacrificial submission are models for us all.

AUTHORITY AND SUBMISSION IN OUR VARIOUS HUMAN RELATIONSHIPS

In our homes, churches, and societies, we live and work within a variety of relationships. In some relationships, we are in authority. In others, we are called to submit.

The Westminster Larger Catechism uses the fifth commandment, "Honor your father and mother," to explain the responsibilities that we have to each other in all our various relationships—not only our biological ones.[9] When it comes to those who are in authority over us, we are called to submit willingly and thankfully and without envy or contempt. When it comes to those who are under our authority, God calls us to love,

9. See the Westminster Larger Catechism, questions and answers 124–30.

counsel, protect, and provide. We should never demand sinful behavior or expect things that others aren't capable of doing. Submission doesn't mean mindlessly obeying reckless authority or sinful instructions. Having authority doesn't mean riding roughshod over others, getting our own way, or being harsh and demanding. It's about taking care of those who have been entrusted to us.

Will we ever submit and lead perfectly? Not this side of heaven. By God's grace and mercy, Christ's life and death cover our failures. But as we look at these different relationships we should remember that, no matter which side of the equation we're on, our authority and submission carry both responsibilities and limitations.

Authority and Submission in the Home

The New Testament contains a handful of passages that describe how believers are to live together in households. Ephesians 5 and 6 is perhaps the most familiar of these passages. In Ephesians 5:21, Paul begins by instructing believers to submit to one another in Christ. Many English translations put a hard break between verse 21 and the rest of the chapter, but the Greek indicates that the passage is connected. Translated literally into English, the Greek text reads,

> v. 21: submitting yourselves to one another in reverence of Christ[10]
> v. 22: Wives to the[ir] own husbands as to the Lord[11]

Verse 22 doesn't have its own verb, meaning that the verses are intended to be understood together.[12] Paul explains that believers are to submit to one another before he outlines specific relationships that include aspects of authority and submission: wives/husbands, children/parents, slaves/masters. In each of these relationships, Paul emphasizes

---

10. See Ephesians 5:21 in the Interlinear Bible, available online from Bible Hub, accessed June 12, 2018, http://biblehub.com/interlinear/ephesians/5-21.htm.

11. See Ephesians 5:22 in the Interlinear Bible, available online from Bible Hub, accessed June 12, 2018, http://biblehub.com/interlinear/ephesians/5-22.htm.

12. See Cynthia Long Westfall, *Paul and Gender: Reclaiming the Apostle's Vision for Men and Women in Christ* (Grand Rapids: Baker Academic, 2016), 100.

service—caring for others by putting their needs first. As we will see, what each person owes another looks different in different types of relationships.

Husbands and wives. Paul writes that wives are to submit to their own husbands "as to the Lord" (Eph. 5:22). Some think this means that a wife should cater to her husband's preferences—for example, that a husband can use his authority to tell his wife how to wash the dishes[13] and that if he wants his wife to get up early and make him breakfast, she should submit to his desire and do so.[14]

This kind of thinking comes from defining authority and submission in military terms.[15] The military operates with rigid and unyielding hierarchy and discipline. Officers give commands and expect to be obeyed.[16] If that's the way that marriage is supposed to work, then it makes sense for wives to cater to their husbands' preferences.

But families aren't armies, and husbands and wives aren't called to imitate military rank and order. Instead, they are to devote themselves to a relationship of love and service.[17] Husbands are to love their wives sacrificially by following Christ's example of self-denial. Wives don't owe their husbands obedience as if they were soldiers.

Authority and submission are one aspect of the husband-and-wife relationship—not the whole. A husband's leadership isn't about power and privilege or about figuring out who's in charge or who should have the final say. A wife's submission isn't about catering to preferences.[18] Submission in marriage is "appropriate, logical, and Christian," because it's "based on a love relationship in which one party yields to another who

13. See Martha Peace, "Soap Bubbles Submission," *Martha Peace* (blog), February 24, 2016, http://marthapeacetew.blogspot.com/2016/02/soap-bubbles-submission.html.

14. See Emily Jensen, "Wives, Honor Your Husband's Preferences," The Council on Biblical Manhood and Womanhood, November 13, 2015, http://cbmw.org/topics/marriage-public-square/wives-honor-your-husbands-preferences/.

15. See Doug Ponder, "The Heart of Femininity," Re | Source, accessed August 23, 2017, http://www.remnantresource.org/the-heart-of-femininity/.

16. See Tracy, "What Does 'Submit in Everything' Really Mean?" 305.

17. See Tracy, 305.

18. See Tracy, 310–11.

uses his power to sacrifice on her behalf."[19] The Bible's emphasis is on how husbands and wives are to serve each other in Christ while working together as co-laborers.

As is the case in all human relationships, both authority and submission in marriage are limited and qualified. A wife submits to her own husband, not just to any man. A husband has no authority over his neighbor's wife down the street. Believers owe ultimate obedience and submission to Christ. Wives aren't supposed to submit to anything sinful, and husbands shouldn't ask them to.

Will God-honoring authority and submission look the same in all marriages? Not necessarily. For example, what was appropriate for wives in the early church wouldn't fit all women everywhere. The Bible gives us guidelines but not all the specifics for every marriage.[20] We will look at this more in chapter 12.

Parents and children. In Ephesians 5–6, Paul also addresses parents and children. Referencing the Ten Commandments, he tells children to obey their parents—both fathers and mothers. He urges parents to raise their children with gentleness. As parents, we are called to love and serve our children, which often means putting their needs before our own.

Parental authority is limited and never absolute. Our authority is limited to our own children; it's not over any child anywhere. It's also limited by the age of our children—we don't have the same authority to discipline or direct our children when they're adults as we do when they're younger. Parental authority is also limited when it comes to what we can ask and expect our children to do. We should never ask them to sin or expect them to do things that are beyond their abilities, as the Westminster Larger Catechism reminds us.

Jesus's response to Mary and Joseph when they found Him in the temple (see Luke 2:41–51) is a good example of honoring parents while respecting the limitations of their authority. When Mary and Joseph

19. Tracy, 307.

20. See Karen H. Jobes, *1 Peter*, Baker Exegetical Commentary on the New Testament (Grand Rapids: Baker Academic, 2005), 212.

found Him after looking for Him for three days, they were frustrated. Jesus responded by reminding them that God the Father had given Him work that He needed to do. He respected Mary and Joseph's authority and continued to live in submission to them, but He also adjusted their expectations of Him.[21]

Authority and Submission in the Body of Christ

Authority and submission are also an important aspect of the relationship between church leaders and congregations. Being a pastor, elder, or deacon is a respectable position and a high calling, but it comes with a greater weight of responsibility. The church's leadership has an essential role to fulfill.

God gives ordained church leaders the responsibility of the ministry of the Word and sacrament.[22] He also makes them responsible for the care and protection of the members of their congregations. Scripture uses the illustration of shepherds who watch over their sheep (see 1 Peter 5:1–4). Sometimes shepherds gather and feed the sheep with gentleness and love. Other times shepherds drive off wolves who threaten the safety and lives of the flock.

Church members are called to submit to the authority of their ordained leaders. As Hebrews 13:17 says, "Obey your leaders and submit to them, for they keep watch over your souls as those who will give an account. Let them do this with joy and not with grief, for this would be unprofitable for you."

As in other types of relationships, church authority is limited and qualified. Not everyone who wants to go into ministry has been called by God to do so. And not everyone meets the qualifications. The Bible sets a high bar:

If any man is above reproach, the husband of one wife, having children who believe, not accused of dissipation or rebellion. For the

---

21. See Tracy, "What Does 'Submit in Everything' Really Mean?" 307.
22. See Aimee Byrd, *No Little Women: Equipping All Women in the Household of God* (Phillipsburg, NJ: P&R Publishing, 2016), 92.

overseer must be above reproach as God's steward, not self-willed, not quick-tempered, not addicted to wine, not pugnacious, not fond of sordid gain, but hospitable, loving what is good, sensible, just, devout, self-controlled, holding fast the faithful word which is in accordance with the teaching, so that he will be able both to exhort in sound doctrine and to refute those who contradict. (Titus 1:6–9)

Paul writes that ordained leadership in the church is restricted to qualified men. Being a man isn't the *only* qualification, but it *is* a requirement. In 1 Timothy 2:12, Paul explains that women aren't to "teach or exercise authority" over men.[23]

But don't hear what Paul isn't saying. He isn't saying that women can never have authority over men or that men can never learn from women. He simply means that women aren't called to positions of authority in the church that would involve their teaching men authoritatively in the church's public worship.[24] Outside the ordained leadership of the church, women aren't restricted from having authority.

If ordained leadership is male, does that mean that half the church (the women) submits to the other half (the men)? No—church members are male and female, and we're all expected to submit to church leadership. Even ordained leaders are supposed to submit to others in the church. Many churches have some type of ecclesiastical structure that means that no leader has absolute authority. There are layers of authority and submission. In some churches, congregations elect their leaders. In others, the denomination appoints the individual church's leadership. Despite the differences in how leaders are selected, churches often have some system of checks and balances to guard against abuses of power and to protect against erroneous teaching.

Church authority is also limited in scope. Church leaders have authority over only the members of their own congregations. A pastor in Idaho doesn't have authority over a random church member in Texas.

23. I'll discuss this topic further in chapter 15.
24. See Carl Trueman, "1 Timothy 2:11–15" (sermon, Cornerstone Presbyterian Church, Ambler, PA, November 11, 2011), available online at https://web.archive.org /web/20160324093349/http://cornerstoneopc.com/media/2011-11-20.mp3.

And, as enjoyable as listening to online sermons can be, you aren't supposed to submit to the authority of any and every pastor whom you hear on a podcast.

Even within the context of our own churches, church leaders have limited authority. They don't have the authority to tell you how to dress, how to vote, how to eat, where to live, or how to educate your kids. The Westminster Confession reminds us that "God alone is Lord of the conscience."[25] We have liberty as Christians to make decisions about these kinds of things. As with the other examples of submission we have discussed, we are never supposed to obey sinful commands, and our church leaders should never ask us to.

Authority and Submission in Society

Included with the discussion of household relationships in Ephesians 6 is the master/slave relationship. While we don't have masters and slaves today, we do have employers and employees. We also have our civil government and our relationship to it as citizens.

Employers and employees. While Paul doesn't specifically address the modern employee/employer relationship, his instructions to masters and slaves do show us how we should work with and for others. Slaves are to serve their masters with honesty. Masters are to treat those who work for them with "justice and fairness" (Col. 4:1) and not threaten them (see Eph. 6:9). Whether we are the employer or the employee, ultimately our work is in service to Christ (see Col. 3:23–24).

Slaves and masters aren't a perfect analogy for us, of course. Employees have much greater rights and freedoms than slaves ever had, and employers have more restrictions on their authority. But we have an enduring responsibility to work honestly and respectfully. Believers in the workforce must serve Christ and do so honorably, whether as employers or as employees.

An employer's authority is limited to his or her own employees. A boss at one company doesn't have authority over an employee at a

---

25. Westminster Confession of Faith, chapter 20.2.

different company across town. Most companies have layers of authority. You may be both responsible to others and responsible for others. Even the heads of companies are often responsible to stockholders or members of a board.

Can employers tell their employees to do whatever they want? No—an employer's authority is limited to work-related things. Your boss doesn't have the authority to tell you where to go to church or who to marry. And, as we have seen with the other relationships, employers shouldn't ask their employees to sin, and employees shouldn't submit if doing so would cause them to sin.

Civil leaders and citizens. We're all familiar with the authority of civil leadership. As citizens, we have the responsibility to vote for our leaders (if we live in a country where we can vote), to pay our taxes, and to obey our country's laws. As Paul reminds us, government leadership is meant for our good (see Rom. 13:1–3). Government leaders are responsible to God, who gave them their authority. Christians in government should seek to serve others, thereby following Christ's example of servant leadership.

Civil authority is limited, though. If you've ever traveled internationally, you're familiar with the limits of national governments. When you're traveling in Paraguay, German laws don't have authority over you. You're responsible for obeying the laws of the Paraguayan government.

Are you supposed to do anything that a government says no matter what? No—civil authority is limited in scope as well as by location. Your government doesn't have the authority to tell you where to worship or how to decorate your house, for example. We are called to submit to civil authorities unless doing so would mean sinning against God. In such cases, as Peter and the apostles said, "we must obey God rather than men" (Acts 5:29).

WHAT DOES THIS MEAN FOR US?

As we have seen, authority and submission are a function of our relationships. The nature of each relationship determines who should lead and who should submit.

Regardless of which role we have in a relationship, our example is Christ. It doesn't matter whether we're in authority or in submission. Jesus showed us the way to do both well. Whatever we do, whether we lead or submit, we should do all things so that we give glory and honor to God.

God-honoring authority is a blessing, and faithful submission is beautiful. But there is so much more to life than authority and submission. In the next chapter, we will look at how the biblical themes of unity, interdependence, and service help us to look beyond authority and submission in our discussions about women and men so that we can be co-laborers together in all aspects of our lives.

DISCUSSION QUESTIONS

1. Can you think of examples of God-honoring authority in your life?
2. What do you think about submission being a *human* characteristic?
3. What relationships do you have in which you are in authority? In submission?
4. How is Jesus our example for both God-honoring authority and submission?
5. What are examples of the limitations on authority and submission?

2

"HAND IN HAND, EYE TO EYE, HEART IN HEART"

UNITY, INTERDEPENDENCE, AND SERVICE

Sir, we believe and know that the time is fast coming when, men having learnt purity and women courage, the sexes shall live together in harmony, each other's helpers towards all things high and holy; no longer tyrant and victim, oppressor and oppressed, but, hand in hand, eye to eye, heart in heart, building up that nobler world which yet shall be.

ELIZABETH WOLSTENHOLME ELMY[1]

In the 1990s, malls had kiosks set up selling posters that, at first glance, looked like abstract art showing random colors and patterns. But if you looked at them long enough, and from the right distance, you could see a 3D image. The trick was to unfocus your eyes. If you focused on the image, all you would see was the 2D abstract art. But if you let your eyes

---

1. Elizabeth Wolstenholme Elmy, *Women and the Law* (Congleton, UK, 1896), quoted in Mary Lyndon Shanley, *Feminism, Marriage, and the Law in Victorian England, 1850–1895* (Princeton: Princeton University Press, 1989), 189.

relax, the hidden picture snapped into view, and you'd see the image that the artist wanted you to see.

The same is true when we study Scripture. Sometimes we're so intent on finding the answers to our questions that we get caught up on the background and miss the bigger picture. When we study the Bible, it is helpful for us to step back and ask, "What is the Bible's purpose?"

The Westminster Shorter Catechism tells us that the Scriptures teach what we are to "believe concerning God, and what duty God requires of [us]."[2] The purpose of the Bible is to explain who God is, who we are, how we got here, and what we must do in order to be saved. Once we understand the bigger picture, we can search for answers to our other questions within that framework.

BEYOND AUTHORITY AND SUBMISSION

In conservative Christian circles, many conversations about women and men start and end with authority and submission. Who's in charge? Who's allowed to do what? These are reasonable questions to ask. At the same time, the Bible doesn't start and end with authority and submission—it is Jesus's story from first to last. If we miss that message, then it doesn't matter what else we believe. No good deeds or proper understanding of women, men, and gender will save us.

That doesn't mean that authority and submission aren't important. We shouldn't dismiss them—but they aren't the focus of the Bible. When we concentrate on maintaining a hierarchy—or on overthrowing it—we forget our unity and interdependence and our call to mutual service.[3] Women can become completely dependent on men and devoted to serving their interests; men can forget their need for women and can focus more on enforcing submission than on serving their wives and families.

Contrary to what popular culture states, women and men are not

2. Westminster Shorter Catechism, answer 3.

3. Michelle Lee-Barnewall, *Neither Complementarian nor Egalitarian: A Kingdom Corrective to the Evangelical Gender Debate* (Grand Rapids: Baker Academic, 2016), NOOK, addresses the biblical themes of unity (see pp. 24–25) and leading through service (see pp. 108–9).

from different planets. We're complementary—more alike than different. Without denying the differences, we need to stop defining women as the polar opposite of men and vice versa. Such divisive definitions create and encourage unnecessary conflict and set up unrealistic and unbiblical expectations for how women and men should behave.

Paul frequently refers to fellow believers—both men and women—as his co-laborers. The word he uses, *sunergos*, means "a companion in work."[4] As we will see in the next sections, *co-laborer* captures the sense of what we were created to be and what we are called to be in Christ.

UNITY IN CREATION, FALL, AND REDEMPTION

In our society, we often focus on the differences between people—on what divides us. We label ourselves based on our skin color or what country we're from. We divide ourselves based on how much money we make, what kind of house we live in, or what car we drive. We're defined by our associations, who we vote for, where we went to college, what activities our kids do. Are you married or single? Do you have children? How many? Even in the church, we put each other in categories. Calvinist or Arminian? Contemporary or traditional worship? Presbyterian, Baptist, Methodist, or fill-in-the-blank?

In contrast, the Bible teaches us about what *unites* us. Humans, male and female, were created in God's image. God made Adam out of the dust of the earth and breathed life into him. He made Eve from one of Adam's ribs. In our very nature, men and women are equally made in the image of God. This is who we are.

There is a profound unity in humanity. You and I, and everyone else, come from the first man, Adam. Even Eve was created from Adam. We have the same human nature, no matter what country we're from or what our bodies look like on the outside. That unity is what Adam emphasized when he first saw Eve: "This is now bone of my bones, and flesh of my flesh" (Gen. 2:23). I'm sure Adam noticed the physical differences

---

4. Thayer's Greek Lexicon, s.v. "sunergos," available online from Bible Hub, accessed June 18, 2018, http://biblehub.com/greek/4904.htm, Strong's number 4904.

between himself and Eve, but they weren't what he dwelt on. He was struck by what united the two of them.[5]

The same unity that Adam and Eve shared in their creation was reinforced in their marriage. God instituted marriage after Adam and Eve were created, and in marriage a husband and wife "become one flesh" (Gen. 2:24). Adam and Eve were made from one flesh, and through marriage they became one flesh again. Isn't that imagery beautiful?

Humanity is also united in the work that God gave us to do (see Gen. 1:28). After God created us and everything else, there was order and unity in the world and communion between God and humanity.

If God made us to be united, why are we so divided now? Sin and death entered the world when Adam and Eve sinned. We are all fallen and are born sinners. Now chaos seems to reign, and relationships are broken—between God and us and between us and others.

Thankfully, that's not the end of the story. God sent His Son to live and die for us. Through Jesus's life, death, and resurrection, the penalty for our sins has been paid. Jesus bridged the gap between God and us. Through Him, we can have communion with God again. If we believe in Jesus and trust in Him for our salvation, we will be saved. And through the work of the Spirit, we can be reconciled to God and one another.

Because of our union with Christ, men and women who believe share an even deeper unity. Our most fundamental identity isn't whether we are male or female; it's whether or not we belong to Christ. Christians, both women and men, are adopted children of God—joint heirs to the inheritance of eternal life in Christ. Men and women together make up the body of Christ. We are, together, the church—the bride of Christ—co-laborers for the gospel.

Our unity is a common theme in the Bible. In the New Testament, Paul encourages the church to pursue unity: "Make my joy complete by being of the same mind, maintaining the same love, united in spirit, intent on one purpose" (Phil. 2:2). Paul wants believers to be united without divisions—"made complete in the same mind and in the same judgment" (1 Cor. 1:10)—so that together we "may with one voice glorify the God

---

5. See Lee-Barnewall, *Neither Complementarian nor Egalitarian*, 169.

and Father of our Lord Jesus Christ" (Rom. 15:6). In Ephesians, he emphasizes the unity of believers with the repeated use of the word *one*:

> There is *one* body and *one* Spirit, just as also you were called in *one* hope of your calling; *one* Lord, *one* faith, *one* baptism, *one* God and Father of all who is over all and through all and in all. (Eph. 4:4–6)

Peter, too, encourages believers to be united together in love:

> To sum up, all of you be harmonious, sympathetic, brotherly, kind-hearted, and humble in spirit; not returning evil for evil or insult for insult, but giving a blessing instead; for you were called for the very purpose that you might inherit a blessing. (1 Peter 3:8–9)

The Bible testifies to our unity. We don't have one Bible for men and a different one for women. The armor of God isn't just for men, and the fruit of the Spirit doesn't apply only to women. No, we have one Bible for us all, and most of the Bible's commands apply to all of us—male or female, old or young, rich or poor, servant or master.

INTERDEPENDENCE IN CREATION, FALL, AND REDEMPTION

Does the unity that women and men have through creation, in marriage, and in Christ mean that we are interchangeable? Are men and women the same? Of course not.

As a society, we make both too much and too little of *sex* (the biological differences between males and females) and *gender* (the social and cultural differences between males and females).[6] Many in our society believe that gender is fluid and that there are many more genders than male and female. We are told that biology doesn't determine gender and doesn't really matter. But we are also told that if your biology doesn't

---

6. See Oxford Living Dictionaries, s.v. "gender," accessed November 26, 2018, https://en.oxforddictionaries.com/definition/gender.

match your perceived gender, you should be free to change your body to match your perception of yourself.

Because of the fall, all aspects of our bodies, minds, and souls are touched by sin. Even human biology can be distorted, in the area of sex, through no fault of our own. Some babies are born with genetic errors that blur the physical and genetic distinctions between male and female. It doesn't happen all that often, but it does happen. When it does, we should address those concerned with compassion, pastoral wisdom, and grace.

For most people, however, it's not hard to figure out who is female and male. "It's a girl!" or "It's a boy!" is a statement of biological fact. Our biological differences demonstrate our interdependence. Human reproduction requires both a man and a woman. A woman can't be a father, and a man can't be a mother. Two women can't have a baby together, and neither can two men, without the aid and intervention of donors and doctors.

No matter what the headlines say, no man has ever been pregnant. Women who identify as men have reduced the male hormones they were taking, allowing their menstrual cycles to begin again. They have carried and delivered babies, but they are able to do so because they are biologically female and not male.

A man can't become a woman, and a woman can't become a man. A woman who has had a mastectomy and hysterectomy is still a woman. A man who has his male reproductive organs removed through surgery, illness, or injury is still a man. Hormones or surgery can't change what God created us to be: males and females made in His image.

It's important to emphasize that when God made humanity in His image, He did so by making a man and a woman. Women are as much made in the image of God as men are. Men don't have more of God's image because of their masculinity. We are equal in worth, but we're not the same. We are different, but we're also interdependent. We were created to complement each other, and we need each other.

God created Eve because it wasn't good for man to be alone (see Gen. 2:18). Woman was made for man's sake, but all men since Adam have been born of women (see 1 Cor. 11:9–12). Men and women depend on each other, as Paul says: "In the Lord, neither is woman independent of man, nor is man independent of woman" (1 Cor. 11:11).

Women and men were created to work together as co-laborers.[7] This is why Eve was created to be Adam's *ezer kenegdo*, as the original text of Genesis 2:18 reads. John McKinley's translation of this phrase as "necessary ally" emphasizes "the joint mission for which the male and female are created to rule God's earthly kingdom."[8]

Ezer also means "helper." Although we tend to think of helpers as assistants who aren't doing the real work, that isn't what the Bible teaches about Eve or about women in general. *Ezer* means "to help, nourish, sustain, or strengthen."[9] As you may know, the word is often used to describe God: "God is our Help. The Holy Spirit is our Helper. . . . God, Sovereign Lord of the Universe, is our helper, and we, as women, are created in His image."[10] A helper provides what is missing, as God does for us.

While we were created to be interdependent co-laborers, we often spend more time fighting and opposing each other. As we saw with our unity, humanity's fall into sin also broke our relationships. Instead of depending on each other, Adam and Eve turned against each other immediately (see Gen. 3:12–13). But Christ restores us and our reliance on each other by building us together into His body, the church.

Just as our physical bodies have many different parts with different functions, the body of Christ is made up of people who have different purposes. As Paul says in 1 Corinthians, we are not all hands or eyes, but we are all necessary in order for the body to function (see 1 Cor. 12:18–25). God has given each of us different gifts. The church needs all our gifts—yours and mine—and so do our marriages and our society.

As Scripture explains, every gift is important, and we should be content with what God has given us and where He has called us to serve. As believers, we should build each other up and care for each other.

7. See Steven R. Tracy, "What Does 'Submit in Everything' Really Mean? The Nature and Scope of Marital Submission," *Trinity Journal* 29 (2008): 309.

8. John McKinley, "Necessary Allies: God as *Ezer*, Woman as *Ezer*," lecture, Hilton Atlanta, November 17, 2015, mp3 download, 38:35, http://www.wordmp3.com/details.aspx?id=20759, quoted in Aimee Byrd, *No Little Women: Equipping All Women in the Household of God* (Phillipsburg, NJ: P&R Publishing, 2016), 25–26.

9. Wendy Alsup, "The Third Way on Gender," Practical Theology for Women, September 22, 2014, https://theologyforwomen.org/2014/09/the-third-way-on-gender.html.

10. Alsup, "The Third Way on Gender."

SERVICE IN CREATION, FALL, AND REDEMPTION

Do you ever wonder what the purpose of your life is? Philosophers have been attempting to answer that question for ages without success. But those of us who know our catechism can answer that our "chief end is to glorify God and to enjoy him forever."[11]

God created us to serve him and to care for creation and one another (see Gen. 1:28). We've been given an important job as stewards of God's creation. As Psalm 8 says, we were made to rule over the earth and the animals as God's representatives on earth (see vv. 4–8). God put Adam in Eden to "cultivate . . . and keep" the garden (Gen. 2:15). He then created Eve to co-labor with Adam in this work.

Because of sin, we tend to put ourselves first and act selfishly. We don't honor God. We don't think about others and their needs or take our role as stewards of creation seriously. But by God's grace, we aren't left in our sin and selfishness. The Spirit works in us, as God's people, to change our hearts and our actions.

For Christians, service isn't just volunteer work that we do because it looks good on our college applications. Service is our way of life. Why? Because we are called to be like Christ. Jesus gave us a perfect example when he acted like a servant by washing His disciples' feet (see John 13:13–16). If Jesus, the Son of God, washed dirty, smelly feet, how can we refuse to serve each other? The Bible teaches us to put others' needs before our own. We are called to humble ourselves and serve one another sacrificially.[12]

Paul reminds us that service isn't a just New Testament theme. Serving others is the essence of the Old Testament command to "love your neighbor as yourself" (see Gal. 5:13–14, quoting Lev. 19:18). Just as we're united in one body and dependent on each other, we are called to use our various gifts to serve each other (Rom. 12:3–13). My gifts aren't just for my benefit, and yours aren't just for yours. Our gifts are meant to be a blessing to others.

---

11. Westminster Shorter Catechism, answer 1.
12. See Lee-Barnewall, *Neither Complementarian nor Egalitarian*, 31.

The world around us tempts us to focus on our differences, not on our unity. It calls us to pursue *in*dependence instead of *inter*dependence. And it's baffled by the kind of service that the Bible calls us to demonstrate. Our society doesn't understand when those with authority put the needs of those whom they lead before their own. And it certainly doesn't understand when we willingly submit to the leadership of such people.

But God calls us to such service. He created us to serve Him as co-laborers. He calls husbands and wives to serve each other. He calls parents to serve their children; and children, as their parents need their help, should serve them too. God calls church leaders to serve their congregations. He calls church members to serve the church using the gifts He has given them. Employers, employees, government and civic leaders— whatever our profession, God calls each of us to serve others in society as we are able.

WHERE DO WE GO FROM HERE?

The Bible gives us the answers to our most pressing questions. Who's ultimately in charge? God. Who are we? We're men and women who were made in the image of God. Why are we here? We were made to serve God and one another as co-laborers in the work God has given us. How are we saved? By faith in Christ alone. When we focus on the big picture, the message of the Bible snaps into view and keeps us from getting lost in the details.

As we saw in the last chapter, the Bible teaches us about the importance and meaning of authority and submission. But authority and submission aren't the only things that the Bible teaches us about our relationships with each other. When we're so focused on this one topic, we miss the significance of other biblical themes and how they can help to expand and deepen our discussions about women and men.

How can unity, interdependence, and service advance our discussions about women, men, and gender? How can these themes encourage us in our calling as co-laborers? In the chapters that follow, we'll consider what the Bible teaches about women and men and how we can apply those teachings specifically in marriage, the church, and society.

But first we need to take a trip back through history as we begin to peel back the layers of ideas that have shaped our beliefs about women and men. In the next chapter, we'll begin with the Greeks and Romans. You may be surprised to find how much we've borrowed from them—it's not just our ideas about democracy and the benefit of good roads.

DISCUSSION QUESTIONS

1. What does *co-laborer* mean?
2. Can you name some ways you are a co-laborer in your life?
3. What are some examples of what unites women and men?
4. How are women and men interdependent?
5. How can we serve others in our various relationships?

PART 2

WOMEN AND MEN
IN HISTORY

3

"THE GENERAL INFERIORITY
OF THE FEMALE SEX"

WOMEN AND MEN IN GRECO-ROMAN SOCIETY

You are quite right, he replied, in maintaining the general inferiority
of the female sex: although many women are in many things
superior to many men, yet on the whole what you say is true.

PLATO[1]

And what will happen if you allow them . . . to attain equality with
their husbands? Do you imagine that you will find them endurable? The
very moment they begin to be your equals, they will be your superiors.

CATO THE ELDER[2]

When I started college at Texas A&M, one of the first things they taught
us was all the Aggie traditions. All schools have them, of course; but at

1. Plato, *Republic*, bk. 5, sec. 455d, trans. B. Jowett, quoted in *Women's Life in Greece and Rome: A Source Book in Translation*, ed. Mary R. Lefkowitz and Maureen B. Fant (Baltimore: The Johns Hopkins University Press, 1982), 66–67.
2. Quoted in Livy, *Rome and the Mediterranean*, trans. Henry Bettenson (New York: Penguin, 1976), 143.

A&M, traditions are especially important. As the joke goes, if you do something twice at A&M, it's a tradition. Sometimes we were told how the traditions had started, but not always. Other times, when we asked "Why?" the answer was a shrug and "Tradition." Ah, yes. Tradition!

Don't walk under the Century tree unless you're getting engaged. Don't walk on the grass by the student center. Say "Howdy" to everyone you pass. When I tried to explain the traditions to my parents, my dad would sing like Tevye, the main character of *Fiddler on the Roof.* If you're not familiar, Tevye sings about tradition as he explains the way that life works in his village. Everyone knows his or her place in their society, because they follow their traditions. Why do they do what they do? Tradition! Where did these traditions come from? No one knows!

Traditions aren't bad in and of themselves. They can be a way of honoring the past and remembering our history. And those are good things. Sometimes, though, we need to stop and consider why we do what we do. As Christians, we need to be willing to consider our traditions and compare them to what the Bible teaches.

Some of our church traditions are harmless. Coffee and donuts in the narthex? Great idea. Wearing your Sunday best? Can't hurt. Potluck dinners? Wonderful! (Want the inside scoop from a pastor's kid? Get dessert first.) Other traditions aren't so benign and need to be reconsidered in light of Scripture. But any that prove to be consistent with Scripture are worth maintaining—even the Protestant Reformers, as they stripped away layers of unbiblical traditions that kept people from the gospel, didn't get rid of tradition altogether.

Like the Reformers, we need to look at what's being taught in our churches and consider where these beliefs came from. Many of our conservative beliefs are traditional—but not biblical. So where did they come from? Let's peel back the layers of history and see what we find.

THE NATURE OF WOMEN AND MEN

As you may remember from your history classes, western civilization owes quite a bit to the Greeks and the Romans. Western politics, philosophy, art, literature, architecture, math, science, history, astronomy, physics, and medicine all have roots in Greco-Roman culture and civilization. Because of the considerable depth and breadth of this influence, we shouldn't be surprised to find that still other aspects of our culture have roots that reach back to the ancient Greeks and Romans.

What matters for our current discussion is how these ancient cultures have shaped our society's beliefs about women and men. These beliefs are truly traditional; they've been around for thousands of years. Traditional, though, does not mean these ideas are biblical. Not only are they not from the Bible, they are contrary to what the Bible teaches. Unfortunately, these pagan ideas are so incorporated into our thinking that we don't realize they are there. They have become part of the foundations of our society—the root of what's being taught about men and women.

Although God created Eve to be a blessing, throughout history she has been blamed for bringing evil into the world. And Eve isn't the only woman who has been accused of this. According to Greek mythology, Zeus created Pandora, the first woman, to punish men because man had stolen fire. He made Pandora beautiful but very wicked. Her name means "all-gift," because each god contributed to her formation. (Hermes, for example, made her a liar and a thief.) The moral of the story is that women were the "worst plague Zeus has made"[3]—"For previously the tribes of men used to live upon the earth entirely apart from evils, and without grievous toil and distressful diseases, which give death to men. . . . But the woman . . . wrought baneful evils for human beings."[4]

Given these beliefs about women's origins, it probably won't surprise you that the Greeks and Romans considered women to be morally, physically, and emotionally weaker than men. In contrast to the Bible's description of Eve, who was created perfect, the Greeks believed that the female body was an aberration—defective, imperfect, and mutilated.

Galen, an influential philosopher and physician, taught that female reproductive organs were inverted versions of their male counterparts.

3. Semonides of Amorgos, *On Women*, trans. H. Lloyd-Jones, quoted in Lefkowitz and Fant, *Women's Life in Greece & Rome*, 16.

4. Hesiod, "Works and Days," in *Hesiod: Theogony, Works and Days, Testimonia*, ed. and trans. Glenn W. Most (Cambridge: Harvard University Press, 2006), lines 90–95.

This was a defect—though it was also necessary for procreation: "This, though making the animal itself that was being formed less perfect than one that is complete in all respects, provided no small advantage for the race; for there needs must be a female. Indeed, you ought not to think that our Creator would purposely make half the whole race imperfect and, as it were, mutilated, unless there was to be some great advantage in such a mutilation."[5] So women are mutilated and imperfect—but that's not such a bad thing, if you're a man.

According to these beliefs, women and men are completely different and have few overlapping qualities. The male body is perfect and ideal. The female body is mutilated and inverted. Men are rational; women irrational. Men are strong and courageous; women weaker and nervous. Men were made to rule; women to obey. As Aristotle wrote, "The courage of a man is shown in commanding, of a woman in obeying. . . . All classes must be deemed to have their special attributes; as the poet says of women, 'Silence is a woman's glory,' but this is not equally the glory of man."[6]

CHASTITY AND MARRIAGE

Have you ever used the word *hysterical*? The English words *hysteria* and *hysterical* come from the Greek word for the uterus: *hysterika*. Greek physicians such as Hippocrates believed that a woman's uterus would move around in her body if it dried out. A wandering uterus would move up against the rest of a woman's internal organs, causing hysteria—a mental and psychological illness. [7]

Obviously, only women could suffer from hysteria. Greco-Romans considered young women, once they reached puberty, to be unstable

---

5. *Galen on the Usefulness of the Parts of the Body*, trans. Margaret Tallmadge May (Ithaca, NY: Cornell University Press, 1968), 2:630.

6. Aristotle, *Politics*, trans. Benjamin Jowett (repr., Los Angeles: IndoEuropean Publishing, 2009), 17–18.

7. See Vanessa Traniello, "Hysteria and the Wandering Womb," Marquette University History Department, accessed June 7, 2018, http://academic.mu.edu/meissnerd /hysteria.html.

and have uncontrollable sexual desires. They believed that the cure for female instability was marriage, which properly channeled these urges into bearing children. Sexual activity and pregnancy had the added benefit of preventing hysteria.[8]

Since women were considered so evil and defective, men had to be encouraged to marry for the good of society and in order to ensure the inheritance of property. Women might be evil, but they were a necessary evil.[9] Men had to be careful to pick good wives who would be faithful. A young, inexperienced woman was preferable. "Marry a virgin, so you can teach her good habits," one author advised. "The best one to marry is the girl who lives near you; look over her in detail, so you don't marry one who'll bring joy to your neighbours."[10]

Though marriage was a necessary evil for men, it was a life purpose for women. Marriage and motherhood were considered to be the highest aspirations for women in ancient Greece and Rome. As the saying went, "The two best days in a woman's life are when someone marries her and when he carries her dead body to the grave."[11]

Good wives were expected to be faithful, honest, careful with money, and not too concerned with their appearance. Being greedy, angry, or quarrelsome was inappropriate. Instead wives were encouraged to be humble, to take care of their households, and to love their children even more than their own lives.[12]

There was a double standard when it came to morality. While wives were expected to be sexually faithful, husbands were not. The female Greek philosopher Phintys wrote, "A woman's greatest virtue is chastity. ... Courage and intelligence are more appropriately male qualities because

8. See Vanessa Traniello, "Hysteria and the Wandering Womb."

9. See Gellius, *Attic Nights*, trans. S. Dixon, 1.6.2, quoted in Eve D'Ambra, *Roman Women* (New York: Cambridge University Press, 2007), 47.

10. Hesiod, *Works and Days*, trans. Mary R. Lefkowitz, 695–705, quoted in Lefkowitz and Fant, *Women's Life in Greece & Rome*, 14.

11. Hipponax, fragment 68, trans. Martin Litchfield West, quoted in Lefkowitz and Fant, *Women's Life in Greece & Rome*, 16. The point seems to be that those were the only times when women were honored.

12. Gretchen Reydams-Schils, *The Roman Stoics: Self, Responsibility, and Affection* (Chicago: University of Chicago Press, 2005), 154.

of the strength of men's bodies and the power of their minds. Chastity is more appropriately female."[13]

Upper-class or wealthy women stayed at home or went out in public with their male guardians. This served to protect them as well as to limit their mobility in society. However, women weren't all equally protected. Actresses and women who worked in businesses and shops were considered sexually available. Slaves were treated as property and so had no rights or protections—not even a right to consent. And this sexual double standard extended to the consequences of sexual acts. Men could charge their wives with adultery, but wives usually couldn't do the same.[14]

This imbalance of power was an outworking of Greco-Roman beliefs about women and men. Marriage was expected to be harmonious, but ultimately (and naturally), husbands were in charge. Plutarch wrote, "In a good and wise household, while every activity is carried on by the husband and wife in agreement with each other, it will still be evident that it is the husband who leads and makes the final choice."[15]

Greco-Roman beliefs about marriage and sexuality created a system in which women were almost completely dependent on men but men didn't depend much on women, aside from childbearing. Quite a contrast from what we saw in the last chapter about the interdependence of women and men, isn't it?

SEPARATE SPHERES

For the Greeks and the Romans, women and men not only had distinctly different natures sharing little overlap but even occupied completely separate spheres in society. The philosopher Aristotle, in particular, advanced the theory of the *oikos* (the private domestic sphere) and the *polis* (the public sphere). The two spheres were both separate and

13. Treatise by Phintys, in Holger Thesleff, ed., *The Pythagorean Texts of the Hellenistic Period* (Turku, Finland: Åbo Akademi, 1965), 151–54, quoted in Lefkowitz and Fant, *Women's Life in Greece & Rome*, 104.

14. See D'Ambra, *Roman Women*, 49.

15. Plutarch, *Moralia*, vol. 2, trans. Harold Cherniss (Cambridge: Harvard University Press, 1957), lines 138a–46a.

unequal. Women, due to their weakness and inferiority, were best suited to the domestic sphere of the home. Good wives took care of the home and didn't venture out much on their own. Men, in contrast, had the necessary strength and superiority to rule the world outside the home.[16]

Yet even in the home, the husband and father of the family was the ultimate authority. He was the *paterfamilias*, and quite literally, he ruled the household. The father had the authority to choose his children's spouses, have his married children divorce their spouses, and punish behavior that brought dishonor on the family.[17]

The family was "the basic unit of social organization and moral authority"[18] and was central to the well-being of the state. The Roman government attempted, at times, to recover "family values." Since family was the foundation of society, and since marriage and children were necessary for the continuation of the state, the government made laws to encourage marriage and childbearing. However, these laws were considered an intrusion of the public sphere into the private sphere of the family and were hard to enforce.[19]

Education and Work

These separate spheres defined the appropriate roles for both women and men in society. The differences between the domestic and public spheres influenced how men and women were educated and what kinds of employment and activities were considered suitable for them both.

Young girls were often taught the basics, such as reading and writing, at home by their mothers. Some wealthy children might go to school or have a private tutor, but even then, girls weren't educated extensively. Too much education might make women headstrong and neglectful of their families.[20] What education women did receive was designed to make them useful to men and suitable for their roles as wives and mothers.

---

16. See Estelle B. Freedman, *No Turning Back: The History of Feminism and the Future of Women* (New York: Ballantine Books, 2002), 34.

17. See D'Ambra, *Roman Women*, 49.

18. D'Ambra, 43.

19. See D'Ambra, 34.

20. See Reydams-Schils, *The Roman Stoics*, 154.

Learning was intended to make women "socially docile and compliant" by "reinforc[ing] the dominant position of men in public life and the quiet reserve of modest women."[21]

Young men, and especially those of the upper classes, could expect to spend years in study. They would be taught subjects such as math, Greek and/or Latin, philosophy, literature, and rhetoric. The goal was to make men into good citizens of the state. Men of the working classes were apprenticed in various fields in order to prepare them to earn their living.

Most ancient Greek and Roman women worked at raising their children and caring for their households. Some also worked as domestic help in wealthier homes or in family shops and businesses. The work that women were allowed to do was typically considered to be beneath men.[22]

Religious Life

The concept of separate spheres also shaped women's participation in religion. Women guarded society's well-being by caring for their homes and families and through the hearth cults of Vesta or Hestia. The hearth, or fireplace, was the center of the home—the source of warmth—where women cooked family meals. The goddess of the hearth, Hestia for the Greeks or Vesta for the Romans, was central and crucial in the pantheon of Greek and Roman gods. Women honored the goddess by maintaining the hearth fire and practicing hospitality.[23]

Allowing women to participate in the cultic worship of these goddesses was unusual in Greco-Roman culture. Fathers were usually in charge of worship, even of the household gods; not only were fathers the priests in their homes, but "Greco-Roman authors often ascribed to fathers the power over life and death itself."[24] But the cults of Vesta or Hestia were different. In the *oikos*, women honored the goddess of the

---

21. Lynn H. Cohick, *Women in the World of the Earliest Christians: Illuminating Ancient Ways of Life* (Grand Rapids: Baker Academic, 2009), 247.

22. See D'Ambra, *Roman Women*, 94, 106–7.

23. See Evelyn Wolfson, *Roman Mythology* (Berkeley Heights, NJ: Enslow Publishing, 2002), 17.

24. Brittany E. Wilson, *Unmanly Men: Refigurations of Masculinity in Luke-Acts* (New York: Oxford University Press, 2015), 61.

hearth. In Rome, the cult of Vesta included not just the private hearths of individual homes but also the public hearth, which symbolized the health and security of the state.

To protect Rome's well-being, priestesses known as Vestal Virgins were chosen to serve Vesta. Charged with maintaining the fire of Rome's sacred hearth, they also guarded the Palladium, a sacred object believed to ensure Rome's safety.[25] Being a Vestal Virgin was an honor, but it came with a particular risk. Because the safety of Rome was connected to the worship of Vesta, if Rome was in danger, it was assumed that the Vestal Virgins had broken their vows of chastity. To appease the gods, a Vestal might be executed as a scapegoat.[26]

Politics and Legal Rights

When Sarah Palin ran on the Republican ticket with John McCain, some conservatives debated the appropriateness of a woman running for vice president. They asked whether it was right for a wife and mother to seek election to such a high office. What if she became president?[27]

There wasn't much debate in ancient Greece and Rome about women running for government. The emotional instability brought on by hysteria left women weak and unsuited for leadership and public service.[28] Because of their natural inferiority, women couldn't be trusted to make decisions. They also didn't have the courage and intelligence that men were believed to have. Politics and the military, which belonged to the public sphere, were off-limits to women. "Because the ancient Greeks and later Europeans associated the *polis* with male rationality and the *oikos* with female irrationality, they excluded women from politics. Their weaker natures, Plato argued in *The Republic*, meant that women endangered the state."[29]

25. See Cohick, *Women in the World of the Earliest Christians*, 162.
26. See Cohick, 165.
27. For examples, see David Bayly and Tim Bayly, "Governor Palin and the Order of Creation . . ." *Baylyblog*, September 24, 2008, http://baylyblog.com/blog/2008/09/governor-palin-and-order-creation, and "Is Sarah Palin Being Held to an Unfair Standard?" CNN, last updated September 8, 2008, http://www.cnn.com/2008/POLITICS/09/08/palin.standard.irpt/index.html.
28. See Traniello, "Hysteria and the Wandering Womb."
29. Freedman, *No Turning Back*, 34.

A woman ruling men in politics or in the military meant that society was in trouble. It was inappropriate and unwomanly for women to have authority over men. For example, Mark Antony's wife Fulvia was often described as domineering and overbearing. Plutarch wrote that she "took no thought for spinning or housekeeping, nor would she deign to bear sway over a man of private station, but she wished to rule a ruler and command a commander."[30] As we will see, similar arguments are made about Deborah in the discussions about whether or not women should be civil leaders today.

What about a woman's legal rights in Greece and Rome? As far as the law was concerned, women had the same rights as children—almost none. Fathers, husbands, or other male guardians controlled women's legal actions, and the father of the household had ultimate power and control over his wife and children. If their husbands died, women couldn't manage any inherited property on their own. If their husbands divorced them, women had few legal rights regarding their children.[31] Fathers even had the legal right to kill their children. Unwanted babies—often girls— were exposed to the elements. One man's letter to his sister shows how easily this was done: "If—good luck to you!—you bear offspring, if it is a male, let it live; if it is a female, expose it."[32]

Greco-Roman women also had few legal protections in marriage. If a husband committed adultery, a wife might not be able to divorce him; but the double standard of adultery meant that he could divorce her, keep the children, and prevent her from seeing them. Emperor Romulus, for example, made a law that gave a husband "power to divorce [a wife] for the use of drugs or magic on account of children or for counterfeiting the keys or for adultery," while preventing wives from doing likewise.[33]

30. Plutarch, "Antony," in *Plutarch's Lives*, trans. Bernadotte Perrin, vol. 9, *Demetrius and Antony, Pyrrhus and Caius Marius* (London: William Heinemann, 1920).

31. See Judith Evans Grubbs, *Women and the Law in the Roman Empire: A Sourcebook on Marriage, Divorce and Widowhood* (New York: Routledge, 2002), 198–99, 219.

32. George Milligan, *Selections from the Greek Papyri* (Cambridge: Cambridge University Press, 1910), 33.

33. "Laws of the Kings," trans. Salvatore Riccobono, in Allan Chester Johnson, Paul Robinson Coleman-Norton, and Frank Card Bourne, *Ancient Roman Statutes: A Translation with Introduction, Commentary, Glossary, and Index* (Austin: University of Texas Press, 1961), 3.

If a wife offended her husband, he could kill her and even be applauded for it. In his first-century collection of anecdotes, Valerius Maximus recorded an incident in which a man "beat his wife to death with a cudgel simply because she had taken some wine. Nobody prosecuted him for doing this, and nobody even criticized him; everyone thought that [he] had set an excellent example by punishing his wife in this way for violating the rules of sobriety. If any woman is too fond of drinking wine, she definitely closes the door on all the virtues and opens it to all kinds of mischief."[34]

CONTEMPORARY VIEWS OF A WOMAN'S LOT

Imagine you are living in ancient Rome. If you're a man, and wealthy, you were born to lead. You are well-educated. You live and work in the public sphere, directing government, carrying out commerce, and ruling over your family. And if you aren't faithful to your wife? Well, boys will be boys. If your wife doesn't please you, you can always get a different one.

What if you're a woman in this society? You are at the mercy of your inferior nature. It's not your fault you are emotionally, physically, and morally weaker. You're just naturally suited to stay at home and leave the business of running the world to men. Hopefully, your father and husband provide for you well. Better keep your husband happy, though, or you could be abandoned.

We may look at these descriptions and be shocked by the way women were treated, but some modern authors have said that women were happy until the feminist movement came along.[35] Is this true? Not according to this excerpt of Sophocles's play. The female character says of herself,

Now outside [my father's house] I am nothing. Yet I have often observed woman's nature in this regard, how we are nothing. When we are young

---

34. Valerius Maximus, *Memorable Deeds and Sayings: One Thousand Tales from Ancient Rome*, trans. Henry John Walker (Indianapolis: Hackett Publishing Company, 2004), 211–12.

35. See Mary A. Kassian and Nancy Leigh DeMoss, *True Woman 101: Divine Design; An Eight-Week Study on Biblical Womanhood* (Chicago: Moody Publishers, 2012), p. 123, NOOK.

in our father's house, I think we live the sweetest life of all humankind; for ignorance always brings children up delightfully. But when we have reached maturity and can understand, we are thrust out and sold away from the gods of our fathers and our parents, some to foreigners, some to barbarians, some to joyless houses, some full of reproach. And finally, once a single night has united us, we have to praise our lot and pretend that all is well.[36]

In the last chapter, we saw that God created women and men to serve Him and each other. The Bible's emphasis on serving others and putting their needs before your own was missing from Greco-Roman society. Men with money and power weren't expected to sacrifice their desires for the benefit of their wives and dependents. Women and slaves were supposed to serve their husbands and masters, not the reverse. That's part of what made Christianity so striking. The gospel turned the ancient world upside down (see Acts 17:6).

CHRISTIANITY CHANGES THE WORLD

Can you imagine the effect that the message of the Bible had on Roman society? Think about how Scripture defines authority and submission. Those who are in authority lead by serving. Women and men are created to live, work, and serve together. Its teachings on unity and interdependence were revolutionary.

Consider how Jesus treated women. Women followed Jesus, and the Bible calls them by name. Jesus addressed and interacted kindly with women. He healed women. He listened to women. Women were the first witnesses to the resurrection.

Women were patrons and supporters of the early church. In fact, Christianity was so appealing to women that the Roman emperor Valentinian ordered Christian missionaries to stop proselytizing pagan women.[37]

36. Sophocles, *Tereus*, trans. Helene P. Foley, in Elaine Fantham, Helene Peet Foley, Natalie Boymel Kampen, Sarah B. Pomeroy, and H. Alan Shapiro, *Women in the Classical World: Image and Text* (Oxford: Oxford University Press, 1994), 70.

37. See Rodney Stark, "Reconstructing the Rise of Christianity: The Role of Women,"

What about Christianity appealed to women? For one thing, the early church prohibited abortion and infanticide. Early Christians rescued many abandoned babies who had been left to die by exposure. By forbidding abortion, which often killed women, and infanticide, Christians protected women more than their pagan counterparts did.[38]

Christianity also held men to the same standard of morality as women. Men were expected to remain faithful to their wives and not to have sex outside marriage. Christians discouraged divorce and made it harder to obtain, which protected women from abandonment.[39]

In addition, the church cared for Christian widows and did not require them to remarry. If a wealthy woman became a widow, she was allowed to manage her husband's estate. If a poor woman became a widow, the church provided for her.[40]

Women were treated with greater respect and honor because of Christian teachings. Christian women also had more freedom than pagan Greek and Roman women. Tertullian, a Christian bishop in the early church, advised his wife not to marry a pagan if he were to die—in part because a pagan husband wouldn't allow his wife the liberty that a Christian woman would expect. Would a pagan man let his wife visit poor brothers in their homes and in prison and stay out all night at church services? How would he feel about her greeting others with a holy kiss?[41] Christianity didn't change everything about how women were treated, but it did improve the status of women in the ancient world.

Greco-Roman beliefs about women and men weren't forgotten, as we will see in the next chapter. Hundreds of years later, the Victorians revived these pagan beliefs and attempted to baptize them as Christian. Using Bible verses as proof texts, Victorians propped up these beliefs about the nature of women and men and the separate spheres. That

---

Sociology of Religion 56, no. 3 (Autumn 1995): 231.

38. See Stark, 232.

39. See Stark, 235–36.

40. See Stark, 236.

41. See Tertullian, "To His Wife," trans. S. Thelwall, in *Ante-Nicene Fathers*, vol. 4, *Tertullian, Part Fourth; Minucius Felix; Commodian; Origen, Part First and Second*, ed. A. Cleveland Coxe, Alexander Roberts, and James Donaldson (Buffalo, NY, 1885), 46.

combination of pagan ideas and misapplied Scriptures is what we will discuss next.

DISCUSSION QUESTIONS

1. What did the Greeks and Romans believe about the nature of women?
2. What did the Greeks and Romans believe about the nature of men?
3. What was the double standard for morality?
4. What was the concept of the separate spheres?
5. How did Christianity change life for women in the ancient world?

4

"THE ANGEL IN THE HOUSE"

WOMEN AND MEN IN THE VICTORIAN ERA

*The Queen is most anxious to enlist every one who can speak or write to
join in checking this mad, wicked folly of "Woman's Rights," with all its
attendant horrors, on which her poor feeble sex is bent, forgetting every
sense of womanly feeling and propriety. . . . It is a subject which makes
the Queen so furious that she cannot contain herself. God created men
and women different—then let them remain each in their own position.*

QUEEN VICTORIA[1]

When I was in my early 20s, I was single and wishing I weren't. I picked
up a book on waiting and patience. Written by older Christian women, the
book attempted to encourage young, single women to live their lives, grow
in faith, and not be the least bit worried about the lack of young men who
were asking them out. The authors seemed to have forgotten what it was
like to be young and unmarried. They lacked compassion and empathy.
I got so fed up that I threw the book across the room.

1. Queen Victoria to Sir Theodore Martin, 29 May 1870, quoted in Frank Hardie,
The Political Influence of Queen Victoria: 1861–1901 (repr., London: Frank Cass and Co,
1963), 140.

As I've become more familiar with the books and conferences that are marketed to Christian women, I have seen this kind of disconnect between authors and their intended audiences in other ways. For example, some Christian authors have built their platform by teaching women not to work outside the home or pursue careers but to find contentment as wives and mothers . . . and they've done so by pursuing careers as authors and conference speakers who work outside their homes.

That same "Do as I say, not as I do" attitude is evident in Queen Victoria's objection to the "mad, wicked folly of 'Women's Rights.'" Victoria was the leader of a nation and the head of the Church of England. Why wouldn't she support "women's rights"? Because the movement for women's rights went against what many Victorians believed about the nature of women and their proper sphere.

The Victorian era, which spanned the reign of Queen Victoria (1837–1901), is a favorite for historical fiction. Books and movies depict ladies in dresses with impossibly tiny waists, fine-mannered gentlemen in suits, lists of societal rules to follow. Many of the plots revolve around a woman's reputation—sometimes being protected, sometimes being destroyed. It can seem so glamorous and pretty on the outside. But underneath the glamour lay pagan beliefs about the nature of women and men.

A lot had happened over the centuries. With the rise of Christianity and the fall of Rome, the influence of Greco-Roman culture had waned. By the end of the Middle Ages, orthodox biblical teaching had also waned.

Two distinct movements brought about drastic changes in western civilization and the church. The Protestant Reformation, which began in the 1500s, set about to restore what the Bible actually teaches about salvation and faith. And, starting in the 1300s, the Renaissance, like the Reformation, returned to earlier ideas. But it wasn't about rediscovering Scripture. During the Renaissance, scholars began to study older Greco-Roman texts. The influence of ancient Greece and Rome appeared everywhere—in artwork, literature, mythology, philosophy, and even medicine. Old, pagan themes about women, men, and gender resurfaced—such as the separate spheres, the dangers of educating women, the defective female body and mind, the unsuitableness of women for working in the public sphere, and the devaluation of work that was done by women.

Victorian beliefs about men and women are worth focusing on because the Victorian era, more than any other, was a unique blend of several streams of thought. Victorians combined the Greco-Roman philosophy of the Renaissance, the technological advancements of the Industrial Revolution, and the evolutionary science of Darwinism. All of this they added to existing Christian religious and moral beliefs.

WHY? BECAUSE SCIENCE!

Victorian beliefs about women and men weren't new, but there was something novel about them. The Victorians had an additional support for their beliefs: science!

When Charles Darwin published his famous book *On the Origin of Species* in 1859, it made a splash. Not everyone agreed with his evolutionary theory, but his theory was useful—especially if you believed men were naturally stronger and smarter than women. According to Darwin, evolution resulted in different natures for men and women—and, not surprisingly, men were superior. Darwin wrote that "man is more courageous, pugnacious, and energetic than woman, and has a more inventive genius" and that man has achieved "a higher eminence, in whatever he takes up, than woman can attain."[2]

Not only did women have inferior natures, but their bodies and brains were smaller than men's. According to evolutionary thinkers of the day, having a smaller brain meant that women were less evolved than, less intelligent than, and inferior to men. During a medical lecture, one man explained that women simply didn't have the capacity for intelligence: "Woman has a head almost too small for intellect but just big enough for love."[3] Gustave Le Bon, a contemporary psychologist and sociologist, explained, "[Women] represent the most inferior forms of human

2. Charles Darwin, *The Descent of Man and Selection in Relation to Sex* (New York, 1871), 2:301, 311, quoted in Estelle B. Freedman, *No Turning Back: The History of Feminism and the Future of Women* (New York: Ballantine Books, 2002), 37–38.

3. Charles Meigs, *Lecture on Some of the Distinctive Characteristics of the Female* (Philadelphia, 1847), 17, quoted in Barbara Welter, "The Cult of True Womanhood: 1820–1860," *Atlantic Monthly* 18, no. 2 (Summer 1966): 160.

evolution and . . . are closer to children and savages than to an adult, civilized man. They excel in fickleness, inconstancy, absence of thought and logic, and incapacity to reason." Although he acknowledged that "some distinguished women" may surpass "the average man," he concluded that "they are as exceptional as the birth of any monstrosity, as, for example, of a gorilla with two heads; consequently, we may neglect them entirely."[4] Yes, he really did compare intelligent women to two-headed gorillas, right before he dismissed such women completely. Can you imagine being his wife? Or the wife of any man who believed the same about women?

Since women were smaller and less evolved, they were basically children. That was all the more reason for men to be in charge. Women's magazines, written by both women and men, encouraged women to show a childlike dependence on men. And if men abused or mistreated them, well, it was best to keep quiet about that:

> True feminine genius is ever timid, doubtful, and clingingly dependent; a perpetual childhood.[5]

> If [your husband] is abusive, never retort.[6]

> To suffer and be silent under suffering, seems the great command [a woman] has to obey.[7]

Victorian science taught that women weren't as healthy as men. Women fainted more often than men. Women had monthly periods that

---

4. Gustave Le Bon, "Anatomical and Mathematical Researches into the Laws of the Variations of Brain Volume and their Relation to Intelligence" (1879), quoted in Stephen Jay Gould, *The Panda's Thumb: More Reflections in Natural History* (New York: W. W. Norton, 1980), 155.

5. Grace Greenwood to an unrecognized poetess, June 1846, in *Greenwood Leaves: A Collection of Sketches and Letters*, 2nd ed. (Boston, 1850), 310, quoted in Welter, "The Cult of True Womanhood," 160.

6. Colesworth Pinckney, ed., *The Lady's Token: or Gift of Friendship* (Nashua, NH, 1848), 120, quoted in Welter, "The Cult of True Womanhood," 161.

7. "Woman," *Godey's Lady's Book*, 3 (July 1831), 110, quoted in Welter, "The Cult of True Womanhood," 162.

obviously weakened them. Like Galen, Victorian doctors believed that the uterus and menstrual cycles were the root of most, if not all, of women's illnesses. Men had heart disease, lung disease, and stomach disorders, but women had "female complaints"[8] that were "merely the sympathetic reactions or the symptoms of one disease, namely, a disease of the womb."[9]

Female complaints and weakened health started with puberty. Since women were at the mercy of their reproductive systems, they were delicate, weak, irritable, and easily tired, which made them prone to hysteria. If women weren't careful, they might overextend themselves and end up nervous wrecks. What was worse, they might pass their weakness and nervous conditions along to their children. To be on the safe side, women were encouraged to focus their limited energies on bearing strong and healthy children.[10]

BAPTIZING PAGAN IDEAS

The Victorian era is a significant link between ancient Greece and Roman and our society today. Some of the greatest damage the Victorians did was through attempting to incorporate the older pagan ideas with Christianity. After the Victorian era, ancient Greek and Roman beliefs about women and men were taught as if they were biblical.

How did the Victorians combine Christianity with the older pagan ideas about gender? One way was by misapplying Scripture. The authors of Victorian literature and magazines took Bible verses out of context to reinforce their beliefs about the nature of women and men and their proper spheres. For example, one book for young brides taught that women were softer than men and were dependent on them by God's design.

Woman inherits the greater portion of the curse pronounced in Eden's garden—"I will greatly multiply thy sorrow," the Lord hath said and

8. Catherine J. Lavender, "Notes on The Cult of Domesticity and True Womanhood," The College of Staten Island, accessed July 10, 2018, https://csivc.csi.cuny.edu/history/files/lavender/386/truewoman.pdf, p. 5.

9. M. E. Dirix, *Woman's Complete Guide to Health* (New York, 1869).

10. See Lavender, "Notes on The Cult of Domesticity," 5.

shall he not do it? But he is also a safe refuge in distress, and in his mercy he has given you many seasons and opportunities of retirement and communion with him, which the ordinary occupations of man deny; he has also, generally speaking, given you a softness of heart, a liveliness of affection, a desire of dependence, a reliance upon aid in difficulties, peculiarly favourable to that state of mind which disposes you to seek assistance from, and to repose trust in him.[11]

The Victorians found support for their belief that women belonged in the home in Paul's encouragement that young women be "keepers at home" (Titus 2:5 KJV). William Alcott, an influential Victorian author and a cousin of Louisa May Alcott, explained that a woman "cannot discharge the duties of a wife, much less those of a mother, unless she prefers home to all other places, and is only led abroad from a sense of duty, and not from choice."[12]

Staying at home was the duty of a wife—a duty that was owed to God. "Ask not, 'Why should I keep at home?' the answer is, because it is your duty to your servant—your children—your husband—your God!"[13] To be a "true woman," to desire nothing more than to have a husband and children to care for, was the "holiest design a woman can entertain."[14]

TRUE WOMANHOOD VERSUS VICTORIAN MASCULINITY

A few years ago, I read a book called *True Woman 101: Divine Design; An Eight-Week Study on Biblical Womanhood*. Maybe you've read it or another book like it. Or maybe you've seen the *True Woman* conferences

11. Arthur Freeling, *The Young Bride's Book: Being Hints for Regulating the Conduct of Married Women* (London, 1839), 30–31.

12. William A. Alcott, *The Young Wife, or Duties of Woman in the Marriage Relation*, 4th ed. (Boston, 1838), 83.

13. Freeling, *The Young Bride's Book*, 86.

14. *Fascinating Womanhood, or the Art of Attracting Men: A Practical Course of Lessons in the Underlying Principles by Which Women Attract Men—Leading to the Proposal and Culminating in Marriage* (St. Louis: The Psychology Press, 1922), 1:24.

or blog. There's even a "True Woman Manifesto" you may have signed. The concept of true womanhood is everywhere in Christian circles.

But there was an earlier true woman movement. The Victorians elevated true womanhood to an art form. In order to be truly feminine, Victorian women had to be pure, pious, submissive, and domestic. If they were successful in this, men would also succeed. If they failed, society would collapse. The women's magazines and religious literature of the 1800s taught women about these virtues and how to achieve them.[15]

The Victorians defined women and men in terms of opposites. Instead of purity, piety, submission, and domesticity, Victorian masculinity was defined by activity, independence, rationality, and dominance.[16] Men were providers, protectors, and leaders of both home and country.

Submission versus Authority

As we saw in the first chapter, submission and authority are part of who we are as humans created in God's image. By the time of the Victorians, the emphasis on submission as a Christian virtue had waned. Submission became a feminine trait, while reason and intellect were considered masculine.[17]

Victorians believed that submission was at the heart of feminine nature because God had made women to submit. A true woman was submissive. If not, she was going against the created order.[18] As one popular women's magazine explained, "In whatever situation of life a woman is placed, from her cradle to her grave, a spirit of obedience and submission, pliability of temper, and humility of mind, are required of her."[19]

Authority was a masculine attribute. Men naturally had authority in all relationships, and especially in the family. A husband, as the ruler, had the last word in all decisions. "In the domestic constitution this superiority

---

15. See Barbara Welter, "The Cult of True Womanhood."

16. See E. Anthony Rotundo, *American Manhood: Transformations in Masculinity from the Revolution to the Modern Era* (New York: HarperCollins, 1993), 145.

17. See Rotundo, 11.

18. See Welter, "The Cult of True Womanhood," 159.

19. *The Young Lady's Book: A Manual of Elegant Recreations, Exercises, and Pursuits* (New York, 1830), 28, quoted in Welter, "The Cult of True Womanhood," 159.

vests in the husband: he is the head, the lawgiver, the ruler," wrote John Angell James, another well-respected Victorian author. "In all matters touching the little world in the house, he is to direct, not indeed without taking counsel with his wife, but in all discordancy of view, *he*, unless he choose to waive his right, is to decide; and to his decision the wife should yield, and yield with grace and cheerfulness."[20]

When a woman married, she became legally part of her husband. This, known as *coverture*, was the legal aspect of the "one flesh" of marriage. Just as a husband and wife became one flesh in marriage, they became one person legally. Naturally, that one person was represented by the husband.[21]

Women were treated like perpetual children and were expected to depend on men to care for them. Women couldn't own property, manage money, or run a business independently. It wasn't in a woman's nature to worry about such things, and women's smaller brains couldn't be expected to handle money well. It would be too much for them. A similar argument was made for why women couldn't vote. Their husbands' votes represented theirs anyway.[22]

True womanhood was about submission. Victorian masculinity was about dominance.

Piety versus Muscular Christianity

Submission wasn't the only virtue that changed over time. If you remember, the Greeks and the Romans believed that men were morally superior to women. But the Victorians turned this upside down. Being morally superior might keep men from being ambitious, assertive, and powerful.[23] So women were given a new responsibility: upholding the virtue of society. Historian Barbara Welter describes the thinking: "Religion or piety was the core of woman's virtue, the source of her strength. . . . Religion belonged to woman by divine right, a gift of God and nature.

---

20. John Angell James, *The Family Monitor, or A Help to Domestic Happiness* (Birmingham, 1828), 56, emphasis in original.

21. See Mary Lyndon Shanley, *Feminism, Marriage, and the Law in Victorian England, 1850–1895* (Princeton: Princeton University Press, 1989), 8.

22. We'll return to this topic in later chapters.

23. See Rotundo, *American Manhood*, 16.

. . . She would be another, better Eve, working in cooperation with the Redeemer. . . . The world would be reclaimed for God through her suffering."[24] Women were still considered mentally and emotionally inferior to men, but now they were considered more moral. Their morality and virtue maintained the health of the nation—from the safe confines of the home, of course. Sounds like an improvement, doesn't it? Surely it's better than being considered the source of evil in the world. Well, yes and no.[25]

As the ancient Greeks and Romans did, Victorians considered women to be the keepers of the hearth, whose virtue protected and saved their husbands and society. Welter writes, "This 'peculiar susceptibility' to religion was given her for a reason: 'the vestal flame of piety, lighted up by Heaven in the breast of woman' would throw its beams into the naughty world of men. So far would its candle power reach that the 'Universe might be Enlightened, Improved, and Harmonized by WOMAN!!' . . . bringing the world back 'from its revolt and sin.'"[26] Since women were guarding society with their piety, men were free to behave as they needed to in the world. The double standard of behavior that Christianity had overturned reappeared during the Victorian era.

In place of traditional Christian observances such as church attendance, which were deemed feminine, men embraced a "muscular Christianity"—"Using metaphors of fitness and body-building, Christian thinkers imagined a strong, forceful Jesus with a religion to match. In 1896, *Century Magazine* called for a 'vigorous, robust, muscular Christianity . . . devoid of all the etcetera of creed,' a Christianity 'which shows the character and manliness of Christ.' This hardy Jesus with rippling muscles was 'no prince of peace-at-any-price.' He was an enforcer who 'turned again and again on the snarling pack of His pious enemies and made them slink away.'"[27] Does this sound familiar? It might, if you've listened to Mark Driscoll. True womanhood required piety. Victorian masculinity required strength and muscles.

24. Welter, "The Cult of True Womanhood," 152.
25. See Susan Hill Lindley, *"You Have Stept Out of Your Place": A History of Women and Religion in America* (Louisville: Westminster John Knox Press, 1996), 52.
26. Welter, "The Cult of True Womanhood," 152.
27. Rotundo, *American Manhood*, 224.

Purity versus Independence

Christianity had made a significant change in terms of what was expected of men. Sexual purity wasn't just for women. However, as the Victorians shifted virtues like submission and piety to women, purity became an exclusively feminine trait. Men couldn't be expected to be pure; they were powerless against their strong male urges. That meant that women had to protect their own purity and save men from themselves. If a woman was successful, then she could present her greatest gift, her virginity, to her husband on her wedding night.[28]

As in the plots of the historical fictions we mentioned earlier, to be a "fallen woman" was a fate worse than death. This was why women—at least the upper-class ones—were so carefully chaperoned. Even speaking to a man without a proper chaperone could endanger a woman's reputation, putting her at the mercy of ruthless men who would take advantage of her unprotected state. And since men couldn't control themselves, if anything happened, guess whose fault it was?

As for the men, they had to prove they could provide sufficiently for a wife before they married. For some, that could take years. What could a man do until then? The answer wasn't patience and celibacy. The answer was prostitutes. Not all women were expected to stay at home and pursue purity. Men, married or not, had needs—needs that virtuous ladies couldn't always fulfill—and so prostitution was considered a necessary evil in Victorian society. Prostitution was in everyone's best interest—or so the argument went. If men didn't have access to prostitutes, they might "be tempted to seduce young ladies of their acquaintance."[29]

As in the double standard of the Greeks and Romans, Victorian men weren't expected to be faithful to their wives, before or after marriage. If a man visited brothels or took a mistress, his wife couldn't do much about it. She couldn't divorce him. But if a woman was unfaithful, her husband could divorce her. He could even sue the other man for damages, since he had lost valuable property—his wife and her affections.[30]

28. See Welter, "The Cult of True Womanhood," 154–55.

29. Editorial, the New Orleans *Mascot*, June 1892, 37, quoted in Freedman, *No Turning Back*, 141.

30. See Shanley, *Feminism, Marriage, and the Law in Victorian England*, 24.

Women didn't have many options for leaving a bad marriage. If a woman's husband was violent, she might be allowed to live separately from him, but she couldn't divorce him. Even if she were able to get a separation, the cards were stacked against her. Women didn't have legal rights to their children, so she would have to leave her children behind.[31] She couldn't provide for her children if she could take them with her. If she left, she'd be without home, family, protection, money, resources, and employment. Given this, what woman would leave?[32]

True womanhood meant purity and faithfulness. Victorian masculinity meant independence and freedom from restrictions.

Domestic Sphere versus Public Sphere

After the fall of Rome and the rise of Christianity, women and men often worked side by side in family businesses and farms. While the separate spheres didn't quite disappear, life and necessity pushed them into the background. People did what they needed to in order to survive.

The Industrial Revolution disconnected work and home. Men and women left the fields and family businesses in order to work in factories and industries in the cities. Urban jobs offered better opportunities. As a result, the family economy changed dramatically. Families didn't work together at home. Work and home became separate worlds. Men left home to work and earn wages. Women, who were paid less and given fewer opportunities than men, tended to stay home. Some women, usually working-class women, worked in factories or in other homes as domestic help, but only if they weren't married. Married women were expected to take care of their own houses and children and to leave the paid work to their husbands.[33]

You can imagine the changes this made to the family economy. Middle-class families weren't growing their food and producing the goods that they needed; men worked for money that bought food and goods. The meaning of work also changed. Work became valuable based

31. See Shanley, 131.
32. See Shanley, 170.
33. See Shanley, 6–7.

on how much money it made. Men were "breadwinners" who earned the money to support a family. The work that women did in their own homes was unpaid and increasingly less valuable. Women, if they had to work, were seen as supplementing the family income. It didn't matter if they were actually supporting themselves and a family on their own. Well-paying jobs were for men. It wasn't in a woman's nature to provide for her family.[34]

As work and home became disconnected from each other, the separate spheres moved back into the foreground. Victorians believed that men, with their ambition, authority, independence, and rationality, were naturally suited to inhabit the public sphere of business and politics. Women, with their natural piety, purity, and submission, belonged to the domestic sphere of the home.

Home was the sanctuary where men could find peace and rest from the harsh world. Just like the ancient Greeks and Romans, the Victorians believed that the home was sacred: "It is the place of Peace; the shelter, not only from all injury, but from all terror, doubt, and division. . . . But so far as it is a sacred place, a vestal temple, a temple of the hearth watched over by Household Gods, before those faces none may come but those whom they can receive with love."[35] Women were the "Angel in the House" who brought men closer to God.[36] From the domestic fireside, women could reform the world.[37]

Marriage and motherhood were a woman's purpose and highest end. Education was acceptable as long as it helped women to be good wives and mothers. But educating women could be dangerous—it could overtax their weaker bodies and ruin their chances of having children.[38] And if

34. See Freedman, *No Turning Back*, 124.

35. John Ruskin, "Of Queens' Gardens," in *Sesame and Lilies: Two Lectures Delivered at Manchester in 1864* (London, 1865), 148.

36. See Coventry Patmore, *The Angel in the House* (London, 1854).

37. See T. S. Arthur, *The Lady at Home: or, Leaves from the Every-Day Book of an American Woman* (Philadelphia, 1847), 177–78, quoted in Welter, "The Cult of True Womanhood," 162–63.

38. See Kathryn Hughes, "Gender Roles in the 19th Century," the British Library, May 15, 2014, http://www.bl.uk/romantics-and-victorians/articles/gender-roles-in-the-19th-century.

women were educated like men, they might go to work, and civilization as the Victorians knew it would end. As Gustave LeBon explained, "The day when, misunderstanding the inferior occupations which nature has given her, women leave the home and take part in our battles; on this day a social revolution will begin, and everything that maintains the sacred ties of the family will disappear."[39] So perhaps it's not surprising that women were taught mostly housekeeping, needlework, piano, painting, and similar "domestic accomplishments."

Did Victorian women ever work outside the home? As much as true womanhood was supposed to be a universal standard for all women, very few women could actually achieve it—especially the domestic part of it.[40] Middle-class women wanted to stay home, although not all of them could. Unmarried or widowed women sometimes had to support themselves or their families. Working-class women had to help to provide for their families and didn't expect to stay at home.

Ironically, in order for the Victorian system to work, some women *had* to work outside their own homes. Upper-class women relied on nannies, governesses, cooks, and maids to maintain their domestic standard. True women were models of domesticity, but most true women had other women who did the actual domestic work. For the most part, society ignored the contradiction of women working to support women who were not working.

Some types of jobs were strictly off-limits for women, however. Science, engineering, medicine, and the law were fields for men only, since such careers went against a woman's very nature. For a woman to be successful in such a harsh environment, she would have to become less feminine, less desirable to men, and less suitable as a wife and mother. It was for the best for women to stay at home and leave the important jobs to men.[41]

Society's survival depended on true womanhood and Victorian masculinity. Men ruled the world, and women upheld society. Welter sums

39. Le Bon, "Anatomical and Mathematical Researches," quoted in Gould, *The Panda's Thumb*, 155.
40. See Lindley, *"You Have Stept Out of Your Place,"* 56.
41. See Rotundo, *American Manhood*, 213–14.

it up: "If anyone, male or female, dared to tamper with the complex of virtues which made up True Womanhood, he was damned immediately as an enemy of God, of civilization and of the Republic. It was a fearful obligation, a solemn responsibility, which the nineteenth-century American woman had—to uphold the pillars of the temple with her frail white hand."[42]

IN THEIR OWN WORDS

Not all men appreciated women for being angels in the house and keepers of the hearth. Like today, some men complained that society was too feminized. They believed that women, at home and in schools, were raising boys to be weak and nervous. They wanted a return to real masculinity.[43] As Henry James wrote in his 1886 novel *The Bostonians*, "The whole generation is womanized; the masculine tone is passing out of the world; it's a feminine, a nervous, hysterical, chattering, canting age, an age of hollow phrases and false delicacy and exaggerated solicitudes and coddled sensibilities, which, if we don't soon look out, will usher in the reign of mediocrity, of the feeblest and flattest and the most pretentious that has ever been."[44]

And what about women? Were they happy and content with their lives? Charlotte Bronte, alias Currer Bell,[45] spoke about the Victorian expectations for women through her heroine, Jane Eyre:

> Women are supposed to be very calm generally: but women feel just as men feel; they need exercise for their faculties, and a field for their efforts as much as their brothers do; they suffer from too rigid a restraint, too absolute a stagnation, precisely as men would suffer; and it is narrow-minded in their more privileged fellow-creatures to say

42. Welter, "The Cult of True Womanhood," 152.

43. See Rotundo, *American Manhood*, 252.

44. Henry James, *The Bostonians* (Baltimore: Penguin Books, 1966), 290, quoted in Rotundo, *American Manhood*, 252.

45. Many women published under male pseudonyms, since writing and publishing for profit weren't entirely respectable for women.

that they ought to confine themselves to making puddings and knitting stockings, to playing on the piano and embroidering bags. It is thoughtless to condemn them, or laugh at them if they seek to do more or learn more than custom has pronounced necessary for their sex.[46]

By the end of the Victorian era, women were beginning to speak up about their concerns. They also began to call for changes. You've probably heard of the suffrage movement. But there was so much more at stake than women voting. In the next chapter, we'll look at the how the feminist movement began. Who were the first-wave feminists, and what did they want?

DISCUSSION QUESTIONS

1. Were you surprised by the quote by Queen Victoria? Why or why not?
2. How did Darwinian evolution give support to pre-existing ideas about women and men?
3. How did the Victorians combine Christianity with Greco-Roman ideas about gender?
4. What was the Victorian meaning of *true womanhood*?
5. What was the meaning of *Victorian masculinity*?

46. Charlotte Bronte, *Jane Eyre* (New York, 1847), 42–43.

5

"VOTES FOR WOMEN AND CHASTITY FOR MEN"

Would men but generously snap our chains, and be content with rational fellowship instead of slavish obedience, they would find us more observant daughters, more affectionate sisters, more faithful wives, more reasonable mothers—in a word, better citizens. . . . The affection of husbands and wives cannot be pure when they have so few sentiments in common, and when so little confidence is established at home, as must be the case when their pursuits are so different. That intimacy from which tenderness should flow, will not, cannot subsist between the vicious.

MARY WOLLSTONECRAFT[1]

What comes to mind when you hear the word *feminist*? Maybe you think of women protesting and wearing pink knit hats. Maybe you think of organizations like the National Organization for Women (NOW) and

---

1. Mary Wollstonecraft, *A Vindication of the Rights of Women: with Strictures on Political and Moral Subjects*, 3rd ed. (London, 1796), 342, 448.

the abortion-rights group NARAL. Maybe you think of the famous quote "A woman needs a man like a fish needs a bicycle."[2]

The first-wave feminist movement began in earnest in the 1800s. At the beginning, it was a movement to reform society and to promote the fundamental equality of women and men. When feminists spoke of equality, they weren't saying that men and women were the same and should be interchangeable. Early feminists thought that women should be wives and mothers—the ones who were most responsible for the home and children. But they wanted changes. They wanted women to be treated better and have better opportunities.

Despite claims to the contrary, the feminist movement didn't make women angry and discontent. Women had been expressing their frustrations and concerns with how they were being treated for hundreds of years. Nor did first-wave feminists want to make women independent and men unnecessary. Instead, they believed that their changes would be good for society—for both women *and* men. If their reforms were enacted, men and women could work together as equals and live together as partners.[3]

As we saw, Victorian society held that women were morally superior to men. First-wave feminists appealed to that belief in support of their reforms. Since women were supposed to be the keepers of morality and to be responsible for upholding society, then they should have a voice in political and social decisions.

In 1848, the first US women's rights convention was held in Seneca Falls, New York. At the convention, Elizabeth Cady Stanton read a "Declaration of Sentiments" that described the goals of this new feminist movement. The goals included the right for women to vote (suffrage), the end of coverture, the right for women to own and manage their own property, access to better educational and employment opportunities for

2. This quote was made famous by Gloria Steinem, but it was actually coined by Irina Dunn in 1970. See "The meaning and origin of the expression: A woman needs a man like a fish needs a bicycle," The Phrase Finder, accessed June 19, 2018, http://www.phrases.org.uk/meanings/414150.html.

3. See Elizabeth Wolstenholme Elmy, *Women and the Law* (Congleton, UK, 1896), quoted in Mary Lyndon Shanley, *Feminism, Marriage, and the Law in Victorian England, 1850–1895* (Princeton: Princeton University Press, 1989), 189.

women, legal rights for women in divorce including custody of their children, an end to the double standard of morality, an end to the separate spheres, and improvements in women's role in the church.[4]

IMPROVING THE LEGAL RIGHTS OF WOMEN

Many women had worked alongside men in the fight to end slavery. Once slavery was abolished in many countries, women continued to have limited rights. Although they had more legal protections than slaves, early feminists drew parallels between slavery and women's lack of rights. As John Stuart Mill, a British philosopher and economist, wrote,

> The wife is the actual bond-servant of her husband: no less so, as far as legal obligation goes, than slaves commonly so called. She vows a lifelong obedience to him at the altar, and is held to it all through her life by law. . . . The two are called "one person in law," for the purpose of inferring that whatever is hers is his, but the parallel inference is never drawn that whatever is his is hers; the maxim is not applied against the man, except to make him responsible to third parties for her acts, as a master is for the acts of his slaves or his cattle.[5]

While first-wave feminists were concerned with many legal issues, the ones they are known for are women's suffrage, the end of coverture, and the temperance movement. Behind the drive for each of these was a desire to improve the lives of women. Women needed a voice in government. They needed greater freedom to represent themselves legally, and they needed protection from abusive men.

Women's Suffrage

Suffrage is probably the best known of first-wave feminism's goals. Some feminists argued that women *must* have the vote because they

4. See Elizabeth Cady Stanton, "Declaration of Sentiments," in *The Selected Papers of Elizabeth Cady Stanton & Susan B. Anthony*, vol. 1, *In the School of Anti-Slavery: 1840 to 1866*, ed. Ann D. Gordon (New Brunswick, NJ: Rutgers University Press, 1997), 78–82.

5. John Stuart Mill, *The Subjection of Women* (London, 1869), 55–56.

were morally superior to men. How else could society get rid of corrupt politicians? Other feminists argued that women needed to vote so they could improve women's status in society—especially in legal matters. The suffragist movement appealed to women's inherent right, as citizens, to vote. Women were citizens, subject to the nation's laws and taxes, but with no say in political matters. That was taxation without representation! Denying women their right to vote was undemocratic.

Ending Coverture

First-wave feminists were also very concerned about coverture. As we have seen, coverture meant that women were represented by their husbands in all legal matters. Women couldn't own property or manage their own money. In good marriages and with kind husbands, this might not might not be so bad, although it was still limiting. But women who had cruel or immoral husbands could end up with nothing and with no means of providing for or protecting themselves or their children.[6] The legal system trapped abused and mistreated women and children under the control of their abusers.

> It is this which frustrates all attempts to maintain the power but protect the woman against its abuses. In no other case (except that of a child) is the person who has been proved judicially to have suffered an injury, replaced under the physical power of the culprit who inflicted it. Accordingly wives, even in the most extreme and protracted cases of bodily ill usage, hardly ever dare avail themselves of the laws made for their protection: and if, in a moment of irrepressible indignation, or by the interference of neighbours, they are induced to do so, their whole effort afterwards is to disclose as little as they can, and to beg off their tyrant from his merited chastisement.[7]

In order to protect women and children, feminists argued that married women needed to be able to own property, to separate from or

6. See Shanley, *Feminism, Marriage, and the Law*, 68.
7. Mill, *The Subjection of Women*, 26.

divorce abusive husbands, and to initiate divorce proceedings if their husbands committed adultery. Women also needed to have custody of their children.[8]

ADDRESSING THE DOUBLE STANDARD OF MORALITY

First-wave feminists also wanted to put an end to the double standard of morality. They wanted men to be held to the same high standards that women were. An early feminist slogan combined female suffrage with male morality: "Votes for Women and Chastity for Men." Men who were unfaithful to their wives often exploited women through prostitution. In doing so, they contracted sexually transmitted diseases such as syphilis that they passed on to their innocent wives and children.[9] If men were held to the same high standard as women, then women and children would benefit.

The many feminists who were against the sale of alcohol weren't being meddlesome busybodies. The temperance movement began because of this same concern for women and children. It wasn't prudishness that made women speak about the "evils of drink." Many feminists had seen or experienced the abuse that women and children suffered at the hands of drunk men. As Susan B. Anthony wrote,

> Though, as a class, women are much less frequently given to the vices of drunkenness and prostitution than men, it is freely conceded that they are by far the greater sufferers—compelled, by their position in society, to depend on men for subsistence, for food, clothes, and shelter, for every chance, even, to earn a dollar, they have no way of escape from the besotted victims of appetite and passion with whom their lot shall chance to be cast. They must endure, if not actually embrace, those twin vices embodied, as they so often are in the person of husband and lover,

8. See Shanley, *Feminism, Marriage, and the Law*, 17.

9. See Jan Marsh, "Gender Ideology & Separate Spheres in the 19th Century," Victoria and Albert Museum, accessed June 19, 2018, http://www.vam.ac.uk/content/articles /g/gender-ideology-and-separate-spheres-19th-century/.

father and brother, employer and employe [sic], and no one doubts that the suffering of the sober, virtuous woman in legal subjection to the presence and mastership of a drunken libertine, husband and father over herself and her children, not only from physical abuse, but from spiritual shame and mortification must be such as wretched man himself cannot possibly comprehend.[10]

IMPROVING EDUCATION AND EMPLOYMENT OPPORTUNITIES FOR WOMEN

Today we may take for granted that women can attend college, get a degree, get a job, and start a career. But it wasn't always that way. The early feminists worked hard to make higher education and better employment opportunities possible for women.

Women who needed to provide for themselves also needed better options for work. So that they wouldn't be lured into prostitution, women needed to be given better education. Susan B. Anthony argued that women needed to be educated and given equal access to "lucrative employment."[11] Elizabeth Cady Stanton wrote that education would allow a woman to do "whatever special work she may be compelled to do."[12]

Having better educational and employment opportunities for women was about more than helping them to earn money or provide for themselves and their families. It was about allowing them to pursue their gifts and abilities. Harriet Taylor Mill, wife of John Stuart Mill, argued that women shouldn't be told that something wasn't their "proper sphere." Instead, men and women should be free to pursue whatever occupation suited them best: "Let every occupation be open to all, without favour or

10. Susan B. Anthony, "Social Purity" (lecture, Mercantile Library, St. Louis, March 14, 1875), in *The Selected Papers of Elizabeth Cady Stanton & Susan B. Anthony*, vol. 3, *National Protection for National Citizens: 1873 to 1880*, ed. Ann D. Gordon (New Brunswick, NJ: Rutgers University Press, 2003), 156.

11. Anthony, 162.

12. Elizabeth Cady Stanton, "The Solitude of Self," in *The Selected Papers of Elizabeth Cady Stanton & Susan B. Anthony*, vol. 5, *Their Place Inside the Body-Politic: 1887 to 1895*, ed. Ann D. Gordon (New Brunswick, NJ: Rutgers University Press, 2009), 425.

discouragement to any, and employments will fall into the hands or those men or women who are found by experience to be most capable of worthily exercising them. There need be no fear that women will take out of the hands of men any occupation which men perform better than they."[13]

MARRIAGE AND COMPANIONSHIP

First-wave feminists believed that marriage should be about more than economics or procreation. Marriage should be about partnership, love, friendship, and companionship as well.

In some ways, all first-wave feminist goals led to this end. If men and women had equal legal rights, if men and women had equal opportunities for education and employment, if men and women had the same standards for morality and marital faithfulness, then women and men could be friends and co-laborers in marriage. A woman wouldn't have to marry a man just because he could provide for her. An educated woman with her own work experiences could be an intellectual partner with her husband. As Mary Wollstonecraft said, women would be "more observant daughters, more affectionate sisters, more faithful wives, more reasonable mothers—in a word, better citizens."[14] Instead of living in separate spheres and leading separate lives, women and men could live and work together as partners who were equally valuable.

THE ROLE OF WOMEN IN THE CHURCH

Today most people agree that women's voting rights, legal protections, improved education, and better employment opportunities were useful goals. But today we associate other, more controversial things with the feminist movement—for example, women's ordination. Yet ordination was a topic of disagreement even within the first-wave feminist movement. Similarly, when Elizabeth Cady Stanton put together a group

---

13. Harriet Taylor Mill, "The Enfranchisement of Women," in *The Essential Feminist Reader*, ed. Estelle B. Freedman (New York: Modern Library, 2007), 69–70.
14. Wollstonecraft, *A Vindication of the Rights of Women*, 342.

of women scholars to write commentary on the Bible, particularly as it related to women, the resulting *Women's Bible* wasn't widely accepted by the first-wave feminist movement. It was even condemned by the National American Woman Suffrage Association (NAWSA). Not many women sought ordination, and this wasn't one of early feminism's major goals.[15]

ABORTION

For many people today, feminism has become synonymous with abortion, but it wasn't always that way. First-wave feminists were horrified by abortion, which they believed was murder. "The gross perversion and destruction of motherhood by the abortionist filled me with indignation, and awakened active antagonism," wrote Elizabeth Blackwell, the first woman to earn an MD in the United States. "That the honorable term 'female physician' should be exclusively applied to those women who carried on this shocking trade seemed to me a horror. It was an utter degradation of what might and should become a noble position for women."[16]

Abortion was contrary to first-wave feminist goals. Early feminists wanted to protect women and children. Abortion destroyed lives. Sisters Victoria Claflin Woodhull and Tennessee Claflin wrote against abortion in their suffragist newspaper. "Wives deliberately permit themselves to become pregnant of children and then, to prevent becoming mothers, as deliberately murder them while yet in their wombs. Can there be a more demoralized condition than this? . . . We are aware that many women attempt to excuse themselves for procuring abortions, upon the ground that it is not murder. But the fact of resort to so weak an argument only shows the more palpably that they fully realize the enormity of the crime."[17]

Toward the very end of the first-wave feminist movement, Margaret Sanger opened the first clinic for birth control in 1916. She went on to

15. See Susan Hill Lindley, *"You Have Stept Out of Your Place": A History of Women and Religion in America* (Louisville: Westminster John Knox Press, 1996), 117, 290, 292.

16. Elizabeth Blackwell, *Pioneer Work in Opening the Medical Profession to Women: Autobiographical Sketches* (London, 1895), 30.

17. "Slaughter of the Innocents," *Woodhull & Claflin's Weekly*, June 20, 1874, p. 9.

found what would become Planned Parenthood.[18] I would never defend Sanger and her abhorrent views on race, eugenics, and abortion.[19] She said and did awful things—but even she, *at first*, was against abortion. In her autobiography, Sanger wrote that her birth-control clinic encouraged contraception and not abortion: "To each group we explained simply what contraception was, that abortion was the wrong way—no matter how early it was performed it was taking life, that contraception was the better way, the safer way—it took a little time, a little trouble, but was well worth while in the long run, because life had not yet begun."[20]

First-wave feminists would be troubled by what the pro-abortion feminist movement has become today.

SOCIETY'S RESPONSE TO THE FEMINIST MOVEMENT

As we see from ads and political cartoons of the time, society's response to feminism was mixed and frequently negative. Anti-suffrage ads and cartoons depicted feminists as large, burly, unattractive women. The scenes show neglected children and pitiful husbands left to fend for themselves. Accompanying these images are slogans such as "Everybody works but Mother. She's a suffragette. I want to vote, but my wife won't let me,"[21] or "Female Suffrage, Male Suffering: John Bell thinks it scarcely necessary that ladies who are already all mouth should have any more voice in public matters."[22]

Other ads argued against the dangers of giving women the vote. If women voted, they'd control the government: "Vote NO on Woman

18. See Estelle B. Freedman, *No Turning Back: The History of Feminism and the Future of Women* (New York: Ballantine Books, 2002), 234.

19. See Jennifer Latson, "What Margaret Sanger Really Said About Eugenics and Race," *TIME*, October 14, 2016, http://time.com/4081760/margaret-sanger-history-eugenics/.

20. Margaret Sanger, *An Autobiography* (New York: W.W. Norton, 1938), 217.

21. Postcard by Dunston Weiler Lithograph Co., 1909, available online at http://www.crusadeforthevote.org/naows-opposition.

22. Political cartoon, June 12, 1875, available online at http://historyoffeminism.com/wp-content/uploads/hist_uk_20_suffra_car_suffragettes_fun_1875.jpg.

Suffrage. . . . Because in some States more voting women than voting men will place the Government under petticoat rule."[23] They'd emasculate men: "What Will Men Wear When Women Wear [Pants]?"[24]

Some ads suggested ways to get women back under control: "The Ducking-Stool and a nice deep pool were our fore-fathers' plan for a scold: and could I have my way, each Suffragette to-day, should 'take the chair' and find the water cold."[25]

Why were people so against women voting? Some believed that society and women would be destroyed if women voted. Women would become calloused and amoral once they were dirtied by politics. Others worried that man's position as head of the household would be endangered. Did women really need to vote anyway? Either women would just vote the way their husbands did or they'd effectively cancel out their husbands' votes. Marriages would be destroyed. Women's voting would be the end of all that was good and right in society.[26]

Nonetheless, the first wave of the feminist movement saw moderate success over time. Educational opportunities improved as more colleges and universities began to admit women. This helped to pave the way for women in fields such as medicine and law. The American Medical Association admitted the first woman doctor in 1915,[27] and the first women were admitted to the American Bar Association in 1918.[28] Women also enjoyed greater legal rights. Legislation was passed allowing them to control and inherit money and property and also to have legal

23. See the pamphlet *Household Hints* (New York: National Association Opposed to Woman Suffrage, n.d.), available online at https://jwa.org/media/pamphlet-distributed -by-national-association-opposed-to-woman-suffrage.

24. Postcard, ca. 1915, available online at http://historyoffeminism.com/wp-content /uploads/suffrage-pants-what-will-men-wear.jpg.

25. "For a Suffragette," postcard, ca. 1909, available online at https://theweek.com /articles/461455/12-cruel-antisuffragette-cartoons.

26. See E. Anthony Rotundo, *American Manhood: Transformations in Masculinity from the Revolution to the Modern Era* (New York: HarperCollins, 1993), 219–20.

27. See Albert S. Lyons, "Medical History—Women in Medicine," HealthGuidance .org, accessed June 18, 2018, http://www.healthguidance.org/entry/6355/1/medical -history-women-in-medicine.html.

28. See "ABA Timeline," American Bar Association, accessed May 27, 2019, https:// www.americanbar.org/about_the_aba/timeline/.

rights over their children.[29] In 1920, the United States ratified the 19th Amendment, giving women the right to vote. These were all good things and improvements for women.

THE GOOD OLD DAYS

If the first-wave feminist movement made such a difference for women, how did we get to *Leave it to Beaver*, with moms vacuuming at home in dresses and pearls while dads went off to work? Close to the end of the first-wave feminist movement, World War I began, and society was never the same: "Men in the trenches experienced a nightmare world of mud, night, blood, and death. On their return they confronted women who had experienced a world in which they had struggled on their own to hold the remaining family together, care for children and relatives, and keep food on the table. . . . When the war ended, men and women confronted each other across an unbridgeable gulf."[30] Even those who wanted to go back to the good old days before the war weren't always able to. Millions of young men had died, leaving a surplus of unmarried young women, particularly in Europe. Many of these women never married and had to provide for themselves.[31]

Things changed even more after World War II. When the war ended in 1945, many people wanted to resume the lives they had put on hold. A period of prosperity began in the United States. Men were back from war and ready to start working and making money. Women, who had been working to keep the country going during the war, were encouraged to quit and go back to having children and caring for the home. And they did. Fewer women went to college, and many got married right out of high school, if not sooner. Birthrates and the economy boomed.

29. See "Married Women's Property Laws" under "State Law Resources," Library of Congress, accessed June 4, 2019, https://guides.loc.gov/american-women-law/state-laws.

30. Charles Sowerwine with Patricia Grimshaw, "Equality and Difference in the Twentieth-Century West: North America, Western Europe, Australia, and New Zealand," in *A Companion to Gender History*, ed. Teresa A. Meade and Merry E. Wiesner-Hanks (Malden, MA: Blackwell Publishing, 2004), 589.

31. See Sowerwine and Grimshaw, 589.

Many of the rights that first-wave feminists had fought for were abandoned following World War II. Women were expected to stay home while men went to work, although working-class women, and especially women of color, still had to work, and many continued to work for other women as domestic help.

In the next chapter, we'll discuss how the feminist movement became what it is today and how Christians have responded to it. In the rush to condemn the evils of the sexual revolution and of pro-abortion feminism, many conservative Christians have overlooked the necessary improvements that were brought about by the early feminists. As did the post–World War II generation, they express a longing to return to the way things used to be before the feminist movement changed everything.

DISCUSSION QUESTIONS

1. How did the first-wave feminist movement start?
2. What were some of the goals of the early feminists?
3. What did the early feminists believe about abortion?
4. How did society respond to the first-wave feminist movement?
5. What good things did the first-wave feminists achieve?

6

"THE 1960S' WOMEN'S MOVEMENT WAS HIJACKED"

LATER FEMINISM AND THE

CONSERVATIVE CHRISTIAN RESPONSE

In 1987, CBMW was established primarily to help the church defend against the accommodation of secular feminism. . . . As evangelical feminism continues to spread, the evangelical community needs to be aware that this debate reaches ultimately to the heart of the gospel.

THE COUNCIL ON BIBLICAL MANHOOD AND WOMANHOOD[1]

Have you ever been skating? Growing up before inline skates were a thing, I loved to go to the skating rink. It was thrilling. The rink floor was polished as smooth as ice. Once you got moving, there wasn't much to stop you, unless you fell or hit one of the dividers. And that was so much better than skating on the rough, uneven sidewalks or streets near my house. It took a lot of work to keep moving on the sidewalk, and if you hit a seam in

---

1. "Mission & Vision," The Council on Biblical Manhood and Womanhood, accessed June 6, 2018, https://cbmw.org/about/mission-vision/.

the concrete . . . well, let's just say that I learned about the laws of motion the hard way.

But the laws of motion don't just help us to understand how objects move. They can help us to make sense of the world around us in other ways. For every action, there's an equal and opposite reaction; and, as the saying goes, nothing happens in a vacuum. Events don't just arise out of nowhere. Our actions are often a response to other actions.

The feminist movement began in response to the way that women were treated during the Victorian era. In response to the upheaval of World War II and the peace and prosperity that followed, society's pendulum swung back toward a belief in separate spheres for women and men. The next wave of the feminist movement started in the 1960s, in many ways as a response to that shift. And by the 1980s, conservative Christian groups were responding to the actions of those second-wave feminists.

THE SECOND-WAVE FEMINIST MOVEMENT

When conservative Christians talk about the feminist movement, they're almost always talking about the second-wave feminist movement, the sexual revolution of the 1960s, and the modern feminists who followed. In particular, they think of abortion. How did the feminist movement become practically synonymous with the sexual revolution and abortion?

In the 1950s, women were busy with domestic life. The war was over. Seemingly happy housewives sent their husbands off to work with a kiss and went about their domestic duties smilingly, without a care in the world. "Their only dream was to be perfect wives and mothers; their highest ambition to have five children and a beautiful house, their only fight to get and keep their husbands," wrote Betty Friedan in *The Feminine Mystique*. "They had no thought for the unfeminine problems of the world outside the home; they wanted the men to make the major decisions. They gloried in their role as women."[2] These were the good old days that conservatives often seem to long for. Men and women followed their

2. Betty Friedan, *The Feminine Mystique* (New York: W.W. Norton, 1963), 14.

distinct roles, with no confusion about who was in charge. Women were content and fulfilled in their separate sphere.

. . . Or maybe they weren't. Behind these pretty pictures of domestic bliss lay an ugly reality. Women weren't happy. Popular culture told them that if they lost weight and bleached their hair, they would be happy. So they bleached their hair, took diet pills, and smoked to keep their figures trim. But they weren't happy. Doctors told them that they needed a little "pick me up." So they took uppers ("mother's little helper"[3]) during the day and sleeping pills at night. A home, a husband, a family, all the modern conveniences—and yet women weren't happy. "If the secret of feminine fulfillment is having children, never have so many women, with the freedom to choose, had so many children, in so few years, so willingly. If the answer is love, never have women searched for love with such determination."[4]

Friedan was right that there was a problem. Women were discontent. Her solution, though, was incomplete. Friedan believed that women would be fulfilled if they had careers that engaged their minds and abilities outside the domestic sphere. What Friedan rightly recognized was that women shouldn't be restricted the way that they were in the society of the 1950s.

Educational opportunities for women had declined after World War II. Significantly fewer women were attending college in the 1950s than in the 1920s.[5] Women had fewer employment options and faced a number of legal challenges in business and society. At first, the second wave of feminism focused particularly on these concerns.

IMPROVEMENTS IN LEGAL RIGHTS AND EMPLOYMENT OPPORTUNITIES

Imagine that you're a young woman with a degree in science who is being interviewed for a job. The interviewer has a couple of questions for you: How fast can you type? And when was your last menstrual period?

3. The Rolling Stones popularized this term for uppers in their 1966 song of the same name—see "Mother's Little Helper," by Mick Jagger and Keith Richards, recorded March 1966, track 1 on *Aftermath* (UK edition), Decca, 1966.

4. Friedan, *The Feminine Mystique*, 24.

5. See Thomas D. Snyder, ed., *120 Years of American Education: A Statistical Portrait*

Does that surprise you? Why would the interviewer ask those questions? The first is to see whether you can do secretarial jobs, since those are what you'll likely be hired to do, regardless of your education. The second is to make sure you aren't pregnant. Everyone knew that pregnant women wouldn't stay after their babies were born.

Imagine that you get the job and now have to hide your pregnancy as long as possible at work, because you'll be fired when your employer finds out. And even if he doesn't fire you as soon as he finds out, there's no guarantee that you'll still have a job after you've had the baby.

Imagine that you've been working for several years. Your husband is in grad school, and you've been able to juggle having a couple of kids. Your boss comes to tell you that a man who you trained has just been given the promotion you were hoping for. Why? Because *he* has a family to support.

It may seem odd to you, but this was the reality for women in the workforce. Employment opportunities were divided between men and women. Women worked, but the jobs they could get didn't pay well. Companies could legally discriminate against women in their hiring practices and the salaries they paid. And yes, interviewers could, and did, ask when a woman's last period was.

Do you have a credit card? If you were a woman in the 1960s, the only credit card you could have would be one in your husband's name. Are you a scientist, engineer, doctor, or lawyer? Women in the 1960s were unlikely to be hired in these fields. Do you want to work for an airline? Airlines did hire women as stewardesses, but only if they fit the profile: single, slender, and under 30.[6] You want to be a pilot? Sorry—that's a job for men.

Second-wave feminists wanted to change how women were treated in the workforce. Title VII of the 1964 Civil Rights Act and The Pregnancy Discrimination Act of 1978 stopped employers from discriminating on the basis of sex. Many women wanted "equal pay for equal work." It became illegal to ask the questions that had once been routine in job interviews.

(Washington, D.C.: National Center for Education Statistics, 1993), 69.

6. See Sue Ellen Browder, *Subverted: How I Helped the Sexual Revolution Hijack the Women's Movement* (San Francisco: Ignatius Press, 2015), chap. 2, loc. 270–75 of 3814, Kindle.

Employers couldn't ask whether a woman was married or pregnant or had children, nor could they deny a woman her job back after she had a baby.[7]

In addition to reforms in the area of employment, second-wave feminists wanted to improve women's economic options. Married women couldn't get credit cards or loans on their own. Without a credit history, it was almost impossible for women to start their own businesses or build credit if their husbands left them. The 1974 Credit Opportunity Act required banks to grant loans to women independently of their husbands.[8] These legislative acts provided greater legal and economic equality and access for women.

FEMALE ORDINATION AND SPIRITUALITY

The second-wave feminist movement accomplished legal, economic, and employment reforms, but it wasn't all positive. Other aspects of second-wave feminism often overshadow the good that it produced.

The second-wave feminist movement produced growing pressure for women to be ordained, although still not all feminists agreed with this. In addition, some second-wave feminists wanted to change the way that the church thought about God. Some in the feminist spirituality movement believed that the language used to describe God shouldn't be restricted to masculine names and concepts. Instead, feminine or gender-inclusive language should be used[9]—for example, God as "Mother" and "She" and Jesus as the "Divine Child" instead of the Son of God.

Other women went further and left Christianity altogether. The new religious movement known as Wicca attracted some women through its emphasis on the feminine, which was also seen in the "goddess movement."[10]

Many mainline denominations and churches embraced a new feminist

7. See Estelle B. Freedman, *No Turning Back: The History of Feminism and the Future of Women* (New York: Ballantine Books, 2002), 178–79, 191.

8. See Freedman, 184.

9. See John W. Cooper, *Our Father in Heaven: Christian Faith and Inclusive Language for God* (Grand Rapids: Baker, 1998).

10. See Cynthia Eller, *The Myth of Matriarchal Prehistory: Why an Invented Past Won't Give Women a Future* (Boston: Beacon Press, 2000), 36.

spirituality—some by adding inclusive language and female ordination to liberal theology and a few by going so far as to incorporate some of the pagan practices from Wicca and goddess worship. Conservative Christians, however, condemned the ordination of women, gender-inclusive language that changed the divine names, witchcraft, and goddess worship.

SEXUAL REVOLUTION AND ABORTION

As we saw in the previous chapter, abortion wasn't originally part of the feminist movement. It wasn't until the sexual revolution began in the 1960s that legalized abortion became a feminist goal. Even then, there wasn't a consensus over abortion at first.

Second-wave feminists split over moral issues. Some saw pornography and prostitution as exploitation, as earlier feminists had. Others saw pornography and prostitution as part of the free love and sexual choice of the sexual revolution.

The sexual revolution encouraged young people to have sex whenever and with whomever they wanted. All the old sexual morality they had grown up with was tossed aside. Guess what happened as a result of all that free love. When people have sex, they often end up with babies. People wanted to enjoy themselves without facing any consequences. The solution was abortion on demand.

Sue Ellen Browder, a former *Cosmopolitan* journalist, addresses how the sexual revolution took over the feminist movement. Larry Lader, founder of what would become NARAL—the National Abortion Rights Action League—convinced Betty Friedan to add abortion as a platform of the National Organization for Women. "That's right. The 1960s' women's movement was hijacked largely due to the tireless efforts of one man, whose greatest passion was to make abortion legal."[11] You may think it's odd that men would be so interested in abortion. But abortion freed men more than it ever helped women. Men led the legal push for abortion because it allowed them to have sex with fewer responsibilities.

Publicly, abortion on demand was declared necessary for women.

11. Browder, *Subverted*, chap. 1, loc. 85–93.

Women needed to be saved from back-alley abortions. They needed to be free to make the choices that were necessary for their careers. But it was all a lie. Abortion exploits women. It abuses women—both born and unborn. Abortion hurts women physically, emotionally, and spiritually.

While everyone was expected to be sexually active, legalized abortion shifted the consequences almost entirely onto women. Before abortion was legal, a man might be held responsible for providing for, or even marrying, a woman whose children he had fathered. After abortion was legalized, if a woman got pregnant while being sexually free, it was her own fault for being careless and not taking precautions. If a man offered to pay for the abortion, what more could he be expected to do? He could even claim that he might not be the father.

The sexual revolution hurt everyone, but ultimately women paid the higher price for sexual freedom. A woman had a choice. She could choose abortion—the preferred choice—but, if she chose not to have an abortion, the baby was her choice and her responsibility. If she took maternity leave and lost out on advancement opportunities, that was her choice too. If she made her family a priority over her job, that was a choice that might cost her, but it was still her choice. Women had to choose between motherhood and a career—or they were guilted into trying to have it all.[12]

Abortion isn't the only way that second-wave feminism and the sexual revolution undermined the goals of the early feminists. First-wave feminists wanted equality with men. They wanted marriage to be a partnership of companions. They believed that men and women needed each other. But a vocal strand of second-wave feminists rejected the unity and interdependence of men and women. They encouraged both an independence of women from men and also a superiority of women over men.

THE MODERN FEMINIST MOVEMENT

The modern feminist movement continues to evolve, and various subcultures of it have developed. Some of its newer concerns include homosexuality, intersectionality, transgenderism, and the #MeToo movement.

12. See Browder, chap. 5, loc. 1201–8.

Beginning in the early 2000s, rights for lesbian and bisexual women have been incorporated into feminism.[13] However, the issue of whether, or how, to include transgender women—those who are born biologically male—is causing the feminist movement to splinter. Some argue that including transgender women undermines the goals of the feminist movement.[14] Others argue that the feminist movement should include the fight for transgender rights. They say feminism is for all who identify as women.[15] Some go so far as to say that those who don't include transgender women aren't really feminists.[16]

While distinct from the feminist movement, the #MeToo movement also illustrates fault lines within modern feminism. #MeToo began as a way to show support for those who have been sexually assaulted or harassed. But not all feminists are on board with #MeToo. Some—particularly those who were part of second-wave feminism—think that the movement has reduced the meaning of harassment and assault to absurdly trivial levels. Others—especially those who are from more recent waves—think that more needs to be done to address any underlying misogyny and sexism that encourage harassment and assault.[17]

Women were once expected to be more virtuous and moral than men. Early feminists wanted men to be held to the same high standard of morality that women were. Second-wave feminists, inspired by the sexual revolution, brought women and men down to a lower standard of morality, and the modern feminist movement is burying us all in the muck.

13. See Jennifer Baumgardner and Amy Richards, *Manifesta: Young Women, Feminism, and the Future* (New York: Farrar, Straus and Giroux, 2000), 279.

14. See Sarah Ditum, "Trans Rights Should Not Come at the Cost of Women's Fragile Gains," *The Economist*, July 5, 2018, https://www.economist.com/open-future /2018/07/05/trans-rights-should-not-come-at-the-cost-of-womens-fragile-gains.

15. See Sara Wilkinson, "Feminism and Transgender Rights," Maryland National Organization for Woman, February 16, 2014, https://marylandnow.org/feminism-and -transgender-rights/.

16. See Brynn Tannehill, "'Feminists' Who Exclude Trans Women Aren't Feminists At All," *HuffPost*, July 10, 2018, https://www.huffpost.com/entry/opinion-tannehill -terfs-right-wing_n_5b44eeeae4b0c523e2637878.

17. See Moira Donegan, "How #MeToo Revealed the Central Rift within Feminism Today," *The Guardian*, May 11, 2018, https://www.theguardian.com/news/2018/may /11/how-metoo-revealed-the-central-rift-within-feminism-social-individualist.

You can see this shift in focus in popular culture, as well. More emphasis is on women being intellectually and emotionally superior to men. Men are the punchline for jokes in movies and television—too dumb to know better. Women often act sexually aggressive in ways that were once reserved for men.

The modern feminist movement remains staunchly pro-abortion. Abortion isn't considered a choice that women agonize over. Whereas the slogan for abortion used to be "Safe, legal, and rare," abortion is now described, in the words of Rev. Carter Hayward, as a "sacrament": "I suspect that for many women today, and for their spouses, lovers, families and communities, abortion is celebrated as . . . an occasion of deep and serious and sacred meaning."[18] Amy Hagstrom Miller, abortion advocate and founder of a clinic that performs abortions, calls abortion a "rite of passage" in which "women take a look at the values that they have inherited from their family/church/culture/education and decide which ones are applicable or meaningful to them, and which ones are not."[19]

The 2017 Women's March had an explicitly pro-abortion and pro-LGBTQ platform and intentionally excluded pro-life women—both Christian and secular. In order to be part of the march, participants were expected to support "open access to safe, legal, affordable abortion and birth control for all people" and freedom from "gender norms, expectations and stereotypes."[20]

Not all modern feminists believe that women are superior to men. And not all of them support abortion and the continued sexual revolution. There are even pro-life feminist groups.[21] Unfortunately, pro-life feminists are often ignored by both mainstream feminists and conservative Christians who are responding to feminism.

18. Quoted in Thomas J. Euteneuer, "The 'Sacrament' of Abortion," *Human Life International e-Newsletter* 1, no. 79 (August 2007), available online at http://www.lifeissues.net/writers/eut/eut_48abortion.html.

19. "Read Amy Hagstrom Miller's REA Speech," Lilith Fund, September 23, 2012, https://www.lilithfund.org/read-amy-hagstrom-millers-rea-speech/.

20. "Mission and Principles," Women's March, accessed June 19, 2018, https://womensmarch.com/mission-and-principles#mandpprinciples.

21. One example of a secular pro-life group is the Feminists for Life—see http://www.feministsforlife.org/.

A CONSERVATIVE CHRISTIAN RESPONSE

As the second wave of feminism gained momentum, conservative Christians grew more concerned about what was happening. The sexual revolution had changed society. Divorce, sexual promiscuity, abortion, and homosexuality had been taboo—but they were becoming more common and accepted.

By the 1980s, home life had also changed. More women were working full-time. Children were spending their early years in daycare, and many older children were latchkey kids who came home to an empty house after school. Fewer families were living the 1950s ideal of women staying at home while men went off to work.

Meanwhile, many churches were ordaining women as pastors and elders. Mainline churches in particular had reinterpreted the passages of the Bible that restricted ordination to qualified men. Churches were also changing their views on issues such as sex outside marriage, divorce, abortion, and homosexuality.

In response, some concerned Christians founded the Council for Biblical Manhood and Womanhood (CBMW). They chose the term *complementarian* to describe their beliefs because it "suggests both equality and beneficial differences between men and women."[22]

The Danvers Statement, which was published in January 1989, outlines CBMW's philosophy. CBMW's founders were concerned about cultural confusion over the difference between masculinity and femininity. They were troubled by the damages that this confusion was having on marriage. They believed that feminist egalitarianism distorted the leadership of husbands and the submission of wives, which was leading to an increasing indifference toward motherhood and domesticity and a decline of biblical sexual morality. Domestic abuse was on the rise. In

---

22. John Piper and Wayne Grudem, eds., *Recovering Biblical Manhood and Womanhood: A Response to Evangelical Feminism* (repr., Wheaton, IL: Crossway Books, 2006), xv. They rejected *traditionalist* because it "implies an unwillingness to let Scripture challenge traditional patterns of behavior" and *hierarchicalist* because it "overemphasizes structured authority while giving no suggestion of equality or the beauty of mutual interdependence."

the area of the church, they were concerned about women in church leadership roles, the undermining of biblical authority and hermeneutics, and the attempts by churches to accommodate the culture rather than to remain faithful to Scripture.[23]

In addition to the Danvers Statement, CBMW published a collection of essays on complementarianism in 1991. The collection, which was edited by Wayne Grudem and John Piper, was published as *Recovering Biblical Manhood and Womanhood: A Response to Evangelical Feminism*. Together, the Danvers Statement and this publication define complementarianism as a movement.

CBMW's founders blamed feminism for the problems that they saw in the home, the church, and society. Feminism's push for equality between men and women was flattening out and destroying the fundamental differences between men and women.[24]

According to complementarian teaching, our society doesn't understand what it means to be male and female, and this is feminism's fault. The movement's solution is a return of the proper complementarian definitions of masculinity and femininity and of the appropriate roles for men and women in marriage, church, and society. For CBMW, these masculine and feminine roles and differences aren't simply about biological differences; instead, "they go to the root of our personhood."[25]

HOW *FEMINISM* BECAME A BAD WORD FOR CONSERVATIVE CHRISTIANS

For conservative Christians today, *feminist* has almost exclusively negative connotations. It's used as an accusation against those who question aspects of complementarian teaching. Some Christians equate feminism

23. See "The Danvers Statement," The Council on Biblical Manhood and Womanhood, June 26, 2007, https://cbmw.org/uncategorized/the-danvers-statement/.

24. See Elisabeth Elliot, "The Essence of Femininity: A Personal Perspective," in Piper and Grudem, *Recovering Biblical Manhood and Womanhood*, 396.

25. John Piper, "A Vision of Biblical Complementarity: Manhood and Womanhood Defined According to the Bible," in Piper and Grudem, *Recovering Biblical Manhood and Womanhood*, 32.

with rebellion,[26] saying that "all women are rebellious feminists at heart."[27] Feminism is the boogeyman—a root cause of the moral decay of society. "It encourages anger, bitterness, resentment, self-reliance, independence, arrogance, and a pitting of woman against man. . . . Power, prestige, personal attainment, and financial gain are exalted over service, sacrifice, and humility. Manhood is devalued. Morality is devalued. Marriage is devalued. Motherhood is devalued. In sum, feminism promotes ways of thinking that stand in direct opposition to the Word of God and to the beauty of His created order."[28]

Some of these concerns are understandable. The modern feminist movement has strong connections with abortion, the sexual revolution, same-sex marriage, and LGBTQ lifestyles. Aspects of the antagonism that conservative Christians show toward feminism, though, are more closely related to the societal attitudes and responses that we saw at the end of the last chapter.

It's not that conservative Christians believe that the feminist movement didn't do any good. They do—but they also believe that women were content until the feminist movement. As one complementarian book explains, "Male-dominated culture, or patriarchy, isn't the problem that feminism made it out to be. It's not the real reason women were unhappy, if they really were unhappy. Why not? Because if it were, women would be happier after the feminist movement's successes, but they aren't."[29]

Much of what's being taught about the nature of women and men and gender roles in marriage, church, and society started out as a response to the feminist movement—or at least to aspects of it. For example, the belief that feminism makes men effeminate and turns women into "'men'

26. Voddie Baucham Jr., *Family Shepherds: Calling and Equipping Men to Lead Their Homes* (Wheaton, IL: Crossway, 2011), chap. 9, loc. 1542 of 3015, Kindle.

27. Anna Sofia Botkin and Elizabeth Botkin, *So Much More: The Remarkable Influence of Visionary Daughters on the Kingdom of God* (San Antonio: Vision Forum, 2005), 31.

28. Mary A. Kassian and Nancy Leigh DeMoss, *True Woman 101: Divine Design; An Eight-Week Study on Biblical Womanhood* (Chicago: Moody Publishers, 2012), p. 121, NOOK.

29. Kassian and DeMoss, 137.

who happen to be biologically capable of having children"[30] has led to particular definitions of masculinity and femininity.

As the anti-suffrage postcards did, some conservatives today depict feminists as being loud and aggressive, demanding of their own way, ambitious, and career-oriented. This goes against what they believe women were created to be, as we will see in the next chapter.[31] Let's see how this reaction to feminism has influenced conservative Christian teaching on the nature of women and men.

DISCUSSION QUESTIONS

1. What happened after WWII that prompted the second-wave feminist movement?
2. What good goals did the second-wave feminists have?
3. What surprised you about how women were treated in the workforce?
4. How did the sexual revolution change the feminist movement?
5. What was the conservative Christian response to the later waves of feminism?

30. Voddie Baucham Jr., *What He Must Be: . . . If He Wants to Marry My Daughter* (Wheaton, IL: Crossway, 2009), 152.
31. See Kassian and DeMoss, *True Woman 101*, 118–20.

PART 3

THE NATURE OF
WOMEN AND MEN

7

"SHE WAS NOT HIS EQUAL"

PREVALENT TEACHING ON THE

NATURE OF WOMEN AND MEN

*So, was Eve Adam's equal? Yes and no. She was his spiritual
equal and, unlike the animals, "suitable for him." But she was
not his equal in that she was his "helper." God did not create
man and woman in an undifferentiated way, and their mere
maleness and femaleness identify their respective roles. A man,
just by virtue of his manhood, is called to lead for God. A woman,
just by virtue of her womanhood, is called to help for God.*

RAYMOND ORTLUND[1]

When we bought our house in Houston, we paid for an inspection so we
would know what we were getting ourselves into. If you've ever seen the
movie *The Money Pit*, you know the danger of not getting an inspection.
As the couple did in the movie, you might buy a house that looks great

---

1. Raymond C. Ortlund Jr., "Male-Female Equality and Male Headship: Genesis 1–3,"
in *Recovering Biblical Manhood and Womanhood: A Response to Evangelical Feminism*, ed.
John Piper and Wayne Grudem (repr., Wheaton, IL: Crossway Books, 2006), 102.

but is actually falling apart. Thankfully, the inspector assured us that there weren't any major concerns—though he warned us that in Houston there are two kinds of houses: those with foundation problems and those that are going to have foundation problems.

You see, in Houston we don't build on rock or stone. We pour concrete foundations on top of clay soil. And that soil is a problem. It expands and contracts as it absorbs water and dries out. Eventually, this can damage a house's foundation.

A beautiful house may have a faulty foundation. If the foundation isn't fixed, the house won't last. But an ugly house may have a solid foundation. The house may need a lot of work, but it's worth it because the foundation is good. As the contractor in *The Money Pit* says, as long as the foundation is okay, "everything else can be fixed."[2]

The same is true when it comes to theology. If beliefs have a solid foundation, then misapplications and other issues can be addressed. But whatever has been built on a bad theological foundation will eventually fall apart, no matter how good it seems to be (see Matt. 7:24–27).

Many conservative Christian churches teach good things. Men and women, created in the image of God and equal in Christ, are different and interdependent. Men can't become women, and women can't become men. Sex is a blessing that's intended to be enjoyed in marriage. Marriage should be between one man and one woman—ideally for life. Husbands should love their wives as Christ loves the church. Wives should submit to their husbands. Only qualified men should be ordained leaders in the church.

These are all solid, biblical beliefs—but some of the other seemingly good things that are taught in conservative Christian churches are built on a faulty foundation. Some of these are actually based on the same unbiblical and extrabiblical teachings about the nature of women and men that we've discussed in the last few chapters.

2. "A Good Foundation," *The Money Pit*, directed by Richard Benjamin (1986; Universal City, CA: Universal Pictures Home Entertainment, 2002), DVD.

THE NATURE OF WOMEN AND MEN

As we saw in the last chapter, the complementarian movement began in response to the feminist movement and the sexual revolution. Some of what complementarians teach about the nature of women and men is good, but other aspects of it are more reactionary. Unfortunately, instead of being rooted in the Bible, many conservative Christian beliefs about women and men trace back to the Greeks, Romans, and Victorians.

These older cultures had similar ideas about the inherent characteristics, or essence, of women and men. They defined men and women in terms of opposites—as being opposing halves of humanity. The feminist movement challenged those definitions of masculinity and femininity. Many complementarians, however, are teaching ideas that move back toward the pagan understanding of women and men.

Complementarian definitions of masculinity and femininity are more than just generalities, as we will see. As the Greeks, Romans, and Victorians did, many conservative Christians consider such definitions to be the essence of women and men. Men, by nature, are strong—they are leaders, providers, and protectors. Women, by nature, are softer—they are submissive, helpers, and keepers of the home. Some even teach that the image of God is only partially displayed in both men and women—women reflect certain aspects and men others, and so it takes both women and men to reflect the full image of God.[3]

Some conservative Christians are concerned that people today don't understand what it means to be male and female. They believe that, as a result of this confusion, men are increasingly effeminate and women increasingly masculine. This same confusion contributes to same-sex marriage, divorce, and people's confusion over their identity and sexuality. Because men are failing to lead, provide, and protect, women are leading in homes, churches, businesses, and the government.[4]

3. See Elisabeth Elliot, "The Essence of Femininity: A Personal Perspective," in Piper and Grudem, *Recovering Biblical Manhood and Womanhood*, 397, and Mary A. Kassian and Nancy Leigh DeMoss, *True Woman 101: Divine Design* (Chicago: Moody Publishers, 2012), p. 33, NOOK.

4. See Owen Strachan and Gavin Peacock, *The Grand Design: Male and Female He*

Many conservative Christians teach that in order to save society from destruction, men and women need to return to following God-ordained definitions of masculinity and femininity in all aspects of life: "When men or women—married or single—are distinctively masculine or feminine with other men and women in the workplace, they serve as a clarion call for people to be saved by Christ in order to live as God intended and nature urges."[5] God will bless us if we fulfill our designated roles as men and women. He will bless men for being initiators, leaders, providers, and protectors and women for being helpers, mothers, and keepers of the home.[6]

The Nature of Men and Masculinity

According to many complementarians, God made men to be leaders, providers, and protectors. This is man's nature—what it means to be a man.[7] The definition of masculinity is having authority and taking initiative.[8] It means being "decisive, steadfast, and aggressive."[9] Men need these characteristics in order to fulfill their roles as providers and leaders. Masculine men are assertive, confident, and not afraid of taking risks.[10] Some describe this understanding of masculinity as "sanctified testosterone."[11]

Godly men are brave, courageous, decisive, and strong. Owen Strachan, a seminary professor and fellow at CBMW, and Gavin Peacock, a pastor and director of CBMW's international outreach, believe that Paul's encouragement for believers to "act like men" and "be strong" (1 Cor.

Made Them (Fearn, UK: Christian Focus Publications, 2016), p. 14, NOOK.

5. Strachan and Peacock, 91.

6. See David Schrock, "Gender Specific Blessings: Bolstering a Biblical Theology of Gender Roles," *The Journal for Biblical Manhood and Womanhood* 21, no. 1 (Spring 2016), available online at http://cbmw.org/topics/complementarianism/jbmw-21-1-gender-specific-blessings-bolstering-a-biblical-theology-of-gender-roles/.

7. See Strachan and Peacock, *The Grand Design*, 41.

8. See Douglas Wilson, *Fidelity: What It Means to Be a One-Woman Man* (Moscow, ID: Canon Press, 2011), chap. 2, loc. 165–67 of 1956, Kindle.

9. Helen Andelin, *Fascinating Womanhood*, updated ed. (New York: Bantam Books, 2013), p. 93, Kindle.

10. See Douglas Wilson, *Her Hand in Marriage: Biblical Courtship in the Modern World* (Moscow, ID: Canon Press, 2010), chap. 2, loc. 391–92 of 1057, Kindle.

11. "Complementarity and the Disappearance of Men," accessed June 9, 2017, http://cbmw.org/topics/news-and-announcements/cbmw-pre-conference-day-one-summaries/.

16:13) gives us a definition of masculinity. Strachan and Peacock apply the passage specifically to males, telling them to be brave, strong, courageous, and decisive and not weak, selfish, or passive.[12]

Strachan and Peacock explain that, in order to be men, boys should be taught to shake hands firmly and look people directly in the eyes, to enjoy physical pursuits, to dress and behave in masculine ways, to play masculine games, and to offer assistance when women need it.[13] According to John Piper, being masculine may mean driving the car, opening doors for women, ordering for both yourself and your date at a restaurant, and protecting your date by walking down the sidewalk closer to the cars.[14]

The popular complementarian definition of masculinity and the nature of men is that masculine men are strong, brave, courageous, and decisive. They are leaders, providers, and protectors. While most complementarians appeal to the Scriptures to defend this description of masculinity, we have seen that these definitions actually come from the Greeks, Romans, and Victorians.

The Nature of Women and Femininity

Many complementarians describe women as being in contrast to men. Women have a set of roles that fill in the space left by the roles played by men, and the definition of femininity is the mirror opposite of that of masculinity. If men are strong and brave leaders, initiators, providers, and protectors, women are the opposite: soft and submissive helpers, mothers, and keepers of the home.

Some conservative Christians teach that women are inherently weaker than men. They understand Peter's command for husbands to treat their wives as the "weaker vessel" (1 Peter 3:7 ESV) to be a statement of women's nature. Women's weakness is simply part of God's design—a God-ordained difference between women and men.[15]

12. See Strachan and Peacock, *The Grand Design*, 54, 61.

13. See Strachan and Peacock, 110.

14. See John Piper, "A Vision of Biblical Complementarity: Manhood and Womanhood Defined According to the Bible," in Piper and Grudem, *Recovering Biblical Manhood and Womanhood*, 41.

15. See Douglas Wilson, *Reforming Marriage* (Moscow, ID: Canon Press, 1995), 38.

Do you remember how the Greeks and Romans believed that women were inverted versions of men? Some complementarians use the same language to contrast man's strength with woman's weakness: "Strength refers to a man's manhood—his potency, virility, and procreative power (Ps. 105:36; Prov. 31:3; Gen. 49:3). By contrast, a woman's 'softness' has to do with her pregnability, penetrability, and vulnerability (in a very positive sense). . . . The bodies of male and female reflect this idea. A man's body is built to move toward the woman. A woman's body is built to receive the man. But the pattern goes beyond the mere physical difference between men and women to encompass the totality of their essence."[16] Women's bodies, which are generally softer and smaller than men's, reflect God's design for femininity. Women should have soft, delicate bodies and quiet, gentle, sweet dispositions.[17]

Many conservative Christians teach that godly, feminine women should demonstrate the virtues of Victorian true womanhood: purity, piety, submission, and domesticity. They should never be harsh, demanding, controlling,[18] assertive, loud, or obnoxious.[19] Instead, women should "cultivate an inner beauty of a gentle and quiet spirit."[20] Such inner beauty should be demonstrated by a demeanor of peace and calm.

As the Greeks, Romans, and Victorians did, some complementarians teach that women are weaker emotionally as well as physically. Whereas men are governed by their minds, women are governed by their emotions. Women, therefore, have a natural, feminine vulnerability.[21]

You might wonder whether women are also considered spiritually weaker, as the Greeks and Romans believed. Some conservative Christians blame Adam's fall, in part, on Eve's spiritual weakness: "Satan knew that the man could not be deceived, but the woman could. . . . But Lucifer could see that this soft, sweet female was vulnerable.

---

16. Mary Kassian, "Steel Magnolia," *True Woman* (blog), Revive Our Hearts, April 13, 2009, https://www.reviveourhearts.com/true-woman/blog/steel-magnolia/.

17. See Kassian and DeMoss, *True Woman 101*, 61–63.

18. See Kassian and DeMoss, 156.

19. See Strachan and Peacock, *The Grand Design*, 77.

20. Wilson, *Her Hand in Marriage*, chap. 3, 532–33.

21. See Andelin, *Fascinating Womanhood*, 396.

God had made her by nature to be responsive, and she was trusting and naïve."[22]

Many complementarians believe that God ordained men to be leaders because women, like Eve, are spiritually weaker than men are. Men are like an umbrella of protection for women. As fathers, husbands, and church leaders, men provide a spiritual covering for women. If a woman rejects God's design for her protection, then she puts herself at risk like Dinah did.[23] As Nancy DeMoss Wolgemuth, cofounder of the True Woman movement, explains, "I believe the failure of many Christian wives to place themselves under their husbands' authority accounts for the extent to which so many women are vulnerable to Satan's attack on their minds, wills, and emotions. When we come out from under authority—whether in big matters or in seemingly insignificant areas— we become 'fair game' for the Enemy."[24]

Despite these weaknesses, women are necessary as mothers and life-givers. But being a life-giver goes beyond physically bearing children. All women should be spiritual life-givers. Bringing forth new life and nurturing children, physically and spiritually, is a core characteristic of womanhood.[25]

As we've discussed, God created women to be helpers or co-laborers with men. In contrast, some conservative Christians define being a helper as a subordinate role. Women are men's "loyal and suitable assistant[s]"[26]—men's "second in command"[27]—created to help men to fulfill *their* purpose: glorifying God and serving Him.[28]

22. Debi Pearl, *Created to Be His Help Meet: Discover How God Can Make Your Marriage Glorious* (Pleasantville, TN: No Greater Joy Ministries, 2010), pp. 107–8, Kindle.

23. See Douglas Wilson, "Courtship and Rape Culture," Blog & Mablog, February 4, 2016, https://dougwils.com/books-and-culture/s7-engaging-the-culture/110222.html.

24. Nancy Leigh DeMoss, *Lies Women Believe and the Truth that Sets Them Free* (2001; repr., Chicago: Moody Publishers, 2007), 148.

25. See Kassian and DeMoss, *True Woman 101*, 174.

26. John Piper and Wayne Grudem, "Charity, Clarity, and Hope: The Controversy and the Cause of Christ," in Piper and Grudem, *Recovering Biblical Manhood and Womanhood*, 409.

27. Strachan and Peacock, *The Grand Design*, 55.

28. See Kassian and DeMoss, *True Woman 101*, 76.

The popular complementarian definition of femininity and of the nature of women is that feminine women are gentle, quiet, soft, submissive helpers and mothers. As we discussed regarding the nature of men, these common beliefs about the nature of women owe less to the Bible than to Greek, Roman, and Victorian cultures.

THE FUNDAMENTAL DIFFERENCE: AUTHORITY AND SUBMISSION

Of all the differences between men and women, the one that conservative Christians focus the most on is the difference of authority and submission. Many conservative Christians believe that when God created Adam and Eve, He instituted an unbreakable structure of authority and submission between men and women. Adam, along with all men after him, have authority over women because Adam was created first and given the authority to name the animals and Eve.

Pastor Stu Weber explains that a man's body illustrates his nature as an initiator and leader: "Among the ancient Hebrew words for man is one meaning 'piercer.' Its feminine counterpart is 'pierced one.' While the anatomical or sexual elements are clear, the force of the words is much larger in scope. The physical is a parable of the spiritual. . . . At his core a man is an initiator—a piercer, one who penetrates, moves forward, advances toward the horizon, leads. At the core of masculinity is initiation—the provision of direction, security, stability, and connection."[29]

For many conservative Christians, the counterparts to masculine initiative and authority are feminine responsiveness and submission—characteristics that define womanhood. Women submit *because* they are women. Godly women should have a "posture of deep respect"[30] and an overall inclination to defer to male leadership. We have seen that wives are called to submit to their husbands, but according to this view, all women were created to submit to male leadership in all aspects of life.[31]

---

29. Stu Weber, *Tender Warrior: Every Man's Purpose, Every Woman's Dream, Every Child's Hope* (repr., Colorado Springs: Multnomah, 2009), 48.

30. Strachan and Peacock, *The Grand Design*, 79.

31. See Kassian and DeMoss, *True Woman 101*, 70, 152.

According to this framework, the fall confirmed the natural authority/ submission relationship that God had instituted at creation. While there are several interpretations of the curses that Adam and Eve received in Genesis 3, a common explanation is that Adam and Eve both sinned by not following the creation order. Eve attempted to usurp leadership from Adam and led him into sin. Adam abdicated his leadership role over Eve and creation (i.e., the serpent) and so sinned and brought all of humanity into sin with him.[32]

Susan Foh, a student at Westminster Theological Seminary in the 1970s, wrote an article in response to the feminist movement on the meaning of "desire" in Genesis 3:16. By comparing the parallels between Genesis 3:16, "your desire will be for your husband, and he will rule over you," and Genesis 4:7, "[sin's] desire is for you [Cain], but you must master it," Foh explained that Eve's desire for Adam was the same as sin's desire for Cain: "a desire to possess or control."[33]

Just as Cain is told to master sin, Adam is supposed to rule Eve. Therefore, Foh interprets the woman's desire in Genesis 3:16 to be a desire to usurp or control her husband. "These words mark the beginning of the battle of the sexes. . . . The woman's desire is . . . to usurp his divinely appointed headship, and he must master her, if he can. So the rule of love founded in paradise is replaced by struggle, tyranny and domination."[34] According to Foh, all women will desire to usurp authority from men, and men must not allow that to happen.[35]

Foh's interpretation of Genesis 3:16 has become the seemingly default position of many complementarian resources, including the ESV Bible.[36] As of 2016, the ESV text of Genesis 3:16 reads, "Your desire shall be *contrary to* your husband, *but* he shall rule over you." The words in

---

32. Strachan and Peacock, *The Grand Design*, 43.

33. Susan T. Foh, "What is the Woman's Desire?" *The Westminster Theological Journal* 37 (1974): 381.

34. Foh, 382.

35. See Foh, 383.

36. Many conservative Bible commentaries teach Foh's interpretation, as well as do many books for men and women. For examples see Voddie Baucham Jr., *Family Shepherds: Calling and Equipping Men to Lead Their Homes* (Wheaton, IL: Crossway, 2011), chap. 9, loc. 1488–93 of 3015, Kindle, and Kassian and Demoss, *True Woman 101*, 107.

italics are the ones that have been changed. In earlier editions of the ESV, the verse had been translated "Your desire shall be *for* your husband, *and* he shall rule over you."

As we discussed, the difference between men and women regarding authority and submission is often applied to all aspects of life. Many conservative Christians consider it to be part of who men and women are from the very beginning. Some believe that it will still apply in the new heavens and new earth. As Pastor Mark David Walton wrote in CBMW's *Journal for Biblical Manhood and Womanhood,*

> There is every reason to believe, then, that male headship will continue as the divine order for male-female relationships. . . .
>
> With both man and woman thus perfected and transformed, are we to suppose that the new creation will abandon the order established in God's original creation? I think not. Rather, such relations will bring to each true joy, and to God, more glory than before. . . .
>
> We can be confident, though, that "God must have some very profound eternal purpose for manhood and womanhood."[37] There is every reason to believe that gender-based distinction of roles will remain.[38]

EQUAL AND SUBORDINATE

While these beliefs about masculine authority and feminine submission may make you wonder whether women are considered to be inferior to men, most complementarians insist that they aren't teaching that. However, if authority and submission are part of the nature of men and women, then women are inherently subordinate to men. That's not the same as teaching that a wife should submit to her husband. It's also not the same as believing that only qualified men should be ordained leaders in the church.

37. Daniel R. Heimbach, "The Unchangeable Difference: Eternally Fixed Sexual Identity for an Age of Plastic Sexuality," in *Biblical Foundations for Manhood and Womanhood,* ed. Wayne Grudem (Wheaton, IL: Crossway Books, 2002), 286.

38. Mark David Walton, "Relationships and Roles in the New Creation," *Journal for Biblical Manhood and Womanhood* 11, no. 1 (Spring 2006): 15, 17, available online at

Some complementarians use the relationship between God the Father and God the Son as a model for the relationship between men and women. If they can show that there is both equality and hierarchy within the Godhead, then there can be both equality and hierarchy between men and women. As pastor Jared Moore explains, "If complementarians can prove that there is a hierarchy in the immanent (ontological) Trinity,[39] then they win, for if a hierarchy exists among the Three Persons of God, and these Three Persons are equally God, then surely God can create men and women equal yet with differing roles in the church and home. . . . The hierarchy in the home and church, and the submission of women to men in the church and home does not necessarily mean that women are less valuable than men."[40]

The teaching that there's a difference of authority and submission within the Trinity is called the *eternal subordination of the Son* (ESS).[41] Proponents of ESS teach that while God the Father and God the Son are equally God, from all eternity the Son submits to the will of the Father. According to Wayne Grudem, co-founder of CBMW and author of a best-selling systematic theology, authority and submission are the main distinction between the Father, the Son, and the Spirit: "Authority and submission between the Father and the Son, and between Father and Son and the Holy Spirit, is a fundamental difference (or probably *the* fundamental difference) between the persons of the Trinity."[42]

There are some basic facts about the Trinity that Christians have historically agreed on. Regarding the nature of God, the Father, the Son, and the Spirit are one God and three persons. Father, Son, and Spirit are one in being, work as one, and have one will. They are one in their power,

---

http://cbmw.org/wp-content/uploads/2013/05/11-1.pdf.

39. *Immanent* or *ontological Trinity* refers to the nature, being, or essence of God.

40. Jared Moore, "The Complementarians Win: A Review of *One God in Three Persons*," *All Truth Is God's Truth* (blog), May 18, 2015, http://jaredmoore.exaltchrist.com /christian-truth/the-complementarians-win-a-review-of-one-god-in-three-persons/.

41. Some prefer the name *eternal functional subordination* (EFS) or *eternal relations of authority and submission* (ERAS).

42. Wayne Grudem, *Evangelical Feminism & Biblical Truth: An Analysis of More Than 100 Disputed Questions* (Colorado Springs: Multnomah Publishers, 2004), 47, emphasis in original.

glory, and majesty. In the nature or being of God, there's no hierarchy, no difference in being, no difference in authority. This is *who* God is.

In the life of God, the Scriptures show that there's an order, or *taxis*. Father, Son, and Spirit relate and work in a consistent way. The Father is the source or origin of the Son—He sends the Son. The Son is the mediator—He accomplishes redemption. The Spirit is the helper, or advocate—He applies redemption to believers. This is *how* God acts in the work of salvation. There's a linear order, but no hierarchy of authority, in how God acts. In the incarnation, Jesus is God and man. As man, He has a human will that submits in obedience to God the Father. As God, He is equal in power, glory, and majesty with the Father.

Instead of teaching that Jesus's submission to the Father is part of the work of redemption and of His role as Mediator between God and man, ESS teaches that within the Trinity, God the Father has supreme authority "because He is Father."[43] As Ware explains, "It is the Father, then, who is supreme in the Godhead—in the triune relationships of Father, Son, and Holy Spirit—and supreme over all the very creation over which the Son rules as its Lord."[44] When they say that God the Father is supreme in authority within the Trinity *because* He is the Father, they are teaching that authority and submission are part of the nature of God.

THE DAMAGE OF ESS

There are consequences to ESS—both for our understanding of the Trinity and for our beliefs about the nature of women and men. To teach that God the Father is the supreme God with the highest authority and supreme glory means that God's nature has to be divided. If the Father

43. Wayne Grudem, in "Marriage and the Trinity," Revive Our Hearts Radio, May 19, 2005, https://www.reviveourhearts.com/radio/revive-our-hearts/marriage-and-the-trinity/.

44. Bruce A. Ware, *Father, Son, and Holy Spirit: Relationships, Roles, and Relevance* (Wheaton, IL: Crossway Books, 2005), 50–51, quoted in Millard J. Erickson, *Who's Tampering with the Trinity? An Assessment of the Subordination Debate* (Grand Rapids: Kregel Academic & Professional, 2009), 233.

is supreme, then the Son and the Spirit are not co-equal with Him. And if Jesus, as the God-man, isn't the exact imprint of the Father—if He's missing something of the essence of God—then He's not truly God, and His death and resurrection can't save us.

On the practical side, ESS matters because it affects what is taught about the nature of men and women. ESS envisions a hierarchy of authority within the persons of the Trinity, which is then used as the foundation for a similar hierarchy between men and women. If a woman submits to male authority just because she is a woman, then she has no choice. She submits *because* she's female. Contrary to this hierarchical view of women and men, submission in marriage and in the church is an example of equals agreeing to submit to the authority of leaders they have chosen for themselves. There is order, but not subordination.

The influence of these teachings is wide-reaching. ESS, and its applications for men and women, are found in numerous articles and resources that are published and promoted by conservative Christian organizations.[45] It's in books written for women,[46] for children,[47] and about marriage,[48] in the ESV Study Bible notes,[49] and in a best-selling systematic theology.[50] It's also in training materials that have been used for women's ministries in Reformed denominations.[51]

45. Many CBMW authors promote ESS.

46. See Kassian and DeMoss, *True Woman 101*.

47. See Bruce A. Ware, *Big Truths for Young Hearts: Teaching and Learning the Greatness of God* (Wheaton, IL: Crossway Books, 2009).

48. See Strachan and Peacock, *The Grand Design*.

49. See Rachel Green Miller, "Eternal Subordination of the Son and the ESV Study Bible," *A Daughter of the Reformation* (blog), July 7, 2016, https://adaughterofthe reformation.wordpress.com/2016/07/07/eternal-subordination-of-the-son-and-the -esv-study-bible/.

50. See Wayne Grudem, *Systematic Theology: An Introduction to Biblical Doctrine* (Grand Rapids: Zondervan, 1994).

51. See "Thinking Biblically and Living Covenantally: A Biblical Apologetic for Women," Christian Education and Publications, last modified 2014, https://web.archive .org/web/20140801133748/http://www.pcacep.org/wp-content/uploads/2014/02 /WM-Training-Manual-Mar-2014.pdf, 45.

ENMITY BETWEEN WOMEN AND MEN

Foh's interpretation of Genesis 3:16, too, has had extensive influence on conservative Christian beliefs about women and men. As we have seen, some teach that women are vulnerable and open to deception. They also teach that because women are like Eve, they will attempt to usurp masculine authority: "Women are tempted to usurp God-constituted authority, to grasp for leadership in certain spheres that the Lord has allotted, in His infinite wisdom, to men."[52] Therefore, men are supposed to lead spiritually and to keep women from rebelling. This masculine leadership goes beyond the ordained roles of pastors, elders, and so on. Some conservative Christians teach that only men should teach God's people, formally or informally—whether inside or outside the church.[53]

The problem is that Foh's interpretation presumes that all wives want to control and usurp their husbands' leadership, which misses the context of the curse: the frustration of existing conditions. She states that a husband's headship, in itself, is not part of the curse.[54] That's certainly true—but neither is a wife's desire. Like childbirth and work, a wife's desire and a husband's headship are pre-fall realities. All men and women have been affected by the fall. Childbirth is painful, work is hard, wives desire their husbands, and husbands rule over them. It's inconsistent to argue that, of all four statements in Genesis 3:16, only the wife's desire is new and the result of sin.

Eve had just been told that childbearing would now be painful. Despite that, and despite the broken relationship between her and Adam, who had just blamed her for his own sin, she would continue to desire her husband. And he would rule over her. This is a descriptive statement of the future of Eve and her daughters, not a prescriptive one. Interpreting "desire" this way fits the passage better and is consistent with the experience of women across the centuries.

---

52. Strachan and Peacock, *The Grand Design*, 117.
53. Strachan and Peacock, 86.
54. See Foh, "What Is the Woman's Desire?" 378.

When conservative Christians teach men to suspect women's counsel because women are prone to deception and will try to usurp their leadership, interactions become antagonistic. If women can't be trusted to make wise decisions, and if men have to be careful not to let women lead them, then men and women are pitted against each other. These teachings undermine the unity, interdependence, service, and co-laboring that should define Christian behavior. On the one hand, men won't trust women—particularly their wives—or benefit from their insight. On the other, wives will doubt themselves and the love that their husbands are supposed to have for them. How can husbands love their wives as Christ loved the church when they see them as adversaries?

TWISTING OURSELVES UP INTO KNOTS

The hyper focus on authority and submission, and the wooden definitions of masculinity and femininity that we've discussed, have also created a good deal of confusion within conservative Christian circles. Many good Christian women and men are struggling to apply these beliefs in their lives. They want to know if it's wrong for a wife to make more money than her husband. They ask if husbands should tell their wives how to vote. They wonder if paying the bills and keeping the finances are areas of masculine authority or feminine domesticity. Maybe you've had similar questions yourself.

From this focus on authority and submission, the greatest concern becomes figuring out who's in charge, which can lead to confusing guidelines for how men and women should interact. Women are told that they shouldn't submit to just any man, but men have a responsibility to lead. As such, men are responsible for taking initiative and exercising authority in all of life. This doesn't mean that women never initiate or lead, but men should set the "tone and pattern" of leadership and initiation.[55] For example, suppose that a woman has information that a man needs—directions to the hospital, let's say. A woman can give a man driving directions, but

---

55. See Piper, "A Vision of Biblical Complementarity," in Piper and Grudem, *Recovering Biblical Manhood and Womanhood*, 36–39.

she should do it in a way that doesn't compromise her femininity by leading or his masculinity as he follows her direction.[56]

According to many complementarians, men demonstrate masculine authority by leading their wives and families in everything. They should discuss important decisions with their wives, but ultimately, the final decision is their responsibility. This is especially true if husbands and wives disagree. Men are the tiebreakers.[57]

Based on these complementarian definitions, is a man who works as a nurse or a teacher feminine? What about a man who loves art or fashion or shopping or baking—is he less masculine? Or is a woman who's an engineer, a scientist, or a cop masculine? What if she loves sports or hunting or working on cars or is the CEO of a company—is she less feminine?

DEFINING MASCULINITY AND FEMININITY

It's no secret that men and women are different. Even our mixed-up culture recognizes that we're not exactly the same. But there's no consensus on how we are different. Some say that women and men are from different planets. Others say that we're polar opposites: feminine versus masculine, yin versus yang, order versus chaos, sugar, spice, and everything nice versus snips, snails, and puppy dog tails. Still others believe that gender is like a continuum, with masculinity on one end and femininity on the other. Some men are considered more masculine than others. Some women are considered more feminine.

Some believe that the image of God in humanity is divided between men and women. This belief is extremely dangerous. If the image of God is only partially represented in both men and women, and if Christ represents males in particular, this raises questions about how Jesus's life, death, and resurrection apply to women. If Jesus is the perfect male, then women must need someone else to imitate. Because, as Brandon O'Brien explains, "if Christ is the model of masculinity, then women can't imitate

---

56. See Piper, 50.
57. See Strachan and Peacock, *The Grand Design*, 76.

him. They can pursue him as the lover of their souls. They can imitate his devotion to the Father in their relationships with their husbands. But they can't become like him in any essential way."[58]

In geometry, complementarity is when two separate angles add up to a 90-degree angle. One writer observed that if this definition applies to men and women, then women and men make up a complete picture of humanity but without any overlap.[59] In contrast, author Wendy Alsup compares masculinity and femininity to a Venn diagram with a large overlapping middle part.[60] This description comes the closest to what we have seen about women and men in the Bible.

Without denying the differences between women and men, the Bible focuses on our similarities. As we have discussed, we are co-laborers—united in creation and in Christ. We are all made in the image of God. Our human nature is united in our creation and represented in Adam, and it is fully represented in Christ's humanity. He's the only hope for both men *and* women. We have one Mediator, one Savior, one gospel, and one way of salvation. We are interdependent and made to serve each other. The world seeks to divide what God has brought together. And, unfortunately, the church often follows suit.

Godly women and men are twisting themselves up in knots trying to be faithful. But what if we're going about this the wrong way? Instead of rules and lists, the Bible gives us general guidelines and Christian liberty—even on the topic of gender. Let's step back from our questions and examine what the Bible teaches about the nature of women and men and the meaning of masculinity and femininity.

58. Brandon O'Brien, "A Jesus for Real Men," *Christianity Today*, April 18, 2008, http://www.christianitytoday.com/ct/2008/april/27.48.html.

59. See Angela Whitehorn (@ImAngelaPangela), "Can we talk about the word 'complementarian?'" Twitter, February 3, 2018, 8:20 p.m., https://twitter.com/ImAngela Pangela/status/960005170112450561?s=03.

60. See Wendy Alsup, *Is the Bible Good for Women? Seeking Clarity and Confidence Through a Jesus-Centered Understanding of Scripture* (Colorado Springs: Multnomah, 2017), 5.

DISCUSSION QUESTIONS

1. How are conservative beliefs about the nature of men and masculinity similar to those of the Greeks, Romans, and Victorians?
2. How are conservative beliefs about the nature of women and femininity similar to those of the Greeks, Romans, and Victorians?
3. How do these beliefs about women and men influence interpretations of Genesis 3:16?
4. How have some conservatives attempted to use the relationship between God the Father and God the Son as a model for men and women?
5. What are some examples of authority and submission being the lens through which we view men and women?

8

"SHE GIRDS HERSELF
WITH STRENGTH"

THE BIBLE ON THE NATURE OF WOMEN

*The fundamental thing is that women are more
like men than anything else in the world.*

DOROTHY SAYERS[1]

When I was a teen, and into my early 20s, I struggled with my self-image—especially in the area of being feminine. I had always wanted to be a wife and mother. I loved wearing pretty clothes and makeup. I wanted to date guys, but I wasn't getting asked out much. As an introspective person, I began to wonder what was wrong with me.

I'd always known that I didn't quite fit feminine stereotypes. As much as I loved being a woman, I didn't look much like the willowy, slender heroines who were popular in many books and movies. There was never any doubt that I was a woman, but I was muscular and strong. I loved science and math, and I was in the top of my class. Until I realized that I didn't

---

1. Dorothy Sayers, *Are Women Human?* (Grand Rapids: Eerdmans, 1971), 53, quoted in Aimee Byrd, *No Little Women: Equipping All Women in the Household of God* (Phillipsburg, NJ: P&R Publishing, 2016), 260.

love calculus, I wanted to be an engineer and to work for NASA like my granddad. Eventually I chose to study history—another male-dominated field. My plan was to be a professor like my mom.

Was I feminine enough for guys to be interested in me? Maybe I was too intelligent, too intimidating—too something. How was I different from the girls who were getting asked out? I started reading some of the books that my friends were reading about "kissing dating goodbye" and being a "lady-in-waiting" and pursuing "passion and purity." But the books left me with more questions than answers.

After my husband and I started dating, I regained my confidence as I saw myself through his eyes. He thought that I was beautiful and feminine. Eventually it dawned on me that maybe there wasn't something wrong with me. Maybe the definitions I'd read of what it means to be "appropriately feminine" were too narrow. Maybe there was something missing from those books about dating and how to be a good Christian woman.

THE MEANING OF MASCULINITY AND FEMININITY, AND WHY IT MATTERS

Conservative Christians often discuss what it means to be a godly man or woman. Most are committed to orthodoxy and want to be biblical. But they aren't sure how to apply what the Bible teaches to the lives they live as men and women. When we talk about the nature of women and men and the meaning of femininity and masculinity, we need to be clear what we mean by these terms.

As terms, *masculinity* and *femininity* tend to be somewhat nebulous in our minds. We have a sense of what the words mean, but when asked to describe them, we fall back on the old saying "We know it when we see it." Merriam-Webster defines *masculine* as "having qualities appropriate to or usually associated with a man"[2] and *feminine* as "characteristic of or appropriate or unique to women."[3] And those definitions help, to a point.

2. *Merriam-Webster*, s.v. "masculine (*adj.*)," accessed December 21, 2018, https://www.merriam-webster.com/dictionary/masculine.

3. *Merriam-Webster*, s.v. "feminine (*adj.*)," accessed December 21, 2018, https://www.merriam-webster.com/dictionary/feminine.

The definition for *feminine* carries the sense of the biological differences between women and men. The characteristics that are unique to women and to men include the ways that our bodies are distinct from each other. We also see the cultural aspects of masculinity and femininity in these dictionary definitions. The definitions mention qualities that are appropriate for men or women or are "traditionally associated with"[4] each gender.

Masculinity and femininity, then, have to do with who we are and how our culture expects us to behave. The cultural component can be the tricky part. Many beliefs about masculinity and femininity are rooted in cultural and ethnic ideas about men and women. What's appropriately feminine in the twenty-first-century United States isn't necessarily what was expected of women in sixth-century China. And what was considered masculine for the Greeks, Romans, and Victorians isn't necessarily the best guideline for men today.

As we saw in the last chapter, many conservative Christians define men and women in terms of opposites, based on older cultural definitions that we've discussed. They define femininity as being submissive, gentle, quiet, responsive, soft, life-giving, and helping. They define masculinity as strength, authority, initiation, provision, protection, and theological discernment. But do these definitions represent the full diversity of expression that is seen in Scripture?

In this chapter and the next, we will compare these common definitions of masculinity and femininity to examples of women and men from Scripture. Looking at these examples will help to expand our understanding of what it means to be feminine and masculine. The Bible's teaching about the nature of women and men gives us more freedom than we realize.

Of course, we always need to be careful not to assume that God approves of the behaviors that the Bible describes. By using Scripture to interpret Scripture, we can compare what people are described as doing with what God has commanded. For example, several of the Old Testament patriarchs and kings had multiple wives, but we know from

---

4. Oxford Living Dictionaries, s.v. "feminine (*adj.*)," accessed December 21, 2018, https://en.oxforddictionaries.com/definition/feminine.

Genesis 2:24 and Matthew 19:4–6 that marriage was created to be between one man and one woman. The examples we will study are ones in which people are commended for their actions or act in ways that aren't otherwise condemned in Scripture.

In this chapter, we will look at biblical women who performed behaviors that are often defined as masculine: leading, initiating, providing, protecting, demonstrating strength, and having theological discernment. In the next, we'll consider examples of men who performed behaviors that are commonly defined as feminine: helping, giving life, responding, and being gentle, quiet, soft, and tender.

WOMEN LEAD AND INITIATE

When I was growing up, I was told stories about heroes from the Bible: David, Samson, Joshua, Gideon, Deborah. As a grown woman, however, I began to notice a difference in the way that some people talked about Deborah. They made comments like "Sure, she was a leader and a judge, but that was bad. She was only a leader because no men were willing to lead. It was a judgment on Israel to have a woman leader. Look at that weak man, Barak. He was a coward who wasn't willing to go into battle without Deborah—a woman! Deborah isn't an example of good leadership. She's 'non-normative.'"

Some say that Deborah was a "living indictment" of the men in Israel.[5] Others say that her leadership was a "shame to the nation of Israel."[6] Some warn against modern Deborahs, saying, "If our society ever sinks to the level where *one* Deborah is necessary, it will be a sign that God is phenomenally displeased with our culture and is inflicting a colossal curse on it."[7] Others believe that Deborah's story should motivate godly

---

5. John Piper and Wayne Grudem, "An Overview of Central Concerns: Questions and Answers," in *Recovering Biblical Manhood and Womanhood*, ed. John Piper and Wayne Grudem (repr., Wheaton, IL: Crossway Books, 2006), 72.

6. Debi Pearl, *Created to Be His Help Meet: Discover How God Can Make Your Marriage Glorious* (Pleasantville, TN: No Greater Joy Ministries, 2010), p. 120, Kindle.

7. Anna Sofia Botkin and Elizabeth Botkin, *So Much More: The Remarkable Influence of Visionary Daughters on the Kingdom of God* (San Antonio: Vision Forum, 2005), 128, emphasis in original.

women to encourage men to lead: "The Bible views Deborah's judgeship as a rebuke against the absence of male leadership. . . . Something is abnormal, something is wrong—there are no men to function as judge! . . . *The story of Deborah should motivate women in such situations to do what Deborah did: encourage and exhort a man to take the leadership role to which God has called him.*"[8]

But what does the Bible say? According to Judges 4, Deborah was a prophetess who judged the people of Israel during the oppressive rule of Jabin, the king of Canaan, and Sisera, his army commander. One day, she summoned Barak and gave him a command from God to take his army and fight Sisera. God promised them victory over their enemies. Barak replied that he would go only if Deborah went with him. Deborah promised to go but warned him that the honor of the victory wouldn't be his. God would deliver Sisera into "the hands of a woman" (v. 9). That is exactly what happened.

Deborah went with Barak and the army. Barak led the army as God routed Sisera. Sisera's army was destroyed, and Sisera himself was killed by the enterprising Jael, who drove a tent peg into his head while he slept. Deborah and Barak then sang a song praising God for saving them.

As we see from the passage, Deborah and Barak's song praises the leaders and the people of Israel for their action: "The leaders led in Israel" and "The people volunteered, bless the LORD!" (Judg. 5:2). Their song goes on to praise the leaders, officers, and princes from the various tribes of Israel who joined forces and fought, as well as praising their "great resolves of heart" (see Judg. 5:14–15). Deborah wasn't the only motivated or faithful person left in Israel.

The Bible praises Deborah for her role as a "mother in Israel" (Judg. 5:7). She's an example of a godly woman who was a civil leader.

John Gill, an eighteenth-century Baptist theologian and pastor, elaborates on Deborah's role as a judge and a leader: "To teach and instruct them in the mind and will of God, to administer judgment and justice

---

8. Wayne Grudem, *Evangelical Feminism & Biblical Truth: An Analysis of More Than 100 Disputed Questions* (Colorado Springs: Multnomah Publishers, 2004), 134–35, emphasis in original.

to them, to protect and defend them, and in all which she discovered a maternal affection for them."[9] Later, Gill explains that Deborah is named ahead of Barak in Judges 5:1 because she was "the root or foundation" and "the chief person" in the work.[10] While female leaders are rare in the Bible, there's no scriptural evidence that what Deborah did was wrong or shameful. She wasn't a priest or an ordained leader in the church. She didn't dishonor her husband. God blessed her leadership, and the people of Israel praised her for helping to free them from their enemies.

Deborah is probably the most familiar female leader in the Bible, but she isn't the only one. Moses's sister, Miriam, was also a prophetess and a leader in Israel. God tells Israel that He sent Moses, Aaron, *and* Miriam to go before them as He brought them out of Egypt (see Mic. 6:4). For example, Miriam acted as a leader when she led the women of Israel to worship God through singing and dancing (see Ex. 15:20–21).

Deborah and Miriam aren't the only women who lead and take initiative in the Bible. Abigail acts on her own initiative to save herself and her household (see 1 Sam. 25). Jochebed takes it on herself to save her son, Moses (see Ex. 2). Zipporah acts quickly to save Moses from death (see Ex. 4). Esther plans a way to save herself and her people (see Esth. 4). Ruth initiates a relationship with Boaz, effectively proposing to him (see Ruth 3). And then there's the Proverbs 31 woman, who demonstrates initiative in her care for her household and her business ventures.

In the New Testament, several women show the same initiative. A woman was healed after she went to Jesus and touched His cloak, demonstrating her faith in His ability to heal (see Luke 8:43–48). In Matthew, the Syrophoenician woman came to Jesus and refused to be sent away until He healed her daughter (see Matt. 15:21–28). The Samaritan woman at the well ran, on her own initiative, to tell everyone who Jesus was (see John 4:28–29). Lydia was the leader of her household (see Acts 16:14–15).

9. Judges 5:7 in *John Gill's Exposition of the Bible,* available online from Bible Study Tools, accessed June 18, 2018, http://www.biblestudytools.com/commentaries/gills-exposition-of-the-bible/judges-5-7.html.

10. Judges 5:1 in *John Gill's Exposition of the Bible,* available online from Bible Study Tools, accessed May 28, 2019, https://www.biblestudytools.com/commentaries/gills-exposition-of-the-bible/judges-5-1.html.

What does that mean for us? While the Bible calls husbands to lead their families and qualified men to lead in the church, it doesn't present leadership and initiative as being exclusively male characteristics. Given these examples, there's nothing unbiblical about a woman leading in society. Women in the Bible lead and show initiative, even by proposing marriage.

WOMEN PROVIDE

In discussions about how to provide financially for a family, conservative Christians don't all agree. Some say that only men should work outside the home.[11] Others believe that women can work outside the home but that men should have the primary responsibility of providing for the family.[12] Certainly men should be concerned with providing for their families. No one should be lazy. God made us all, male and female, to work.

I didn't grow up on a farm, but my husband did. If you are a farmer or a farmer's kid, you know that there's always work to be done—all day, every day. Chores have to be done. Cows have to be milked and fed, twice a day. Crops have to be planted, grown, and harvested. Food has to be canned and preserved. There's work for everyone in the family. Everyone works, or it doesn't get done.

This life may seem foreign to many of us, but most of the world still lives this way. In farming societies, a family's survival depends on everyone working together. Families raise their own food, make their own clothes and tools, and craft as many of their own goods as they can. Husbands and wives work the fields together, tend livestock together, and care for each other. It's true that men often do the bulk of the fieldwork and that women take primary care of the children, but husbands and wives depend on each other to survive.[13] Our modern preoccupation with "who makes

11. See Botkin and Botkin, *So Much More*, 24, 107.

12. See John Piper, *What's the Difference? Manhood and Womanhood Defined According to the Bible* (Wheaton, IL: Crossway Books, 1990), 38–39.

13. See Estelle B. Freedman, *No Turning Back: The History of Feminism and the Future of Women* (New York: Ballantine Books, 2002), 125.

the money" is relatively recent. "What do we need to do so that we don't starve" was a more pressing concern for people in the past—and still is for much of the world today.

But for our discussion, we will look at women who provided for their families or for others.

Consider how Ruth worked to provide for herself and Naomi by gleaning in the fields for grain (see Ruth 2:17–18). Maybe she provided for herself and Naomi only because they were widowed and had no one else to provide for them, but she isn't the only woman in the Bible who provided for others.

Many women in the Old Testament cared for their families' animals. Livestock weren't a side business. A family's herds were a significant portion of the family's worth or income. And the Scriptures give us many examples of women who took care of their families' herds. For example, Rachel, Jacob's wife, was a shepherdess (see Gen. 29:9). Given that her father, Laban, had sons as well as daughters (see Gen. 31:1), she wasn't working with the herds by default. Zipporah, Moses's wife, also cared for the family's livestock with her sisters (see Ex. 2:16).

The Proverbs 31 woman provided for her family, for her household, and for the needy in many ways, and the Bible praises her for it.

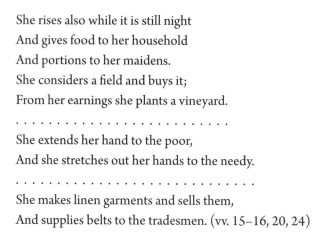

> She rises also while it is still night
> And gives food to her household
> And portions to her maidens.
> She considers a field and buys it;
> From her earnings she plants a vineyard.
>
> . . . .
>
> She extends her hand to the poor,
> And she stretches out her hands to the needy.
>
> . . . .
>
> She makes linen garments and sells them,
> And supplies belts to the tradesmen. (vv. 15–16, 20, 24)

In the New Testament, Lydia was a seller of purple cloth. She apparently had her own household to support (see Acts 16:14–15). Dorcas provided for the needs of the widows in Joppa (see Acts 9:36–39). Priscilla, Aquila's wife, worked alongside her husband in the tentmaking business (see Acts 18:1–3).

Some people have taken 1 Timothy 5:8 to mean that men are intended to be the primary breadwinners of the family. They often quote the verse this way: "But if any man does not provide for his own, and especially for those of his household, he has denied the faith and is worse than an unbeliever."[14] The context of the passage, however, is a discussion of widows in the church and how to care for them. Believers are warned that they need to care for their own families, including any dependent widows.

"If any *man*" is actually an inadequate translation. The word is gender-neutral, and the overall phrase is properly translated "if *anyone* does not provide." Both male and female believers are told to provide for the needs of widows in their families.[15] In fact, 1 Timothy 5:16 specifically tells believing women that they must provide for any dependent widows in their households: "If any woman who is a believer has dependent widows, she must assist them and the church must not be burdened, so that it may assist those who are widows indeed."

As Pastor Nate Pyle points out, this passage isn't focused on ensuring that "all Christian husbands for all generations take on the primary role of breadwinning. . . . [Paul] is exhorting the immediate family of a widow to rise to the occasion and take care of their own family so as to not place undue burden on the church. To imply that Paul is making the case for men being the primary breadwinners is to change the most apparent meaning of the text."[16]

In addition to providing for the needs of their households and contributing to the economy of their families, many women in the Bible

<hr/>

14. See J. D. Gunter, "Men as Providers," The Council on Biblical Manhood and Womanhood, November 11, 2013, https://cbmw.org/topics/leadership-2/men-as-providers/.

15. John Calvin insists that 1 Timothy 5:8 applies both to men and women. See John Calvin, *Commentaries on the First Epistle to Timothy*, trans. William Pringle, in *Galatians–Philemon*, Calvin's Commentaries 21 (repr., Grand Rapids: Baker, 1979), 126.

16. Nate Pyle, *Man Enough: How Jesus Redefines Manhood* (Grand Rapids: Zondervan, 2015), 51.

provided for the needs of those in ministry. The Shunammite woman in 2 Kings provided for the prophet Elisha. On her initiative, she and her husband provided food and a place for Elisha to rest (see 2 Kings 4:8–10).

In the New Testament, women provided for Jesus and the disciples "out of their private means" (Luke 8:3). Other New Testament women provided for the early church and hosted church meetings in their houses. These included Lydia (see Acts 16:40), Priscilla (along with her husband, Aquila—see 1 Cor. 16:19), and Nympha (see Col. 4:15).

What does that mean for us? Being a provider, based on the biblical examples that are shown here, isn't an exclusively masculine responsibility. Both men and women are called to provide for the needs of others. The Bible doesn't address the question of who should make the most money. But we can apply the examples from the Bible to answering questions such as whether it's wrong for a woman to make more money than her husband.

It would be wrong for a man to refuse to work and provide for his family (see 2 Thess. 3:10), but that's not the main question that these passages are answering. According to the Bible, both men and women have a responsibility to provide for others. How that works out in each family is a matter of Christian liberty.

WOMEN PROTECT

As we discussed in the last chapter, masculinity is defined, in part, as protecting others—especially women. But the Scriptures give many examples of women who protected others. In fact, protection is integral to who women are as wives and mothers. We are called to nurture and protect.

We see this in how Moses is protected by women over and over again. Even before his birth, the Hebrew midwives, Shiphrah and Puah, protected the baby boys from Pharaoh's order to kill them (see Ex. 1:15–21). Moses's mother, Jochebed, and sister, Miriam, hid him as an infant and devised and carried out a plan to protect him over the long term. Pharaoh's daughter took him and raised him as her own, providing protection for Moses as he grew up (see Ex. 2:1–10). Later, when the Lord sought to kill Moses, Zipporah, Moses's wife, stepped in and protected his life by circumcising their son (see Ex. 4:24–26).

Abigail, Nabal's wife, is remembered for the quick thinking she showed in order to keep David from killing her household. When Nabal refused to provide for David and his soldiers, Abigail sent provisions for David and his men and pled with David not to destroy her household. In this one act, she took initiative, led her male servants, provided for the needs of David and his men, and protected her household—all against the express wishes of her husband. For her actions, Abigail is commended and becomes David's wife when her husband, Nabal, dies for his wickedness (see 1 Sam. 25:18–42).

Another biblical example of a woman who protected others is Esther. She took her life in her hands to protect her people from being killed. Like Abigail, Esther took initiative, directed men (her cousin Mordecai), and took action to protect many people (see Esth. 4:15–17).

Other examples include Rahab, who protected her family and the Jewish spies (see Josh. 2), Mephibosheth's nurse, who protected him after Saul and Jonathan died (see 2 Sam. 4:4), and Jehosheba, who protected Joash (who later became king) when Athaliah killed all of the royal sons (see 2 Kings 11:2).

What does that mean for us? Many men throughout the Bible protect their families and others. Godly men should certainly protect those in their care, but protecting others is not uniquely masculine. Can women be police officers or in the military? Godly women should protect others in whatever ways they can, as God gives them opportunity and ability.

WOMEN ARE STRONG

Strength is another defining characteristic of masculinity that we have discussed. On average, men are generally bigger and physically stronger than women, but that doesn't mean that women aren't strong in their own way. One of the clearest examples of a strong women in the Bible is Jael, who drove a tent peg into a man's skull (see Judg. 4:21). Jael had the strength of mind and character, as well as the physical strength, to drive a tent peg through Sisera's skull. She's the hero of the story—a strong woman who is praised for her actions and even called "most blessed of women" (Judg. 5:24). The Scriptures also praise the Proverbs 31 woman for her strength: "She girds herself with strength and makes her arms strong" (v. 17); "Strength and dignity are her clothing, and she smiles at the future" (v. 25).

The Psalms often encourage God's people, both male and female, to be strong: "Wait for the LORD; be strong and let your heart take courage; yes, wait for the LORD" (Ps. 27:14); "Be strong and let your heart take courage, all you who hope in the LORD" (Ps. 31:24). In Ephesians 6:10, before describing the armor of God, Paul tells believers to be "strong in the Lord."

In 1 Corinthians 16:13, Paul says, "Be on the alert, stand firm in the faith, act like men, be strong." Some say that Paul is equating strength with masculinity, but let's consider the context. At the beginning of this letter to the Corinthians, Paul compares the believers in Corinth to spiritual infants who can't take solid food (see 1 Cor. 3:1–3). The contrast that Paul is making is between immature and mature believers, not between men and women. John Gill explains that we should "be not like children for non-proficiency, instability, and weakness."[17] At the end of 1 Corinthians, when Paul calls on all believers—male and female—to stand firm, to act like men, to be strong, he is encouraging them to be mature in the faith. He isn't challenging men (or women) in particular to be more masculine.

The strength that Paul is exhorting believers to have isn't so much a physical strength or a personal attribute; it's strength from the Lord. Believers are strong when they recognize their natural weakness and trust in the Lord for His strength. Paul boasts in his own weakness because God uses it to display Christ's power and strength (see 2 Cor. 12:9–10). Believers are called to be strong in their faith and weak in themselves. In the New Testament, the world's expectations and priorities are replaced by the priorities and expectations of the gospel.

Most men have an advantage over women when it comes to physical strength, but strength isn't masculine. A smaller or weaker man isn't less

17. 1 Corinthians 16:13 in *John Gill's Exposition of the Bible*, available online from Bible Study Tools, accessed June 18, 2018, https://www.biblestudytools.com

of a man. A strong, muscular woman isn't less of a woman. Strength and physical ability don't define us as men or women.

Strength also goes beyond a physical ability to lift weights or run fast. Women had to be strong to do all the physical labor that was required to survive in most societies throughout history. Hauling water, washing clothes, cleaning, cooking, working in the fields, and so on required considerable strength and made women physically strong and muscular.

A woman's body has to be strong in order to go through pregnancy, labor, and delivery—both physically and mentally. Emotionally, too. Throughout history, women have faced the likelihood of their own death and/or the deaths of their children. This takes strength—something that men *and* women should have.

WOMEN HAVE THEOLOGICAL DISCERNMENT

Because conservative Christian denominations generally ordain men as leaders in the church, some believe that men naturally have a greater interest in theology or that men should be the "resident theologians" of their homes.[18] The Bible, however, gives us many examples of women encouraging and instructing men in spiritual matters.

Samson's mother showed greater understanding of God and His ways than her husband, Manoah, did, when she advised Manoah after God visited them. Manoah was convinced that God was going to kill them, but she assured him that God meant to bless them (see Judges 13:22–23).

King Josiah sent his men to have Huldah, the prophetess, ask God what he should do after the book of the Law was found (see 2 Kings 22:14–20). Huldah advised the king and told him what God's message was for him.

Lois and Eunice taught Timothy and instructed him in the faith (see 2 Tim. 1:5). Priscilla, along with her husband, Aquila, taught Apollos so that he would understand the gospel more accurately (see Acts 18:24–26). Anna, the prophetess at the temple, shared the good news about Jesus's coming (see Luke 2:36–38).

/commentaries/gills-exposition-of-the-bible/1-corinthians-16-13.html.

18. See Douglas Wilson, *Reforming Marriage* (Moscow, ID: Canon Press, 1995), 38.

All believers, both women and men, should test what they are taught against the Scriptures, as the Berean church did (see Acts 17:10–12). The Bible tells all believers to share their faith and to be able to give a defense for their hope (see 1 Peter 3:15). As Aimee Byrd writes, "Everyone in the church needs to be a good theologian."[19]

What does that mean for us? Questions about women and theology come up all the time in discussions among conservative Christians. From what we have seen, women should be encouraged to read and to study theology. They may be more interested in theology than their husbands are, and that's okay, too. It's good for women to share what they've learned, and it's appropriate for men to learn from women.

We're not talking about who should preach and have authority in the church. Ordination to church leadership should be restricted to qualified men. But outside those ordained roles, there is room for women to have a voice in theological discussions. And there is room for men to learn from women.

DIVERSITY IN THE BIBLICAL DEPICTION OF WOMEN

The Bible gives us positive examples of women who led, initiated, provided, protected, demonstrated strength, and had theological discernment. Making decisions, earning money, running businesses, being physically strong, and being interested in theology don't make women less feminine. The Scriptures give us a much greater range of feminine behavior and actions than the prevalent complementarian definition of femininity does. If we allow the Bible to be our template for appropriate behavior, women will have more freedom to use their gifts and talents in ways that will glorify God.

In the next chapter, we will consider various ways in which godly men in the Bible demonstrate "feminine" behaviors. Men need the freedom and diversity that the Bible provides for our understanding of masculinity.

19. Byrd, *No Little Women*, 34.

DISCUSSION QUESTIONS

1. What are some examples of women in the Bible who led and took initiative?
2. How did women in the Bible work to provide for their families?
3. What are some examples of women who protected others in the Bible?
4. What does strength look like for a woman, based on the biblical examples that were given in this chapter?
5. Should women be less theologically discerning than men?

9

"LET YOUR GENTLE SPIRIT
BE KNOWN TO ALL"

THE BIBLE ON THE NATURE OF MEN

If it is more natural for a man to be aggressive and a woman to be
passive, then a genuine encounter with Christ should challenge a man to
become gentle (Gal. 5:23) and a woman to become bold (2 Tim. 1:7).

BRANDON O'BRIEN[1]

Women aren't the only ones who struggle with cultural stereotypes. In some ways, the definition of masculinity seems to be even more stringent than the meaning of femininity. After all, women don't tell each other that they're going to lose their "woman card" if they go to a baseball game or drive a pickup truck. But if a man goes to a "chick flick" with his wife or drives a minivan? Those are some of the "Top 10 Ways to Lose Your 'Man Card.'"[2] In case you're curious, this list (and others like it) also includes

---

1. Brandon O'Brien, "A Jesus for Real Men," *Christianity Today*, April 18, 2008, http://www.christianitytoday.com/ct/2008/april/27.48.html.
2. Paul Carter, "10 Ways to Lose Your Man Card," Lift-Run-Bang, August 4, 2011, http://www.lift-run-bang.com/2011/08/10-ways-to-lose-your-man-card.html. A word of warning that this webpage contains some very crass language and content.

going shopping with your wife/girlfriend, wearing matching outfits, not driving the car on a date, and knowing what the Tony awards are.[3]

While strength defines masculinity, masculinity itself appears to be easily lost and hard to regain. Even the dictionary definitions that we looked at in the last chapter illustrate the stricter limits that masculinity has. If you remember, Merriam-Webster defines masculine as "having qualities appropriate to or usually associated with a man."[4] We have words for men who aren't masculine enough or who do something that reduces their masculinity—we call them effeminate or emasculated. But there aren't parallel words for women.

I feel for my brothers in Christ who don't fit the masculine mold. There isn't much leeway when it comes to living up to this standard. Pastors who don't like football have a tough road if they're living in the southern United States, where football is everything. The message, even in church communities, is that "real men" do certain things and behave in particular ways. If you are a man who doesn't care much for sports, hunting, cars, or camping (to name a few), you have probably had your masculinity questioned. And heaven forbid that you actually cry at a sad or romantic movie.

Conservative Christians define femininity in terms of helping, giving life, and being gentle, quiet, responsive, and soft. The Bible does give us examples of women who display these traits. But the question is whether these qualities are *exclusively* feminine. Does the Bible give us examples of godly men who display these characteristics?

MEN HELP

Woman was created to be a helper for man, but that doesn't mean that only women are helpers. As we saw, the Bible often describes God as a helper. In the Old Testament, the Psalms praise God for helping His people: "Behold, God is my helper" (Ps. 54:4); "You have been the helper

---

3. Woody, "Top 10 Ways to Lose Your 'Man Card'—According to 102.7 KORD Listeners," KORD, April 25, 2013, http://1027kord.com/top-10-ways-to-lose-your -man-card-according-to-102-7-kord-listeners/.

4. *Merriam-Webster*, s.v. "masculine (*adj.*)" accessed December 21, 2018, https:// www.merriam-webster.com/dictionary/masculine.

of the orphan" (Ps. 10:14). In the New Testament, Jesus calls the Holy Spirit our Helper (see John 16:7).

In the Old Testament, armies and foreign countries are also described as helpers: "They will know that I am the LORD, when I set a fire in Egypt and all her helpers are broken" (Ezek. 30:8); "Ethiopia was her might, and Egypt too, without limits. Put and Lubim were among her helpers" (Nah. 3:9).

In the New Testament, both men and women are described as helpers in the work of the church. In Romans 16:2, Paul says that Phoebe "has also been a helper of many, and of myself as well." In Acts 13:5, Luke writes that Barnabas and Saul "also had John as their helper."

What does that mean for us? Being a helper is an important trait for believers. Because God is often described as a helper, being a helper isn't uniquely feminine. In marriage, the church, and society, men and women should help each other. How that works out in individual situations—for example, in a family—may vary depending on the season of life of the people involved, on God's gifting and calling of them, and on their individual needs.

MEN ARE GENTLE AND QUIET

First Peter 3:4 tells women to adorn themselves not with jewelry but with "the hidden person of the heart, with the imperishable quality of a gentle and quiet spirit, which is precious in the sight of God." Certainly believing women should have a gentle and quiet spirit, and we will see in a moment what that means. But gentleness is not limited to women. Jesus describes Himself as being "gentle and humble in heart" (Matt. 11:29). In Philippians 4:5, Paul encourages all believers to "let your gentle spirit be known to all men." And in 1 Timothy 3:3, one of the qualifications for elders is that they be "gentle, peaceable, free from the love of money." Gentleness is part of the fruit of the Spirit (see Gal. 5:22), and Paul and the other New Testament authors frequently encourage believers to have gentleness or a spirit of gentleness.[5]

---

5. See 1 Cor. 4:21; 2 Cor. 10:1; Gal. 6:1; Eph. 4:2; Col. 3:12; 1 Tim. 6:11; 2 Tim. 2:25; Titus 3:2; James 1:21; 3:13; 1 Peter 3:15.

We sometimes translate the Bible's terms for *gentle* and *gentleness* as "meek," "meekness," or "humility." In English, we associate these words with weakness, but that's a misunderstanding on our part. A better understanding of the Greek terms, *praus* and *praotes*, is "strength under control."[6] When we understand gentleness and meekness in this way, we can grasp how Jesus and Moses could be considered meek or gentle. Godly gentleness can include righteous anger (see Ex. 32:19)—even overturning tables in the temple (see Matt. 21:12–17).

What about a "quiet spirit"? Should men have that as well? Paul uses the same root word for "quiet" that he used in 1 Peter 3:4 to describe the type of life that believers should lead: "make it your ambition to lead a quiet life and attend to your own business and work with your hands" (1 Thess. 4:11). In another letter, he urges believers to pray for authorities "so that we may lead a tranquil and quiet life in all godliness and dignity" (1 Tim. 2:2).

Strong's defines this word for quiet, *hésuchios*, as meaning "peaceable, quiet."[7] The related words *hésuchazó* and *hésuchia* are defined as "cease, hold peace, be quiet, rest"[8] and "quietness, silence."[9] These words are used to describe both men and women. The sense of the words is the "*God-produced calm* which includes an inner tranquility,"[10] as expressed in Psalm 131:2: "Surely I have composed and quieted my soul; like a weaned child rests against his mother, my soul is like a weaned child within me."

What does that mean for us? Greeks, Romans, Victorians, and even modern conservative Christians often say that gentleness and quietness are feminine qualities. But instead of being exclusively feminine

6. William Barclay, *New Testament Words* (repr., Louisville: Westminster John Knox Press, 2000), 242.

7. James Strong, *A Concise Dictionary of the Words in the Greek Testament; with their Renderings in the Authorized English Version*, in *Strong's Exhaustive Concordance of the Bible* (repr., Peabody: Hendrickson Publishers, 1988), Strong's number 2272.

8. Strong, s.v. "*hésuchazó*," Strong's number 2270.

9. Strong, s.v. "*hésuchia*," Strong's number 2271.

10. HELPS Word-studies, s.v. "*hēsyxía*," available online from Bible Hub, accessed June 18, 2018, http://biblehub.com/greek/2271.htm, Strong's number 2271 (italics in original).

characteristics, gentleness and quietness are Christian traits that all believers should have as we exhibit strength under control and inner calm. A quiet or gentle-natured man isn't less masculine.

MEN GIVE LIFE

Biologically, only women can bear children. According to the common complementarian definition of femininity, life-giving is a feminine trait. But both biology and the Scriptures tell us that women don't bring new life into the world on their own. In Hebrew, the word for bearing, begetting, giving birth, and fathering (*yalad*) is used for women and men.[11] Proverbs 23:22 says, "Listen to your father who gave you life" (ESV).

Ultimately, God is *the* life-giver. All life is from Him. He is the Creator and sustainer of all things, and at the beginning, He breathed life into Adam. And not just physical life is from God; spiritual life is from Him as well, through the death and resurrection of Jesus Christ. As Paul writes, "The last Adam became a life-giving spirit" (1 Cor. 15:45).

Today, many people wonder what role fathers have in raising children. Some believe that men aren't equipped to nurture their children. Others go so far as to say that men are emasculated by taking an active role in caring for their children.[12]

Women have a unique role as they carry and labor to deliver babies, but life-giving isn't exclusively feminine. Scripture shows that all new human life comes from the cooperative work of men and women. All spiritual life comes from the completed work of Jesus and the continuing work of the Spirit. Believers, both women and men, are called to participate in the work of raising children and spreading the gospel. What exactly that looks like may vary from person to person and family to family.

11. See *"yalad,"* Bible Hub, accessed June 18, 2018, http://biblehub.com/hebrew/3205.htm, Strong's number 3205.

12. See Voddie Baucham Jr., *What He Must Be: . . . If He Wants to Marry My Daughter* (Wheaton, IL: Crossway, 2009), p. 76, Kindle.

MEN RESPOND

According to the prevalent complementarian definitions, the feminine counterpart to masculine leadership and initiative is responsiveness. But as we saw in chapter 1, responding to leadership is a human characteristic, not exclusively a feminine one. The Bible gives us examples of godly men following a woman's leadership.

Barak responded to Deborah's instructions regarding the attack on Sisera (see Judg. 4:6–8). We saw in the last chapter that some think that Deborah was a judge in Israel only because there weren't any men willing to lead. Barak is often criticized for telling Deborah that he wouldn't go out against Sisera unless she went with him, but Matthew Henry argues against the view that Barak was weak or cowardly. Instead, Barak was a man of conviction—a man who was aware of the necessity of God's presence.

> Barak insisted much upon the necessity of her presence, which would be to him better than a council of war (v 8). . . . Some make this to be the language of a weak faith; he could not take her word unless he had her with him in pawn, as it were, for performance. It seems rather to arise from a conviction of the necessity of God's presence and continual direction, a pledge and earnest of which he would reckon Deborah's presence to be, and therefore begged thus earnestly for it. . . . Nothing would be a greater satisfaction to him than to have the prophetess with him to animate the soldiers and to be consulted as an oracle upon all occasions.[13]

Daniel Block, Professor Emeritus of Old Testament at Wheaton College, compares Barak's reluctance to Moses's and Gideon's calls for authenticating signs. Barak's "protestation is less emphatic than Moses' in Exodus 3–4 and less apologetic than Gideon's in Judg 6:15." He

---

13. Judges 4:4–9 in *Matthew Henry Commentary on the Whole Bible (Complete)*, available online from Bible Study Tools, accessed June 11, 2019, https://www.biblestudytools.com/commentaries/matthew-henry-complete/judges/4.html.

continues, "On the surface his reaction . . . appears cowardly. He will not enter the fray unless he has this woman beside him holding his hand. And this impression is reinforced by Deborah's response. But at a deeper level the objection reflects a recognition of Deborah's status. The request to be accompanied by the prophet is a plea for the presence of God."[14]

Sarah, Abraham's wife, is commended as an example of wifely submission (see 1 Peter 3:6). But there was a time when God told Abraham to follow Sarah's lead. When Sarah wanted to send Hagar and Ishmael away, God told Abraham to listen to, or obey, her (see Gen. 21:12).

When Hannah made a vow to give her son Samuel to God, her husband, Elkanah, went along with her decision (see 1 Sam. 1:21–28). The Shunammite woman made all the important decisions in the Bible's account of her. She decided to build a room for Elisha and was promised a son in return for her kindness. She went to Elisha for help when her son died, directing her husband and her male servant to assist her. Her husband, her servant, and even Elisha all responded to her actions (see 2 Kings 4:8–37).

Proverbs 8 encourages men to respond to the call of Wisdom, who is personified as a woman. Mordecai, Esther's cousin, responded to Esther's commands (see Est. 4:17), and Haman and the king responded to her requests (see Est. 5). Boaz responded to Ruth's initiation when she asked him to be her kinsman-redeemer (see Ruth 3:6–15).

Apollos responded to the instruction of Priscilla and Aquila (see Acts 18:24–26). Military men respond to the commands of their officers, as the centurion said to Jesus (see Luke 7:8). And as we've discussed, all people are called to respond to God, in both the Old and New Testaments (see Ex. 24:3, Matt. 11:28; 2 Cor. 5:20).

God gives wisdom to both men and women. It's appropriate for us to respond to godly leadership. Based on these biblical examples, we can see that responsiveness is not particularly feminine. Instead, it's a trait that all believers should display.

14. Daniel I. Block, *Judges, Ruth*, The New American Commentary 6 (Nashville: Broadman & Holman, 1999), 199.

MEN ARE SOFT AND TENDERHEARTED

The complementarian definitions of men and women typically contrast with each other. If women are soft, then men must be strong. But, while female bodies are often physically softer than male bodies, softness is not a uniquely feminine quality. Consider these biblical examples of godly men who demonstrated softness or tenderness.

When David and Bathsheba's son dies, David demonstrates softness and tenderness as he comforts Bathsheba (see 2 Sam. 12:24). There is a unique tenderness that a husband shows for his wife, especially when she's hurting. The Song of Songs similarly shows the love and tenderness that a man should have with his wife.

In Ephesians 5:25–32, Paul describes how Christ loves the church. He uses this as an example of how husbands should love their wives. The verses depict Christ as loving, washing, nurturing, and cleansing—all words that show softness and tenderness. The description would have shocked the men of Ephesus. As we saw with the Greeks and the Romans, women or slaves did domestic chores and responsibilities like these—never free men.[15]

But this imagery should have been familiar to the Jews because of Old Testament descriptions of God's actions toward Israel.[16] God describes Himself as a groom who cares for His bride. Consider the book of Ezekiel, in which God describes Himself as washing His bride, anointing her with oil, dressing her in silk and linen, and giving her beautiful jewelry (Ezek. 16:9–12). In multiple places in the Scriptures, God also describes Himself as a tender shepherd who gently cares for His sheep: "Like a shepherd He will tend His flock, in His arm He will gather the lambs and carry them in His bosom; He will gently lead the nursing ewes" (Isa. 40:11). In other passages, God describes His actions as those of a mother who nurses and comforts her children (see Isa. 49:15; 66:13; Hos. 11:3–4).

In the New Testament, Paul uses this same metaphor to describe the

---

15. See Cynthia Long Westfall, *Paul and Gender: Reclaiming the Apostle's Vision for Men and Women in Christ* (Grand Rapids: Baker Academic, 2016), 58–59.
16. See Westfall, 57.

tender care he had shown believers in the church: "We proved to be gentle among you, as a nursing mother tenderly cares for her own children" (1 Thess. 2:7). And Jesus compares Himself to a hen who gathers her chicks together in order to protect them (see Matt. 23:37).

You are likely familiar with some ways in which men show tenderness and softness. If you've ever watched a groom's face as his bride walks down the aisle or seen a father hold his newborn baby, you have seen beautiful, masculine tenderness on display. And if you're a father who has ever had a tea party or tied your daughter's ribbons, then you're a good daddy—not an effeminate man.

According to Paul, godly men don't "lose their man cards" for being tender and affectionate with their wives. When believing husbands put their wives first, when they take on the role of a servant in nurturing their wives, they are acting as men of God. They are following Christ's example of service. Expressing emotions (even crying) or showing tenderness, kindness, and deference isn't contrary to masculinity. After all, Jesus wept (see John 11:35), had compassion on the sick and grieving (see Matt. 9:36; 20:34; Luke 7:13), and showed tender care and concern for His mother, Mary, before He died (see John 19:25–27). An interest in cooking, art, clothing, music, or poetry isn't feminine. Consider Jacob, David, and Solomon.

Despite the ways in which our secular and Christian cultures often define masculinity, being gentle, quiet, and responsive to leadership aren't effeminate behaviors. All believers, women *and* men, should display these characteristics.

ARE WOMEN AND MEN DIFFERENT?

As we have seen, godly women should be submissive, gentle, quiet, and responsive. And so should godly men. Women are helpers and life-givers. And so are godly men. Godly men should be leaders, initiators, providers, protectors, should be strong, and should have theological discernment. And so should godly women.

It is not my intention here to flatten out the distinctions between the sexes. God created us, male and female, in His image. Our bodies demonstrate that there are important differences between women and men, and it's appropriate for us to raise our children as male or female based on their biological sex. What we need to be careful about is conforming to narrow or wooden definitions of masculinity and femininity. As professor Gary Welton writes, "The notion of what it means to be female, or what it means to be male, is extremely broad. . . . In fact, there should be no singular conception of what it means to be masculine or feminine."[17]

As we have seen, the Bible gives us a much broader picture of what it means to be masculine and feminine than many conservative Christians do. Jacob and Esau were extreme opposites, but both were masculine. Deborah and Esther were very different, but both were feminine. Our definitions of masculinity and femininity must be biblical and must reflect the diversity of expression that is displayed in Scripture.

Culturally appropriate behavior for women and men often varies. While it is important to be sensitive to these culturally determined guidelines, a Christian's ultimate standard is the Bible. If cultural standards of gender-appropriate behavior are contrary to the Scriptures, then we need to follow the Bible instead of culture. Every culture's beliefs must be weighed against Scripture—especially our own.

Dr. Welton argues that we "need to adjust our thinking about what it means to be masculine and feminine in our modern world."[18] Given a doll, a boy may well use it as a weapon, and a girl may well tuck a toy car into a baby bed. Men may gravitate toward careers in STEM fields; women may prefer careers in nurturing fields. But these preferences don't determine the meaning of masculinity and femininity, and those who have different preferences are no less masculine or feminine. Their preferences are based on the gifts, abilities, and interests that God has given each of us.

If God made you a woman, you are feminine. Not because you're a wife or a mother. Not because you wear your hair long and curly and love flowers and pretty clothes. Not because you fit the complementarian mold—quiet, gentle, soft, responsive, and submissive.

---

17. Gary Welton, "My Human Identity Transcends Gender," The Aquila Report, July 30, 2017, https://www.theaquilareport.com/human-identity-transcends-gender/.
18. Welton, "My Human Identity Transcends Gender."

You are not less feminine if you love math, science, history, and theology. Even if you are the CEO of a company and are responsible for men and women employees. Even if you asked your husband out first. Even if you make more money than he does. Even if you handle the finances. Even if you're a police officer. Even if you lift weights and build muscles. You are feminine because that is what God made you, and nothing can change that.

The same is true for men. If God made you a man, you are masculine. Not because you love football and cars and getting dirty outside. Not because you fit the complementarian mold—a leader, initiator, provider, and protector who is strong and has theological discernment. You aren't less masculine if you love art and music. Even if you work as nurse or even stay at home with your children. Even if your wife is taller or physically stronger than you are. Even if you drive a minivan. You are masculine, and always will be, because God made you a man.

In the next chapter, we will look at how the complementarian beliefs about the nature of women and men have influenced what many conservative Christians teach about marriage. When the emphasis is on authority and submission, women and men both suffer.

DISCUSSION QUESTIONS

1. Is being a helper something that's exclusive to women?
2. What are some biblical examples of men being quiet and gentle?
3. Are men life-givers? What are some examples?
4. Should men lose their "man cards" for being tender or compassionate?
5. How are men and women different?

PART 4

WOMEN AND MEN IN MARRIAGE

10

"KING IN HIS HOME"

PREVALENT TEACHING ON MARRIAGE

*Wives need to be led with a firm hand. A wife will often test her husband
in some area, and be deeply disappointed (and frustrated) if she wins.
It is crucial that a husband give to his wife what the Bible says she needs,
rather than what she says she needs. So a godly husband is a godly lord.
. . . It is tragic that wholesale abdication on the part of modern men
has made the idea of lordship in the home such a laughable thing.*

DOUGLAS WILSON[1]

Have you heard the saying "You are what you eat"? If that's true, I may be
nearly 90 percent tea by this point in my life. But when I was in college,
our campus minister had a different take on this saying. He would say,
"You are what you believe about God."

It may sound a little funny at first, but there's a profound truth in
that statement. Just as what we eat and drink affects our bodies and our
health, our doctrine has far-reaching effects on all aspects of our lives.
That is why our campus minister also taught us that "orthodoxy leads

---

1. Douglas Wilson, *Reforming Marriage* (Moscow, ID: Canon Press, 1995), 80.

to orthopraxy." Good doctrine should have a positive influence on how we live, while false teaching will have a negative impact on our lives. Our beliefs aren't contained in a neat little box that keeps them separate from how we live.

When it comes to what we believe about how women and men should work together, our beliefs about the nature of men and women influence us. If we believe that unity, interdependence, and service are essential biblical themes, we will see how necessary it is for women and men to be co-laborers in all areas of life. But if we believe that men were created to be in authority and that women were created to submit to them, our beliefs about the nature of women and men will have a profound effect on our beliefs about marriage, the church, and society.

SEPARATE SPHERES

If you believe that men and women have truly opposite natures, you will be more likely to buy into the Greco-Roman concept of separate spheres. Some conservative Christians even teach that the public and domestic spheres are part of creation. Because God made Adam first, Adam was given authority over Eve. Therefore, God created men to be dominant leaders[2] and women to defer to male leadership in all aspects of life: family, church, and society.

The reasoning goes like this: Adam was created from the dust and placed in the garden of Eden. This is significant because he wasn't created in the garden but outside it in the field, while Eve was created from Adam's rib in the garden. Therefore, man was created in the public, working sphere and given the primary responsibility of providing for his family. Woman was created in the domestic sphere (since the garden was Adam and Eve's home) and given the primary responsibility of caring for the home and the family.[3] Men are oriented toward work, and women are oriented toward the home.

2. See Douglas Wilson, *Reforming Marriage*, 24.
3. Mary A. Kassian and Nancy Leigh DeMoss, *True Woman 101: Divine Design* (Chicago: Moody Publishers, 2012), pp. 46, 72, NOOK.

Some complementarians believe that it is appropriate for men and women to inhabit separate spheres because these different spheres suit the distinct natures of men and women. Because men are stronger, they are able to withstand the rigors and dangers of the public sphere. Women, who are softer and more yielding by nature, were created to be helpers, mothers, and keepers at home, which is their "God-ordained and proper sphere."[4] In this view, these differences aren't merely roles that men and women fulfill in various relationships. Rather, they are God-ordained distinctions that define the very essence of who and what women and men are. While these distinctions are expressed primarily in home and church life, they "should find an echo in every human heart."[5]

As we have seen, many conservative Christians believe that our culture is falling apart because we've rejected the gender distinctions that God created. If men led and women followed in marriage, the church, and society, God would bless our obedience to the creation order. Author Helen Andelin sums up this belief when she writes, "In a world where men lead we would have less crime and violence, less divorce, and less homosexuality. There would be happier marriages, happier homes, and therefore happier people."[6]

According to this paradigm, in any situation involving a man and a woman, the man is expected to lead. For this reason, some conservative Christians teach their daughters to "honor and defer to their brothers— older and younger—in recognition that even young boys need to be treated as wise leaders by their older sisters in order to gain the confidence to be leaders of their future families."[7]

4. "The Tenets of Biblical Patriarchy," Vision Forum Ministries, accessed June 18, 2018, https://homeschoolersanonymous.files.wordpress.com/2014/04/the-tenets-of-biblical-patriarchy-vision-forum-ministries.pdf.

5. "The Danvers Statement," The Council on Biblical Manhood and Womanhood, June 26, 2007, https://cbmw.org/uncategorized/the-danvers-statement/.

6. Helen Andelin, *Fascinating Womanhood*, updated ed. (New York: Bantam Books, 2013), p. 155, Kindle.

7. Kathryn Joyve, *Quiverfull: Inside the Christian Patriarchy Movement* (Boston: Beacon Press, 2009), 222.

AUTHORITY AND SUBMISSION IN MARRIAGE

This focus on authority and submission in marriage and the family is strikingly similar to what we saw with the Greeks, Romans, and Victorians. While there are differences in how these views are applied, many conservative Christians teach that men have a unique role of authority over their families, like the Roman *paterfamilias* did. This comes from a particular application of Ephesians 5.

Ephesians 5, of course, says that husbands are to love their wives as Christ loves the church and that wives are to submit to their husbands as the church does to Christ. Paul makes an analogy between the relationship of husband and wife and the relationship of Christ and the church. Some Christians believe that the husband thus represents Christ in a special way, and they use Christ's three offices of prophet, priest, and king[8] to expand on this application. As prophets, men bring the Word of God to their families. As priests, they sanctify their families. As king, they lead their families.[9]

Men as Prophets and Priests in the Home

The prophetic and priestly roles that men are given in these conservative Christian teachings involve more than their leadership in the home. As husbands represent Christ, men are taught to do the work that Ephesians 5 describes Christ doing for the church. They should sanctify their wives and families, washing them with the Word, purifying them, and presenting them as spotless: "When we remind our wives not to have a complaining spirit, but to rejoice in all things, we are fulfilling our prophetic role. . . . [W]e are again seeking to wash away the spots and stains, to purify, to beautify the garden that is our family. We are not just cleansing our families, but doing so with the very Word of God. We cleanse from our families those thoughts, words, and deeds that do not match up with what the Word of God commands."[10]

8. See the Westminster Shorter Catechism, answer 23.

9. R.C. Sproul Jr., *Bound for Glory: A Practical Handbook for Raising a Victorious Family* (Dallas, GA: Tolle Lege Press, 2008), chap. 3, loc. 607–9 of 1738, Kindle.

10. Sproul, chap. 3, loc. 618–22.

Those who hold to this view don't intend to teach that men can take Christ's place in making their wives holy. Husbands aren't expected to replace Christ, but they are expected to do what Christ does and to assist in their wives' sanctification by reading and applying Scripture to their wives, correcting their wives when they sin, and lovingly making their wives more and more holy. "The husband, who is to love like Christ, bears a unique responsibility for the moral and spiritual growth of his wife. . . . The wise and loving husband seeks to speak in a way that brings his wife more and more into conformity to Christ."[11]

In these teachings, women aren't given the responsibility to sanctify their husbands. Because the priestly role is part of a man's authority over his wife and family, women are encouraged to submit to their husbands and to wait patiently and quietly for God to address any shortcomings or sinful behaviors in them. If a wife absolutely needs to address a husband's sins, she should do so respectfully and carefully: "When you believe your husband is acting foolishly or unwisely, go away to another room if necessary and ask God to give you the grace not to 'preach' at him. If he asks, gently and respectfully give him your input, looking at your own faults and sins. Are you really better?"[12]

After all, only God can change a husband's sinful behavior: "You must not make the mistake of trying to undertake to deal with [your husband's] sins; you must deal with your own. . . . God is the only One who can bring about change. The Scripture is clear that you may be a potent instrument in God's hand, if you are committed to being the woman described in 1 Peter 3 who wins him without a word."[13]

Men as Kings in the Home

Many conservative Christians also teach that men reflect Christ's kingly role in the home. The father is "king in his home" and is "responsible

---

11. John Piper, "Just Forgive and Forbear?" in John Piper, Francis Chan, et al., *Happily Ever After: Finding Grace in the Messes of Marriage; 30 Devotions for Couples* (Minneapolis: Desiring God, 2017), 94.

12. Nancy Wilson, *The Fruit of Her Hands: Respect and the Christian Woman* (Moscow, ID: Canon Press, 2011), chap. 3, loc. 497–99 of 1215, Kindle.

13. Wilson, chap. 7, loc. 1050–54.

for all that goes on" there.[14] God leads families through the father. As with Greek and Roman fathers, the father's authority, while limited by the laws of church and state, is otherwise ultimate in the home.[15]

This authority is different from servant leadership. Instead of emphasizing that husbands and fathers sacrifice for their families' needs, this view of authority encourages women and children to cater to their husbands' and fathers' preferences. This might mean wearing a particular style or color of clothing.[16] It might mean wearing your hair in a certain way[17] or at a certain length.[18] For daughters, it might mean practicing being helpmeets by waiting on their fathers.[19]

As with the Roman *paterfamilias*, a father's authority extends to his children's courtship or dating. Men are responsible for leading their children, and particularly their daughters, through the courtship process. Douglas Wilson, pastor and author of several books on marriage and the family, writes that "the most important thing is that the authority of the father is represented" in the courtship process.[20] In this vein, many conservative Christian books on dating and courtship teach women not to pursue men or to ask them out on a date. Initiating a relationship isn't appropriately feminine behavior. Instead, these books teach men to pursue young women after getting their fathers' approval, since fathers are the leaders, providers, and protectors of their daughters until they marry.[21]

---

14. Sproul, *Bound for Glory*, chap. 5, loc. 852–54.

15. See Wilson, *The Fruit of Her Hands*, chap. 3, loc. 347–49.

16. See Anna Sofia Botkin and Elizabeth Botkin, *So Much More: The Remarkable Influence of Visionary Daughters on the Kingdom of God* (San Antonio: Vision Forum, 2005), 35.

17. See Isabelle Hoffmann, "The Glory of Hair," Recovering Grace, January 9, 2012, http://www.recoveringgrace.org/2012/01/the-glory-of-hair/.

18. See Douglas Wilson, *Fidelity: What It Means to Be a One-Woman Man* (Moscow, ID: Canon Press, 2011), appendix B, loc. 1944–45 of 1956, Kindle.

19. See Botkin and Botkin, *So Much More*, 48–49.

20. Douglas Wilson, *Her Hand in Marriage: Biblical Courtship in the Modern World* (Moscow, ID: Canon Press, 2010), chap. 3, loc. 688–89 of 1057, Kindle.

21. See Greg Gibson, "Thinking Different about Teenagers and Dating," The Council on Biblical Manhood and Womanhood, February 19, 2015, https://cbmw.org/topics/courtship-dating/thinking-different-about-teenagers-and-dating/.

At the wedding, the father hands off his daughter from his authority and protection to her husband's authority and protection.[22] This smooth transfer of authority ensures that fathers fulfill their responsibility of protecting their daughters' virginity. As Pastor Voddie Baucham explains, "Walking our daughters through the process of finding, vetting, courting, and marrying Mr. Right is a tall order. Along the way we must protect our daughters from male 'predators' so they will marry as virgins, thus bringing honor to our name and purity to their husbands."[23]

Some conservative Christians encourage men to set modesty standards for their wives and daughters.[24] Specific guidelines are strictly for women. There aren't parallel guidelines for male modesty.

A man's kingly authority over his family is also seen in his having the final say on any decisions or promises that his wife or daughter makes.[25] The explanation is that men protect women by keeping them from unwise decisions or rash vows,[26] as Numbers 30:13 says: "Every vow and every binding oath to humble herself, her husband may confirm it or her husband may annul it."

WOMEN AS KEEPERS OF THE HEARTH

Just as prevalent conservative Christian beliefs about men have an effect on marriage, similar beliefs about the nature of women also have an influence on marriage. Appealing to Ephesians 5, many teachings emphasize the wife's role in representing the church's submission. This submission isn't the voluntary yielding of an equal; instead, it is rooted in the belief that it's in a woman's nature to be submissive.

---

22. See Marshall Segal, "Dads, Date Your Daughter's Boyfriend," Desiring God, June 12, 2014, http://www.desiringgod.org/articles/dads-date-your-daughter-s-boyfriend.

23. Voddie Baucham Jr., *What He Must Be: . . . If He Wants to Marry My Daughter* (Wheaton, IL: Crossway, 2009), 54.

24. See John Piper, "Lionhearted and Lamblike: What Does It Mean to Lead? Part 2," Desiring God, March 25, 2007, https://www.desiringgod.org/messages/lionhearted-and-lamblike-the-christian-husband-as-head-part-2.

25. See Wilson, *Her Hand in Marriage*, chap. 1, loc. 295–96.

26. See Baucham, *What He Must Be*, 53.

In marriage, husbands and wives are one flesh. This illustrates the unity and interdependence of men and women. Some conservative Christians take the meaning of "one flesh" further and say that a wife "is a complement to her husband and a necessary completing part of his being."[27] According to this interpretation, a woman's responsibility as a helper for her husband means helping him to achieve *his* calling.[28]

There are many different callings that God may place on men's lives. Men may be called to be pastors, business owners, missionaries, professors, or engineers, or to any other legitimate career. Men may also be fathers in addition to callings such as this. God gives *men* work to do. Women are called to help in that work.[29]

As in the age of coverture, women are an extension of men. They are helpers for their husbands and fathers. They exist in order to further their husbands' and fathers' vision or purpose in life. Even if a woman works in ministry, her work should be an extension of her husband's ministry.[30] In order to help men to fulfill their goals and callings, women should encourage their husbands' or fathers' leadership by submitting to their authority. Women help men by having children, raising them, teaching them, and caring for the home. A woman's goals or priorities shouldn't be separate from her husband's or father's: "Helping her husband fulfill *his* goals and dreams is a wife's main responsibility. Remember that you are to support *his* vision—he establishes the goals and priorities for your family. A foolish wife will crush her husband's spirit by resisting his decisions, and God will hold her accountable for disobedience to His instructions."[31]

---

27. Dorothy Patterson, "The High Calling of Wife and Mother in Biblical Perspective," in *Recovering Biblical Manhood and Womanhood*, ed. John Piper and Wayne Grudem (repr., Wheaton, IL: Crossway Books, 2006), 368.

28. See Raymond C. Ortlund, Jr, "Male-Female Equality and Male Headship: Genesis 1–3," in Piper and Grudem, *Recovering Biblical Manhood and Womanhood*, 103.

29. See Wilson, *Reforming Marriage*, 29.

30. See Wilson, *The Fruit of Her Hands*, chap. 1, loc. 124–25.

31. "How Can I Meet My Husband's Basic Needs?" Institute in Basic Life Principles, accessed June 19, 2018, http://iblp.org/questions/how-can-i-meet-my-husbands-basic -needs, emphasis added.

Though men may have many different callings, women have one main calling: motherhood. This is a woman's highest calling[32] and the place where women find their "greatest fulfillment."[33] At home, women can focus "their energies on raising up godly seed."[34] In this view, working outside the home leads women to abandon their responsibilities and go against the created order that God established from the beginning.[35]

Many conservative Christians agree with the Greek, Roman, and Victorian beliefs that women are best suited to the domestic sphere of child-rearing and domesticity. Mary Kassian writes, "The Bible teaches that God created woman with a uniquely feminine 'bent' for the home."[36] One psalter paraphrase of Psalm 113 emphasizes this with the words "keeping house she finds reward."[37]

This emphasis on the home is partly practical. In order to care for their children, women need to be in the home where the children are. But this emphasis also results from the belief that all women were designed and ordained by God to be keepers at home. Unmarried women and women without children can find fulfillment by creating a welcoming and nurturing environment for their friends.[38] In this view, women's domestic work isn't drudgery or a limitation. Instead, it's a joyful challenge for women that enables them to use all their gifts to fulfill their role in "God's plan for the complementarity of the sexes."[39]

Mirroring Greco-Roman and Victorian beliefs, this view among Christians envisions the home being transformed by domesticity and

---

32. See Kassian and DeMoss, *True Woman 101*, 165.

33. Thomas R. Schreiner, "The Valuable Ministries of Women in the Context of Male Leadership: A Survey of Old and New Testament Examples and Teaching," in Piper and Grudem, *Recovering Biblical Manhood and Womanhood*, 224.

34. Sproul, *Bound For Glory*, chap. 4, loc. 794.

35. See Botkin and Botkin, *So Much More*, 111.

36. Mary A. Kassian, *Girls Gone Wise in a World Gone Wild* (Chicago: Moody Publishers, 2010), 76.

37. "Psalm 113A," in *The Book of Psalms for Singing* (Pittsburgh: Crown & Covenant Publications, 1973).

38. See Kassian and DeMoss, *True Woman 101*, 73–74.

39. Patterson, "The High Calling of Wife and Mother in Biblical Perspective," in Piper and Grudem, *Recovering Biblical Manhood and Womanhood*, 377.

hospitality into a place of peace and rest for others—a haven from the labors of the public sphere. Many conservative Christian books on marriage teach that the home should reflect the order and harmony of God's creative works.[40]

The Victorians' influence on complementarian authors is demonstrated through their use of Victorian sources. Dorothy Patterson, wife of former seminary president Paige Patterson, quotes from the Victorian poem "The Angel in the House" to defend the position that women's domestic work is "God's assignment to the wife" so that they will create a haven for their families.[41] Mary Kassian and Nancy DeMoss quote from the Victorian John Angell James's book *Female Piety* to explain how important it is that women preserve the health of society. Like James, they call on women to "use their influence to impact their communities for good and for godliness."[42]

These books teach women the importance of cooking meals, having a clean, well-decorated home without clutter or mess, and paying attention to a man's needs when he comes home. But not only that—like the Victorians, some conservative Christians teach that women civilize men. Men, on their own, are rude and brutish, but women make men better. The secret to a woman's power is found in her femininity: "Women create, shape, and maintain human culture. Manners exist because women exist. . . . Civilization arises and endures because women have expectations of themselves and of those around them."[43] In particular, women participate in saving society by offering others a place of rest from the world.[44]

This emphasis on men as being primarily providers and women as being primarily homemakers and mothers is an unattainable ideal for many families. Just as the Victorian model of domesticity was achievable

---

40. See, for example, Wilson, *The Fruit of Her Hands*, chap. 6, loc. 893–96.

41. Patterson, "The High Calling of Wife and Mother in Biblical Perspective," in Piper and Grudem, *Recovering Biblical Manhood and Womanhood*, 367.

42. Kassian and DeMoss, *True Woman 101*, 175.

43. Glenn T. Stanton, "Why Man and Woman Are Not Equal," First Things, August 26, 2016, https://www.firstthings.com/blogs/firstthoughts/2016/08/why-man-and-woman-are-not-equal.

44. See Kassian and DeMoss, *True Woman 101*, 167.

only for upper- and middle-income families, many working-class families, particularly immigrants and persons of color, can't survive on one income. Thus, one of the caveats that some conservatives offer regarding the prospect of women working outside the home is the issue of necessity. If it isn't possible for a woman to do otherwise, then having a job outside the home may be acceptable—lamentable, but acceptable—as long as she can honestly say that the work is necessary and won't interfere with her duties as wife and mother.[45]

Even so, working outside the home is considered less than ideal for a wife. It puts stress on husbands who have to pick up the slack at home. It leaves children without adequate care. No one is home to run the household. Wives have to balance what their bosses want from them with what their families need from them. And husbands are demoralized by not being able to provide for their families without the supplemental income from their wives.[46]

Some believe that it would be better if men were hired instead of women. After all, women are "simply supplementing" their husbands' income, as one article explained: "I'm not saying that they don't need the money, I'm not saying they should not work. I'm saying that where a man could support himself and maybe a wife with the job that is simply supplementing a married woman's household income, then the man should get the job, competence being equal."[47]

A SKEWED FOCUS

Marriages and families are damaged when a husband's authority in marriage is overemphasized. This marital authority is presented as being

---

45. See George W. Knight III, "The Family and the Church: How Should Biblical Manhood and Womanhood Work Out in Practice?," in Piper and Grudem, *Recovering Biblical Manhood and Womanhood*, 356.

46. See Patterson, "The High Calling of Wife and Mother in Biblical Perspective," in Piper and Grudem, *Recovering Biblical Manhood and Womanhood*, 375.

47. Rebecca VanDoodewaard, "In Praise of Clerks," The Christian Pundit, October 24, 2012, https://web.archive.org/web/20150204062814/http:/thechristianpundit.org/2012/10/24/in-praise-of-clerks/.

far-reaching. Christian teachers argue that husbands must assert their authority in the home in order to be godly, masculine men. They say that men should control the finances, because women will spend too much if men let them.[48] They admit that wives may manage the home, but they believe that ultimately men are responsible for delegating and overseeing their wives. From the dishes, to a wife's weight and appearance, to questions of theology, no detail is too small. Men must be the authority in all things.

Even the sexual relationship between a husband and wife is taken to be a matter of authority and submission. Douglas Wilson argues, "However we try, the sexual act cannot be made into an egalitarian pleasuring party. A man penetrates, conquers, colonizes, plants. A woman receives, surrenders, accepts. This is of course offensive to all egalitarians, and so our culture has rebelled against the concept of authority and submission in marriage."[49] John Piper explains that even if a wife initiates intimacy with her husband, she's really asking him to lead her: "A feminine initiation is in effect an invitation for the man to do his kind of initiating. . . . The wife is inviting him to lead in a way as only a man can, so that she can respond to him."[50]

Even prevalent teachings about men needing respect while women need love is another way in which authority and submission control the discussions about marriage. In this view, men need respect because they're made to be in authority. "Men, who by nature are more assertive, who arrange their social organization hierarchically, and who seek to elevate their level of control and respect, can find fulfillment and daily stress relief through the admiration of a wife who respects her husband."[51] But this overlooks the Bible's teaching that we should *all* love and respect each other. Wives need to respect and love their husbands. Husbands need to love and respect their wives.

48. See Wilson, *Reforming Marriage*, 89.

49. Wilson, *Fidelity*, chap. 7, loc. 978–81.

50. John Piper, "A Vision of Biblical Complementarity: Manhood and Womanhood Defined According to the Bible," in Piper and Grudem, *Recovering Biblical Manhood and Womanhood*, 40.

51. Gregg Johnson, "The Biblical Basis for Gender-Specific Behavior," in Piper and Grudem, *Recovering Biblical Manhood and Womanhood*, 293.

THE DAMAGE TO THE GOSPEL

Is there any good in these common conservative Christian teachings about marriage? Certainly. It's good to encourage husbands and wives to exhibit Christ's love and the church's submission in their marriages. Not only that, but home and family are truly important. Much of my concern about these areas comes when a truth is misapplied or taken too far.

Equating gender roles with the gospel, equating marriage with the gospel, and putting men in the role of Christ as priest and mediator for their wives and families creates a type of works righteousness: "Do this and live." We're told that these beliefs about gender and gender roles are inseparable from the gospel. "The two are one."[52]

But complementarianism isn't the actual gospel. We're not saved by faith in or faithfulness to a particular understanding of gender, men, and women. We're saved by grace alone, through faith alone, in Christ alone—and to God alone be the glory for the truth of the gospel.

When marriage is emphasized as living out a picture of the gospel and as the highest calling for women, along with bearing children, it tends toward making marriage and family into idols. This is especially harmful for singles and widows and for those who don't fit the neat box of a nuclear family unit.

If marriage is the gospel and (alongside motherhood) is the way for women to fulfill their divine calling, how can single women fulfill the Great Commission and the creation mandate? Marriage, while a good and necessary thing, isn't the gospel. Conflating the two obscures the actual gospel and presents a truncated understanding of what Christ actually accomplished for believers through His death and resurrection.

In the next chapter, we'll look at what the Bible teaches about marriage. We'll look at what marriage should be and how the biblical themes of unity, interdependence, and service can help us to fulfill our callings to be co-laborers together in Christ.

---

52. See Owen Strachan and Gavin Peacock, *The Grand Design: Male and Female He Made Them* (Fearn, UK: Christian Focus Publications, 2016), p. 133, NOOK.

DISCUSSION QUESTIONS

1. How is the concept of the separate spheres used in prevalent conservative teaching?
2. How are conservative beliefs about marriage similar to those of the Greeks, Romans, and Victorians?
3. Does the Bible teach that men are the "prophets, priests, and kings" of their homes? Why or why not?
4. What are some examples of authority and submission being the lens through which we interpret marriage?
5. How do these prevalent teachings damage the gospel?

11

"A TRUE FRIEND"

The wife is to be looked upon, not as a servant, but as a companion
to the husband, with whom he should freely converse and take sweet
counsel, as with a friend, and in whose company he should take delight
more than in any other's; for is she not appointed to be thy companion?

MATTHEW HENRY[1]

During my senior year of college, a group of us were headed in to Dairy Queen when an elderly couple walked out of the restaurant hand in hand. One of my friends said, "That's what I want." I looked at him, not sure what he was talking about.

He gestured toward the couple and explained that theirs was the kind of marriage he hoped he would have. He looked forward to having a relationship with his wife in which they'd still be holding hands and going out for ice cream when they were in their eighties. Of all the things that a guy might look forward to about marriage, he wanted lasting companionship.

---

1. Malachi 2:10–17 in *Matthew Henry Commentary on the Whole Bible (Complete)*, available online from Bible Study Tools, accessed June 11, 2019, https://www.bible studytools.com/commentaries/matthew-henry-complete/malachi/2.html.

The idea of friendship or companionship in marriage sometimes gets short shrift from Christians. Some say that expecting our spouses to be our best friends diminishes the significance of marriage and undercuts the importance of friendships with others. According to some, companionship is a downgrade in marriage.[2] But people who say this have failed to understand the importance of companionship and the significant place it should have in our marriages, as we will see.

Our culture doesn't seem to know what to expect of marriage anymore. Perhaps you've read about the women who married trees.[3] Or about "sologamy"—a woman who married herself.[4] Then there are "throuple" marriages—weddings between multiple people.[5] Even the dictionary definition of marriage isn't as straightforward as you might think. If you look up the word *marriage*, you'll find definitions such as these:

> the state of being united as spouses in a consensual and contractual relationship recognized by law[6]

> The legally or formally recognized union of two people as partners in a personal relationship (historically and in some jurisdictions specifically a union between a man and a woman)[7]

2. See Mark Jones, "'My Spouse is My Best Friend'," *reformation21* (blog), Alliance of Confessing Evangelicals, November 2, 2015, http://www.reformation21.org/blog/2015/11/my-spouse-is-my-best-friend.php.

3. See Alexandra Deabler, "Women Are Marrying Trees to Help Save Them," Fox News, February 28, 2018, http://www.foxnews.com/lifestyle/2018/02/28/women-are-marrying-trees-to-help-save-them.html.

4. See Mark Molloy, "'A Fairytale without the Prince': Italian Woman 'Marries Herself,'" *The Telegraph*, September 27, 2017, https://www.telegraph.co.uk/news/2017/09/27/fairytale-without-prince-italian-woman-marries/.

5. See Jasmine Taylor-Coleman, "Polyamorous Marriage: Is There a Future for Three-Way Weddings?" BBC News, July 21, 2017, https://www.bbc.com/news/world-40655103.

6. *Merriam-Webster*, s.v. "marriage," accessed June 18, 2018, https://www.merriam-webster.com/dictionary/marriage.

7. Oxford Living Dictionaries, s.v. "marriage," accessed June 18, 2018, https://en.oxforddictionaries.com/definition/marriage.

a legally accepted relationship between a man and a woman in which they live as husband and wife[8]

any of the diverse forms of interpersonal union established in various parts of the world to form a familial bond that is recognized legally, religiously, or socially, granting the participating partners mutual conjugal rights and responsibilities and including, for example, opposite-sex marriage, same-sex marriage, plural marriage, and arranged marriage[9]

So, according to our modern culture, marriage is a sometimes-legal relationship between at least two people who may or may not be of the opposite sex. To say that there's confusion over the meaning and purpose of marriage would be an understatement. And this confusion affects the church, too. As Christians, we need to know, and be able to teach, what the Bible teaches about marriage.

MARRIAGE AS A CREATION ORDINANCE

According to Scripture, marriage was instituted by God and given to us as a creation ordinance. That means that marriage began before the fall. Because it existed before sin and death, our understanding of marriage needs to fit the way life was before the fall as well as after.

Christians aren't the only people who get married (although Christianity should lead to a deeper appreciation for marriage).[10] No, marriage is a universal aspect of life. While not everyone gets married, all cultures throughout history have included some type of marriage relationship, and non-Christians can have beautiful marriages that are characterized by love, sacrifice, faithfulness, and joy. Many of us have friends or

8. *Cambridge Dictionary*, s.v. "marriage," accessed June 18, 2018, https://dictionary.cambridge.org/us/dictionary/english/marriage.

9. Dictionary.com, s.v. "marriage," accessed June 18, 2018, http://www.dictionary.com/browse/marriage.

10. See Brian Tallman, "Bringing Marriage Back to Earth," Ligonier Ministries, December 1, 2012, https://www.ligonier.org/learn/articles/bringing-marriage-back-to-earth/.

family members who aren't believers but whose marriages demonstrate tenderness and devotion. This is a testimony to the common grace of marriage. God blesses faithfulness in marriage—even in the marriage of unbelievers.

In Ephesians 5, Paul draws a comparison between marriage and the relationship of Christ with the church. Some press this analogy, saying that the *purpose* of marriage is to act out a parable of Christ and the church. Adam and Eve were "*created* to represent that relationship, and that is what *all marriages* are supposed to do."[11] God designed marriage "to dazzle the cosmos through the covenantal union of Christ the Savior and the church his redeemed possession."[12] Denny Burk writes, "Each and every marriage is supposed to be an enacted parable of the gospel."[13]

It is true that the Bible uses the example of Christ's sacrificial love to demonstrate the kind of love a husband should have for his wife. Paul also compares the submission that a wife should display with the love that the church shows Christ through submission. But, looking at it from the other direction, we see that the relationship between Christ and the church is a great mystery, as Paul says. To help us to understand that mystery, the Bible uses the analogy of marriage. We know what it means to be husband and wife. Marriage, therefore, helps us to understand the relationship between Christ and the church.

Husbands are called to love their wives with the same kind of sacrificial love that Christ showed for the church. Wives are called to respond to their husbands through love and submission as the church loves and submits to Christ. Pastor Todd Bordow summarizes it this way: "Adam and Eve were to love each other as their own flesh. Eve was to serve as a helpmate to Adam. Their mutual intimacy would be a picture of God's love and relationship with his image-bearers. After the fall, the husband's

11. Wayne Grudem, *Evangelical Feminism & Biblical Truth: An Analysis of More Than 100 Disputed Questions* (Colorado Springs: Multnomah Publishers, 2004), 41, emphasis in original.

12. Owen Strachan and Gavin Peacock, *The Grand Design: Male and Female He Made Them* (Fearn, UK: Christian Focus Publications, 2016), p. 104, NOOK.

13. Denny Burk, *What Is the Meaning of Sex?* (Wheaton, IL: Crossway Books, 2013), 106.

love for his wife would come to picture Christ's *love* for his bride, the church, whom he died for, and the wife's response to her husband would picture the church's *love* for Christ."[14]

Our marriages do resemble Christ's union with the church, but that isn't why marriage was instituted by God. Paul quotes Genesis 2:24 in Ephesians 5:31: "For this reason a man shall leave his father and mother and shall be joined to his wife, and the two shall become one flesh." Matthew Henry explains that the words "have also a hidden mystical sense in them, relating to the union between Christ and his church, of which the conjugal union between Adam and the mother of us all was a type: though not instituted or appointed by God to signify this."[15]

So why *was* marriage instituted?

MARRIAGE AND COMPANIONSHIP

The BBC version of Jane Austen's *Pride and Prejudice* ends with a double wedding. The priest reads the wedding service from the 1662 Anglican *Book of Common Prayer*, while a montage of scenes illustrates the three reasons that are given in the *Book of Common Prayer* for marriage.[16] I've always loved that scene and the emphasis that the liturgy puts on the importance of companionship. Marriage was ordained for

1. "the procreation of children, to be brought up in the fear and nurture of the Lord, and to the praise of his holy Name."
2. "a remedy against sin, and to avoid fornication; that such persons as have not the gift of continency might marry, and keep themselves undefiled members of Christ's body."

14. Todd Bordow, *What Did Jesus Really Say about Divorce? An Alternative Interpretation of Matthew 5:31&32 and Its Implications for Counseling Troubled Marriages in the Church* (Saarbrücken, Germany: Blessed Hope Publishing, 2014), 7, emphasis added.

15. Ephesians 5:21–33 in *Matthew Henry Commentary on the Whole Bible (Complete)*, available online from Bible Study Tools, accessed June 11, 2019, https://www.bible studytools.com/commentaries/matthew-henry-complete/ephesians/5.html.

16. See *Pride and Prejudice*, episode 6, directed by Simon Langton, adapted by Andrew Davies, aired October 29, 1995, on BBC.

3. "the mutual society, help, and comfort, that the one ought to have of the other, both in prosperity and adversity."[17]

The *Book of Common Prayer* liturgy demonstrates the shift in beliefs about marriage that took place as a result of the Reformation. That procreation was *the* purpose of marriage was a common belief throughout history. During the Middle Ages, the Roman Catholic Church didn't emphasize the value of marriage beyond that of procreation. Celibacy and single-minded dedication to the church were considered higher callings. Sure, marriage was necessary, since not everyone could be celibate. But aside from providing an approved outlet for sexual desires, the main purpose of marriage was having children.

The view of marriage as being a necessary evil for men and an ultimate goal for women was pretty much what the pagan Greeks and Romans had believed. But the Reformers rejected that view of marriage. Instead, they believed that marriage was important for women *and* men. Marriage honored God—and not only by producing children. Both Luther and Calvin emphasized that marriage was about companionship.[18] Luther wrote, "Woman is necessary, not only for the multiplying of the human race but also for the companionship, help and protection of life."[19] Calvin, too, in his commentary on Genesis 2:23, wrote, "Adam indicates that something had been wanting to him; as if he had said, Now at length I have obtained a suitable companion."[20]

As Genesis 2 says, it isn't good for man, or woman, to be alone. We need companionship, and marriage is one of the ways in which God

17. "The Form of Solemnization of Matrimony," in the 1662 version of the *Book of Common Prayer*, available online at http://justus.anglican.org/resources/bcp/1662/marriage.pdf, p. 1.

18. See Julie Hardwick, "Did Gender Have a Renaissance? Exclusions and Traditions in Early Modern Western Europe," in *A Companion to Gender History*, ed. Teresa A. Meade and Merry E. Wiesner-Hanks (Malden, MA: Blackwell Publishing, 2004), 348–49.

19. Martin Luther, *Luther on the Creation: A Critical and Devotional Commentary on Genesis*, ed. John Nicholas Lenker (Minneapolis: Lutherans in All Lands, 1904), 1:190.

20. John Calvin, *Genesis*, trans. John King, Calvin's Commentaries 1 (repr., Grand Rapids: Baker, 1979), 135.

fulfills that need. We see the same emphasis on companionship in Song of Songs 5:16, which says, "This is my beloved and this is my friend." The prophet Malachi speaks of "the wife of your youth . . . your companion and your wife by covenant" (Mal. 2:14). When Isaac and Rebekah married, the Scriptures say that Isaac loved Rebekah and was "comforted after his mother's death" (Gen. 24:67).

God created marriage for our good, for our happiness, and as a blessing for men and women. Marriage was given to us so that we could fulfill the creation mandate, be fruitful, fill the earth and subdue it, and rule over the creation together.

The Reformers still taught that marriage was for having children and avoiding sexual sin, but they didn't stop there. By reaffirming companionship as a biblical part of marriage, the Reformers improved the value and respectability of marriage and women. Women weren't just objects for having babies and providing sexual release. A wife was meant to be her husband's help and comfort, and vice versa. Being married and serving God as a husband or wife was as important as being celibate and serving God as a priest, monk, or nun.

Not all marriages produce biological children. Some men and women can't have children. Some couples choose to adopt children instead of bearing children. Some couples marry late in life, past childbearing age. Marriages are still genuine marriages, whether or not children are born— but all marriages should demonstrate companionship.

UNITY, INTERDEPENDENCE, AND SERVICE IN MARRIAGE

While marriage appropriately involves a wife's submission to her husband's authority, there is much more to marriage. The idea of companionship incorporates the biblical themes of unity, interdependence, and service in marriage.

Unity in Marriage

The first man and woman were united by God in the first marriage. Jesus states this when He answers the Pharisees' question on divorce.

Haven't you read ... that at the beginning the Creator "made them male and female," and said, "For this reason a man will leave his father and mother and be united to his wife, and the two will become one flesh"? So they are no longer two, but one. Therefore what God has joined together, let man not separate. (Matt. 19:4–6 NIV)

"Man's well-being depended on having a companion who could come to his aid in time of need and unite with him in doing God's will in the world," explains Joel Beeke, president of Puritan Reformed Theological Seminary. "He needed someone 'meet,' or suitable, to who and what he was. This was a true friend."[21]

Marriage, as defined by the Bible, is a joining together of one man and one woman in a union that is intended to be lifelong. Beeke writes, "We were made to have communion with each other, and the closest possible communion is that between husband and wife."[22]

Interdependence in Marriage

In 1 Corinthians 11, when Paul describes the relationship between man and woman, he says that Adam was created first and that Eve was created for Adam (see vv. 8–9). But Paul goes on to explain that all men after Adam have been born from women, and so there is interdependence (see vv. 11–12). Adam and Eve, men and women, husbands and wives need each other. Commentator Simon Kistemaker writes, "The husband has no advantage over the wife because Adam was created before Eve. In the Lord, both parties show reciprocity and complementary dependence and assistance, for all these things have been designed by God himself."[23]

After God created man and woman in His image, He gave them three tasks: to fill the earth, to subdue it, and to rule over the living creatures (see Gen. 1:28). He gave these instructions both to man and woman,

---

21. Joel R. Beeke, *Friends and Lovers: Cultivating Companionship and Intimacy in Marriage* (Hudson, OH: Cruciform Press, 2012), chap. 1, loc. 231 of 1455, Kindle.

22. Beeke, chap. 1, loc. 257.

23. Simon J. Kistemaker, *Exposition of the First Epistle to the Corinthians*, New Testament Commentary (Grand Rapids: Baker Academic, 1993), 378.

because in order to fulfill these responsibilities, women and men need to work together.

It's easy to see how filling the earth is a joint responsibility. You can't have babies without both women and men. While it's less obvious, it's also true that men and women need to work together in order to subdue the earth and to rule. In Proverbs 31, we see a picture of a husband and wife who each work according to their gifts and callings. Priscilla and Aquila worked together as tentmakers to provide for their family (see Acts 18:2–3).

Service in Marriage

Adam needed a helper for himself and for the work that God had commanded. It wasn't good for him to be alone. As Adam saw, the animals weren't suitable helpers. But when God brought Eve to Adam, Adam was struck with how fitting Eve was as his helper—his *ezer*. She alone was bone of his bone and flesh of his flesh. Luther writes, "That very word . . . most beautifully expresses the glad surprise and exulting joy of a noble spirit which had been seeking this delightful meet companion of life and of bed; a companionship full, not only of love, but of holiness."[24]

God created women to be co-laborers in the work that He gave humanity to do. As Steven Tracy writes, Eve was "created . . . to serve with man."[25] This is especially true in marriage. We have to work together in marriage in order to take care of our families, provide for them, and raise our children. Kistemaker explains, in his commentary on 1 Corinthians 11, "As long as the Lord grants them life, let husband and wife be bound in mutual love and service to one another."[26]

One way that believers serve each other in marriage is by building each other up and encouraging each other to grow in grace and faith. Some people go so far as to say that God gave us marriage not to make us happy but to make us holy.[27] However, when God instituted marriage,

---

24. Luther, *Luther on the Creation*, 1:217.
25. Steven R. Tracy, "What Does 'Submit in Everything' Really Mean? The Nature and Scope of Marital Submission," *Trinity Journal* 29 (2008): 309.
26. Kistemaker, *Exposition of the First Epistle to the Corinthians*, 378.
27. See Gary Thomas, *Sacred Marriage: What If God Designed Marriage to Make Us*

Adam and Eve were already righteous. Before the fall, they didn't need to be made holy.

Of course, the fall and our need for salvation and sanctification weren't a surprise to God. Redemption isn't "plan B." God knew what our needs would be when He created us and gave us marriage. But that doesn't mean that He was more concerned about Adam's holiness than about his happiness when He said, "It's not good for man to be alone."

God uses our marriages to sanctify us—just as He uses our families, our jobs, our daily commutes, our friends, our churches, and everything else in our lives. As Romans 8:28 tells us, God works all things together for our good. But not everyone gets married. When we focus on sanctification as the meaning of marriage, we tell singles that they're missing out. We tell them that they can't really be holy or experience sanctification unless they are married. It's not intentional, but it's an unintended consequence that hurts singles in our churches.

Because of the fall and the effects of sin, we work and serve together by the sweat of our brows, beating back entropy one day at a time. Anyone who has done laundry or yard work knows that the fall and entropy affect all kinds of work, both inside and outside the home.

WHY DOES IT MATTER WHAT WE FOCUS ON IN MARRIAGE?

Women and men are created in God's image, united as joint heirs, and called to serve together and serve each other, following Christ's example. This is our identity. This is who and what we are.

By emphasizing unity, interdependence, and service in marriage, we can move beyond authority and submission as the lens through which we understand the relationship between husband and wife.

When we make our *unity* a focal point of marriage, we see our similarities instead of our differences. The differences are still significant, but we highlight the common ground that we have as husbands and wives. Then we can remember that we're meant to be side-by-side allies and not

---

Holy More Than to Make Us Happy? (Grand Rapids: Zondervan, 2000).

face-to-face opponents. As believers, we are brothers and sisters in Christ who are serving the same Master. We have the same goal: glorifying God.

When we remember that women and men are *interdependent* in marriage, then we see how much we need each other. Husbands need their wives. Wives need their husbands. Each of us brings something to our marriages that is lacking in the other. Understanding this interdependence keeps us from thinking that we're more important than our spouses.

When we focus on *service*, husbands will be encouraged to love their wives sacrificially and to put their wives' needs before their own. Wives will be encouraged to submit to their husbands and to love and respect them by putting their husbands' needs first. Focusing on our spouses' needs discourages us from trying to manipulate or dominate them.

What a difference this focus on service, unity, and interdependence makes in our marriages. Wives are called to submit to their husbands, but not because they are women and therefore submissive and responsive by nature. A wife's submission to her husband is the voluntary submission of an equal, out of respect for her husband and in recognition that her ultimate Lord is Christ. This submission isn't the same as the obedience that slaves owe to their masters or even that children give to their parents. It's a "voluntary yielding to another in love."[28]

Husbands are called to love their wives sacrificially and to lead through service. A husband's leadership isn't just because he's a man and therefore a natural leader. It's an act of service and love that carries the recognition that he and his wife both serve the same Master. He doesn't lord it over his wife or attempt to enforce her submission. He respects her, her insight, and her abilities. In marriage, the husband and the wife are each called to put the other first, and *that* makes all the difference in the world.

In our marriages, the possibility of procreation lasts a short time. Even sexual intimacy may diminish in importance over time. But the friendship and companionship of marriage should stand the test of time as we're knit together through love and our shared experiences and struggles. That unity and shared purpose will remain with believers in glory after the other aspects of marriage have served their purpose.

28. Tracy, "What Does 'Submit in Everything' Really Mean?" 306–7.

In the next chapter, we'll look at some specific applications and answer a few questions about marriage and what the Bible teaches us.

DISCUSSION QUESTIONS

1. What does it mean that marriage is a creation ordinance?
2. What is the purpose of marriage?
3. How do we demonstrate our unity in marriage?
4. How do we demonstrate our interdependence in marriage?
5. How can we serve each other in marriage?

12

"BRINGING MARRIAGE BACK TO EARTH"

Eve was not taken out of Adam's head to top him, neither out of his feet to be trampled on by him, but out of his side to be equal with him, under his arm to be protected by him, and near his heart to be loved by him.

MATTHEW HENRY[1]

If you've read Madeleine L'Engle's book *A Wrinkle in Time,* you're familiar with the scene in which Meg, Calvin, and Charles Wallace arrive on Camazotz. The town seems to be fairly unexceptional, but something about it makes them feel uneasy. Rows of identical houses line the street. Down to the last detail, every house and yard are the same.

In the front yard of each house, a child either bounces a ball or skips rope. Charles Wallace realizes that the children are bouncing or skipping at exactly the same time. Then the doors open at the same time and

---

1. Genesis 2:21–25 in *Matthew Henry Commentary on the Whole Bible (Complete),* available online from Bible Study Tools, accessed June 11, 2009, https://www.bible studytools.com/commentaries/matthew-henry-complete/genesis/2.html.

practically identical women step outside and clap to call the children inside. The children, in unison, gather their toys and turn and go inside.[2]

Later, Charles Wallace, while under the influence of the evil ruler of Camazotz, explains, "On Camazotz we are all happy because we are all alike. Differences create problems. . . . In Camazotz all are equal. In Camazotz everybody is the same as everybody else."[3]

Marriage books that are popular within conservative Christian circles tend to take a cookie-cutter approach to marriage. While it may be tempting for us to expect all marriages to look and function the same and to have the same positive end result, our marriages are as distinct as the people in them are. With that in mind, I'd like to consider a few application questions that come up in Christians' conversations about marriage.

SHOULD ALL MARRIAGES LOOK THE SAME?

As we saw in the last chapter, the biblical picture of marriage is beautiful and inspiring. Husbands are to love their wives sacrificially. Wives are to submit to their husbands' leadership. Women and men who are sisters and brothers in Christ are to co-labor together to raise families and serve the Lord in all that they do. But does that mean that all biblical marriages will look the same? Looking around us, we can see they don't.

The Bible gives us some basic guidelines about marriage, but within those guidelines, marriages can look considerably different. God has given each of us various gifts and also distinct needs. Those differences have an effect on how individual marriages work. Our season of life and our responsibilities will also affect our marriages.

Husbands and wives have to make many decisions about who will be responsible for the different tasks that need to happen within family life. Questions are often raised about who "should" do various things, such as taking care of finances, cooking meals, washing dishes, cleaning house, doing the laundry, and taking care of the cars. Some conservative

---

2. See Madeleine L'Engle, *A Wrinkle in Time* (1962; repr., New York: Square Fish, 2007), 115–16.

3. L'Engle, 155, 177.

Christian marriage books assign these tasks on the basis of gender. But these are areas in which we should be fairly flexible.

Maybe your wife is gifted at math, so she pays the bills and the taxes and handles the budget. Maybe your husband is gifted at cooking, so he fixes most of the meals. Maybe you like to cook together. Maybe you trade turns. My mom realized early in her marriage that my dad loves to cook but that he doesn't like doing the dishes. So Dad does most of the cooking, and Mom washes the dishes. Everyone's happy. In our house, the housework is done by all, based on everyone's abilities and available time. For us, that means that my children and I do most of the work, but my husband helps when he's home. When it comes to cars, some men are mechanically inclined, and others aren't. The same is true for women. The work should be done by whoever has the time and abilities to do it—for example, the local auto shop.

A few questions about marriage and family life are more delicate to answer, and some people have strong opinions about the "right" way to do these things. Who should take care of the children, for example, may depend on several factors, such as the age of your children, the financial needs of your family, and the gifts that you and your spouse have. The situation may also change over time. Sometimes my mom was the one who was home with us. Sometimes it was my dad. But we were always loved and cared for.

The question of who makes the most money is a particularly sensitive one. But if we remember that all we have is from God, we'll see that whether money comes through the wife's work or the husband's work or their work together, all of it is His blessing. We should seek God's wisdom about the best way to be good stewards of the gifts and abilities He has given us.

"Beyond Scripture, there is godly wisdom and Christian liberty," writes Michael Horton. "Biblical principles focus on what it means to live in Christ by his Word and Spirit, and even in those few passages that speak directly to men and women, there will be legitimate diversity in application."[4] Marriages aren't going to look the same, and they don't

4. Michael Horton, "Muscular Christianity," *Modern Reformation* 21, no. 3 (2012), 46–47.

need to. God has given us guidelines and principles to follow, but He has also given us liberty to make wise decisions about how to apply those guidelines in our marriages. Husbands and wives will need to consider how best to follow what God has said while not judging others for their decisions. Each of us is responsible to the Lord for how we serve Him.

WHAT ABOUT DIVORCE?

What we believe about marriage influences what we believe about divorce. Because of the confusion within secular society about the meaning and importance of marriage, divorce is often treated lightly. Don't get along well? Get a divorce. Fall in love with someone else? Get a divorce. Fall out of love? Get a divorce. People even talk of "starter marriages"[5]— as if spouses plan to trade up for a better model eventually. Many people have been harmed when these cultural beliefs about marriage and divorce are followed—especially the spouses and children who are left behind.

Two Views on Marriage and Divorce

Within conservative Christianity, certain prevalent beliefs about marriage have caused a different type of damage. In the last chapter, we discussed the view that marriage is meant to be a parable of the gospel. That understanding of marriage has far-reaching consequences, particularly when it comes to teachings on divorce. The two most common conservative Christian views on divorce are the *permanence* view and the *adultery-desertion* view. Both of these take their starting point from the belief that if marriage is a picture of the gospel, then divorce "tell[s] a lie about God's relationship to his people."[6]

The argument is that marriage represents to the world God's love and covenant faithfulness to His people, the church. God would never break His covenant promises. He would never leave or divorce His people.

5. See Deborah Schupack, "'Starter' Marriages: So Early, So Brief," *The New York Times*, July 7, 1994, https://www.nytimes.com/1994/07/07/garden/starter-marriages -so-early-so-brief.html.

6. John Piper, *What Jesus Demands from the World* (Wheaton, IL: Crossway Books, 2006), 303.

Therefore, we should not divorce, because doing so paints a false picture to the world around us about God's love—"that it is conditional, fragile, and unreliable."[7]

John Piper, a proponent of the permanence view, writes, "I don't think the Bible allows divorce and remarriage *ever* while the spouse is living."[8] He argues, "Jesus said, 'What therefore God has joined together, let not man separate' (Mark 10:9). And the deepest reason for that prohibition of breaking a marriage is that marriage was created by God from the beginning as a picture or an expression of the covenant-keeping love of Christ and his church."[9]

Those who promote the adultery-desertion view use similar arguments: "Covenant faithfulness within marriage sends a message to the world about Christ's covenant faithfulness to his bride. For this reason, upholding this icon of the gospel ought to be a matter of first importance to every Christian spouse—even when that spouse has what would otherwise be legitimate grounds for dissolving the marriage."[10]

Unlike the permanence view, proponents of the adultery-desertion view teach that divorce is permissible in some limited cases. Even so, men and women are often encouraged not to divorce. Denny Burk writes, "Taken together, Jesus and Paul teach that divorce is not an option for believers. The only exceptions that they allow are in cases of immorality or desertion. Neither Jesus nor Paul says that a person *must* be divorced if there is *infidelity* or *desertion*. They are simply saying that it can be permissible in those two situations."[11]

Our culture has a very low view of marriage, and it may seem like the permanence and adultery-desertion views are the ones that uphold the highest view of marriage. However, a high view of marriage means

7. Bruce Ashford and Chris Pappalardo *One Nation Under God: A Christian Hope for American Politics* (Nashville: B&H Publishing, 2015), 77.

8. John Piper, "Does the Bible Allow for Divorce in the Case of Adultery?" Desiring God, January 9, 2009, https://www.desiringgod.org/interviews/does-the-bible-allow-for-divorce-in-the-case-of-adultery, emphasis in original.

9. John Piper, "To a Spouse Considering Divorce," Desiring God, July 31, 2014, http://www.desiringgod.org/interviews/to-a-spouse-considering-divorce.

10. Denny Burk, *What Is the Meaning of Sex?* (Wheaton, IL: Crossway, 2013), 135.

11. Burk, 134, emphasis in original.

recognizing that it can be broken. Dr. Geerhardus Vos gives an illustration that helps to explain.

> We may have on our parlor table a beautiful and costly vase. It ought to be handled carefully. It ought not to be broken. It was not made to be smashed; it was made to exist as a thing of beauty and grace. But it is not impossible to break it. And if a member of the family breaks it through carelessness, or in a fit of temper smashes it deliberately, there is nothing to do but sweep up the broken fragments and dispose of them. We will not say, "This vase was not intended to be broken; therefore it is impossible to break it; the vase is unbreakable; therefore in spite of the fact that it lies in shattered fragments on the floor, we will not throw it away; we will keep it forever." No one would say that about a broken vase; yet that is substantially the argument of those who say that the marriage bond is "indissoluble" and "unbreakable."[12]

The Bible on Marriage and Divorce

From the beginning, God created marriage to be a lasting bond between a man and a woman. The reality, however, is that just because "God intended for marriage never to be broken does not mean that the marriage union is unbreakable."[13] In a perfect world, marriage would be lifelong. However, because of the fall, we don't live in a perfect world anymore. Because of sin, we don't always live up to the ideal. Because of our sinful behaviors, we sometimes destroy the good things God has given us.

Even believers sin against each other regularly. And that's especially true in marriage. We sin against our spouses. Most of the time, especially in a marriage between two Christians, those sins are ones that we repent from and forgive each other for on a daily basis: a sharp word in a tense moment, a thoughtless comment, an unintended stepping on

12. Quoted in Loraine Boettner, *Divorce* (Nutley: The Presbyterian and Reformed Publishing Company, 1972), 13, quoted in "Report of the Ad Interim Committee on Divorce and Remarriage" (paper presented to the Twentieth General Assembly of the Presbyterian Church in America, Roanoke, VA, June 1992), http://pcahistory.org/pca/2-203.pdf, p. 208.

13. "Report of the Ad Interim Committee on Divorce and Remarriage," 207.

toes, occasions of forgetting to show the love we owe each other. As the Scriptures say, "love covers a multitude of sins" (1 Peter 4:8), and these sins are the kind that we should willingly and readily forgive.

But other times, sins are grievous. They can demonstrate a persistent pattern of disregard for the marriage and for the vows that were made to God and to a spouse. Such sins are evidence of an unrepentant, hard heart. In such cases, the marriage is in danger. Maybe the marriage is failing. Maybe it is already broken.

There is a third understanding of divorce among conservative Christians that acknowledges this—the *serious-sin* view. For example, the Presbyterian Church in America's "Ad Interim Report on Divorce and Remarriage" takes this approach to divorce by including abuse— particularly physical abuse—in the list of serious sins that break the marriage bond: "A husband's violence . . . seems to us, by any application of Biblical norms, to be as much a ruination of the marriage in fact as adultery or actual departure. This is so precisely because his violence separates them." Even if the wife is not driven to physically leave the home, marital violence creates "profound cleavage between them . . . and is thus an expression of his unwillingness 'to consent' to live with her in marriage (1 Cor. 7:12–13; Eph. 5:28–29)."[14]

Todd Bordow, an Orthodox Presbyterian pastor, takes a slightly different approach. He believes that when Jesus said, "Everyone who divorces his wife, except for the reason of unchastity, makes her commit adultery" (Matt. 5:32), He wasn't giving specific examples of when divorce is permissible. Instead, Bordow argues that Jesus mentioned sexual immorality as a *type* of serious sin that would break the marriage bond. According to Bordow, "The Bible does not actually give us specifics on which sins committed in a failed marriage constitute a justifiable divorce in God's eyes."[15]

Marriage was meant to last. Husbands and wives are called to love each other and to uphold their marriage vows. Those marriage vows are

---

14. "Report of the Ad Interim Committee on Divorce and Remarriage,"229.

15. Todd Bordow, *What Did Jesus Really Say about Divorce? An Alternative Interpretation of Matthew 5:31&32 and Its Implications for Counseling Troubled Marriages in the Church* (Saarbrücken, Germany: Blessed Hope Publishing, 2014), 34.

serious—but when they are broken, we don't affirm the beauty and glory of marriage by denying that they are broken.

"For I Hate Divorce"?

Malachi 2:16 is often quoted as proof that divorce is never a biblical option. It's true that some translations, like the NASB, strongly suggest this: "'For I hate divorce,' says the LORD, the God of Israel, 'and him who covers his garment with wrong,' says the LORD of hosts. 'So take heed to your spirit, that you do not deal treacherously.'"

But the Hebrew may not be as straightforward as these translations make it seem. The ESV, among other translations, reflects a different understanding of the Hebrew: "For the man who does not love his wife but divorces her, says the LORD, the God of Israel, covers his garment with violence, says the LORD of hosts. So guard yourselves in your spirit, and do not be faithless." Bordow agrees with the ESV translation. "The ESV better captures the grammar of verse 16, when instead of using 'God' as the subject, [it] sees 'the man who does not love his wife' as the subject. . . . Malachi rebukes the men for hating and then divorcing their wives for no good reason."[16]

The kind of divorce that God condemns Israel for in Malachi 2 is exactly the same kind of no-fault, easy divorce that all Christians should oppose. But when we rightly protect against this kind of mistreatment of marriage, we should be careful not to go beyond Scripture.

It's important to note that in the serious-sin view, filing for divorce isn't necessarily what breaks the marriage bond. "The one who hardens his heart and breaks the marriage covenant is not always the one who files for divorce. The onus of repentance is placed upon the one who broke the bond of marriage by serious sin, and not necessarily on the one who seeks a public record of the broken marriage covenant."[17]

When we teach that divorce is never an option or is a very bad option, regardless of the situation, we lay a burden on spouses who have been grievously sinned against. We tell them that no matter how their spouses

---

16. Bordow, 13.
17. Bordow, 38.

have broken their marriage vows, no matter how they've been abused and sinned against, no matter what their spouses do to them, they must stay married. Doing so makes the marriage more important than the people who are in it. There is no grace or mercy in that teaching—only hopelessness and despair.

God Himself presented the Israelites with a certificate of divorce for their idolatrous and adulterous behavior (see Jer. 3:8). While it's true that He forgave and preserved a remnant of His people, the individuals who had sinned continuously against Him were sent away. They died and didn't return to the land, just like the people who died in the wilderness because they refused to go into Canaan (see Num. 26:65).

Because we hold a high view of marriage, we need to acknowledge that some sins are so heinous that they destroy a marriage. Hard-hearted sinners who break their marriage vows shouldn't be allowed to make a mockery of marriage through their actions. Marriage is important, but it's not meant to be preserved at all costs.

BRINGING MARRIAGE BACK TO EARTH

We have already seen that the medieval church valued celibacy over marriage, and the Reformers rightly corrected that belief. But the pendulum has swung too far in the opposite direction. Marriage is a great blessing. There's a great need to defend a biblical understanding of marriage. But if conservative Christian teaching makes marriage too hard and expects too much from it, there's a real danger of making marriage into an idol—"a good thing turned into an ultimate thing," in the words of Tim Keller.[18]

Marriage is a good thing, but it's not an ultimate thing. When we make marriage our highest calling—our focus in life and in the church—we set ourselves up for disappointment and heartache. We weigh ourselves and others down with impossible standards and unrealistic expectations.

By God's grace, our salvation is secure in Christ, regardless of our

---

18. Timothy Keller with Katherine Leary Alsdorf, *Every Good Endeavor: Connecting Your Work to God's Work* (New York: Dutton, 2012), 134.

marital status. Marriage isn't the gospel. It isn't what saves us. It isn't what gives our lives meaning. It isn't what makes us holy. It isn't what fulfills us. Whether we are married, divorced, single, widowed, or separated, we are called to serve God and to glorify Him wherever and however we are able.

"In this institution we serve God and our neighbor," Brian Tallman writes. "Maybe it's time we recognize that we are members of Christ and culture. And just maybe, in bringing marriage back to earth, we might come to realize that marriage really isn't all that hard. We might just find that God will bless our marriages and use them to build and shape the culture and as a stage upon which to magnify His grace."[19]

We can bring marriage "back to earth" by focusing on the themes of grace, forgiveness, and mercy. God gave us marriage at the beginning of creation as a blessing for us. As such, marriage is an example of God's common grace. Believers and non-believers can experience this blessing—this grace.

As Christians, we should be better equipped for marriage because of the work of the Spirit in our lives. As Bordow explains, "God's people in the New Covenant will be so filled with the Spirit that marriages of Christians will not only be able to last a lifetime, but will be loving marriages characterized by Christ-like love for one another."[20] That doesn't mean that we won't have difficult marriages at times. We're sinners too. We will sin against each other. Others will sin against us, and life may be painful. But our hope is in forgiveness.

Our sins have been forgiven through Jesus's life, death, and resurrection. Because we have been forgiven, we should be forgiving of others—especially our loved ones. That doesn't mean that we allow ourselves to be abused and mistreated. No—in order for forgiveness to happen, there must be true repentance. And, even then, sins may have far-reaching consequences—including divorce. But in our day-to-day lives, as believers living together, we trust in Christ for our forgiveness, and we repent and forgive, showing our love for each other. In doing so, we demonstrate

19. Brian Tallman, "Bringing Marriage Back to Earth," Ligonier Ministries, December 1, 2012, https://www.ligonier.org/learn/articles/bringing-marriage-back-to-earth/.
20. Bordow, *What Did Jesus Really Say about Divorce?* 33.

mercy. As believers, we should be merciful with each other in marriage and should always be showing compassion. But mercy also goes beyond our own marriages.

We should also have mercy and compassion on all those who are around us. All around us are people who are hurting. Some are in difficult marriages. Some have been or are being abused. Some have been abandoned. Some have lost their spouses. Some are divorced or separated. Some are single and are longing to be married. Some are single and wishing that others wouldn't look down on them for not being married.

It's easy to look at the people around us and to make assumptions and judgments about whether or not they are "doing things the right way." I'm not saying that we shouldn't encourage one another to follow Christ faithfully. There are times when we need to address sinful behavior. But we should be quick to show compassion for those around us. Men and women in our churches and communities shouldn't feel like they are wearing a scarlet D (for *divorced*) or S (for *single*). We are so much more than our marital status.

By focusing on grace, forgiveness, and mercy, we can truly rest in Christ. We can rest because our salvation is secure. We can lay down the burdens we've been carrying—burdens of perfection, rule-following, competition, and attempts to save ourselves. Instead we can turn our attention to the unity that we have in Christ and with each other, the interdependence that we have as men and women, the service that we owe each other, and the love and respect we should show each other.

God has given us liberty in our marriages within the boundaries that Scripture draws. So we should stop trying to press everyone into the same mold. We don't have a license to sin, but we do have freedom to make decisions about how our marriages will work. Regardless of our marital status, we are called to use the gifts God has given us to serve Him and each other.

In the next chapter, we'll consider what is being taught by conservative Christians about how women and men should function in the life of the church.

DISCUSSION QUESTIONS

1. Should all marriages look the same? Why or why not?
2. What are the different conservative views on divorce?
3. What do you think of the statement "A high view of marriage means recognizing that it can be broken"?
4. What are some examples of how marriage can become an idol?
5. How can we bring marriage "back to earth"?

PART 5

WOMEN AND MEN
IN CHURCH

13

"MASCULINE PIETY"

PREVALENT TEACHING ON WOMEN

AND MEN IN THE CHURCH

*Masculinity is not a trait for which we should apologize; it should
ooze out of our lives and out of our sermons. . . . Do men perceive
of you as a godly person or a godly man? Men follow men.*

CRAIG THOMPSON[1]

When you go to church on Sunday morning, chances are you'll see
families sitting together in neat little rows—husbands and wives sitting
together or strategically interspersed among their children. But this hasn't
always been the norm.

When families went to worship at the temple in Israel, men and
women were separated into different courts. The outer ring, the Court
of the Gentiles, was as far as non-Jewish people were allowed. Inside that
was the Court of the Women, where women and children could worship.

---

1. Craig Thompson, "Reaching Men from the Pulpit," *Facts & Trends*, LifeWay Christian Resources, July 7, 2014, https://factsandtrends.net/2014/07/07/reaching-men
-from-the-pulpit/.

The Court of the Israelites was restricted to Jewish men. The inner court was the Court of the Priests, which priests alone could enter and where the altar of sacrifice was located. Women and young children could only watch what happened in the inner court from a distance.[2]

When Jesus died on the cross, the veil in the temple that blocked the entrance to the Holy of Holies was torn from top to bottom (see Mark 15:38). Christ's death and resurrection not only opened the way for us to have direct access to God but also tore down the dividing walls between Jews and Gentiles and men and women (see Gal. 3:28).

Women and men in the early church met and worshipped together. But it wasn't long before women and men were sitting separately in worship.[3] That separation remained common practice until the Protestant Reformation—although the custom still exists in some churches today. In addition to its stemming from different cultural practices, the reasoning behind this custom is that sitting separately reduces distractions and discourages inappropriate and indiscreet behavior.[4]

Perhaps you think that men and women sitting separately sounds like a great idea. Or maybe you're thankful that most modern churches in the West have done away with such ideas. Either way, while women and men aren't physically separated in our churches, they are often functionally separated in the life of the church.

SEPARATE SPHERES IN THE CHURCH

As we discuss what's being taught about women and men in the church, we are talking about more than who can be ordained or become a church leader. We are talking about all the aspects of life within the

2. See "The Court of the Women in the Temple," Bible History Online, accessed January 25, 2019, https://www.bible-history.com/court-of-women/.

3. See Teresa Berger, "Christian Worship and Gender Practices," Oxford Research Encyclopedias, March 2015, http://oxfordre.com/religion/view/10.1093/acrefore/9780199340378.001.0001/acrefore-9780199340378-e-6.

4. See Rajan Zed, "Faith Forum: Should Sexes Sit Together During Services?" *Reno Gazette Journal*, December 24, 2014, https://www.rgj.com/story/life/2014/12/24/faith-forum-sexes-sit-together-services/20885129/.

greater church community. This includes Bible studies, community groups, youth and children programs, and even conferences and para-church organizations. While we will focus on what happens in our local churches, the issues we'll address do affect the broader conservative Christian community.

In many of our conservative Christian churches today, the concept of separate spheres for women and men still influences us. Men and women effectively function in separate and distinct domains. We have men's ministries and women's ministries. We have programs for our senior high girls and guys. The local Christian bookstore even sells different Bibles for women and men.

On the one hand, women in conservative churches teach women's Bible studies and take care of most of the childcare needs, from nursery to children's Sunday School and choirs. They are tasked with most of the hospitality functions in the church: wedding and baby showers, potluck (pot providence?) dinners, coffee and donuts in the narthex. Women also take care of many of the mercy ministry needs, such as meals for the sick or for new mothers. Women's Bible studies are likely to focus on biblical womanhood, motherhood, and hospitality. Typically, lay men, on the other hand, teach men's and coed Bible studies and most youth group programs. Men take care of the maintenance and upkeep of the church. They may also be tasked with assisting in home repairs for widows and for others in need. Men's Bible studies are often focused on doctrinal or theological training and leadership.

AUTHORITY AND SUBMISSION IN THE CHURCH

It's one thing to say that qualified men are called to be ordained leaders in the church. It's another to consider all men as leaders or potential leaders, whether or not they are qualified and called to ministry. When all men in the church are leaders *by virtue of their gender*, the result is a hierarchy of men over women.

When women are considered as being easily deceived and likely to usurp authority over men, men need to stop women from rebelling against authority. Women need a "spiritual covering" beyond Christ. Otherwise, they'll be left spiritually unprotected and in danger. In many conservative churches, men are expected to step up and take responsibility for the spiritual protection of the women around them.

In some conservative Christian churches, this masculine authority extends to church membership. In a household or family membership approach, families are treated as a unit instead of as individuals who have individual membership responsibilities and privileges. Typically, the male head of the household is the one who is interviewed for membership. His wife and children are accepted into the church on his testimony.[5]

Some churches go so far as to restrict women from voting or from participating in church meetings. In these churches, only the male heads of households are allowed to do so. In some cases, the elements of the Lord's Supper are handed to the male heads of households to distribute to their families. If a woman's husband isn't at church that Sunday, her son can pass out the bread and wine, even if he's a child.[6]

This emphasis on masculine authority and feminine submission in the church, even when its applications are less extreme, results in churches that prioritize men and undervalue women just as the Greeks, Romans, and Victorians did.

MEN AS THE PRIORITY IN THE CHURCH

Churches that prioritize men tend to believe that churches should be male-oriented. They believe that pastors should represent the masculinity of Christ. Similar to some men in the Victorian era, some also believe that many pastors and much of church worship have become effeminate. As Douglas Wilson explains, "A standard of feminine piety has been accepted as normative in the Church as the standard for all the saints, both men and women. . . . We have failed because we have forgotten what

---

5. For examples, see "Constitution of Christ the Redeemer Church," Christ the Redeemer Church, accessed June 5, 2019, http://www.ctrchurch-mhk.org/CTR constitution.pdf, and "Constitution of Membership," Christ Reformed Evangelical Church, accessed June 5, 2019, https://www.crecannapolis.com/crec-constitution.pdf.

6. See Andrea, "A Church for Men," *Spirits Reclaimed* (blog), August 14, 2012, https://spiritsreclaimed.wordpress.com/2012/08/14/a-church-for-men/.

masculine piety even looks like."[7] Masculine piety focuses on principles of "truth" instead of on "relationships": "Truth, order, dominion, honor, self-sacrifice, judgment, law, fatherhood, citizenship, duty, truth, war, etc. . . . are just a few of the Scriptural themes men were made to delight in. Give your men such themes to confess, and make sure the musical accompaniment helps them to rejoice in them."[8]

The thinking goes that once we've recovered masculine piety and worship, our pastors will be masculine and their masculinity will draw other men to our churches. "Men follow men. Pastors, we must resist the temptation to sacrifice our masculinity for a gender-inclusive form of Christianity that appeals to women and children but alienates men. Men come in all kinds of shapes and sizes and masculinity is not defined by any one particular trait, but we must embrace it if we are to reach men."[9]

A concern for making masculine men has produced a whole movement of conferences, books, and resources that are aimed at men. Mark Driscoll rose to fame in part because of his association with the masculinity movement: "According to Driscoll, 'real men' avoid the church because it projects a 'Richard Simmons, hippie, queer Christ' that 'is no one to live for [and] is no one to die for.' Driscoll explains, 'Jesus was not a long-haired . . . effeminate-looking dude'; rather, he had 'callused hands and big biceps.' This is the sort of Christ men are drawn to—what Driscoll calls 'Ultimate Fighting Jesus.'"[10]

In masculine churches, men are the priority in the areas of teaching

7. Douglas Wilson, *Mother Kirk: Essays and Forays in Practical Ecclesiology* (Moscow, ID: Canon Press, 2001), 204.

8. Jody Killingsworth, quoted in David Bayly and Tim Bayly, "Masculine Worship: Pounding Guitars and Lots of D Minor?" *Baylyblog*, August 13, 2001, http://baylyblog .com/blog/2011/08/masculine-worship-pounding-guitars-and-lots-d-minor.

9. Craig Thompson, "Reaching Men from the Pulpit," *Facts & Trends*, LifeWay Christian Resources, July 7, 2014, https://factsandtrends.net/2014/07/07/reaching-men -from-the-pulpit/.

10. Brandon O'Brien, "A Jesus for Real Men," *Christianity Today*, April 18, 2008, http://www.christianitytoday.com/ct/2008/april/27.48.html, quoting from Mark Driscoll, "Death by Love" (sermon, Reform and Resurge Conference, Seattle, WA, May 2006), available online at https://web.archive.org/web/20071009190552/http:/the resurgence.com/files/audio/r_r_2006_session_11_audio_driscoll.mp3.

and discipleship. This is no accident: "The Church needs an intentional strategy to reach men because if you reach a man, you reach his whole family. A changed man will influence a marriage and a family. A changed family will influence a neighborhood and a community. A changed community will influence a state and a nation. A changed nation will help change the world. It all begins with a changed man."[11] Discipleship aims to equip fathers, who will then teach their families. "We don't have specialized ministries designed to aim targeted discipleship at every age and/or constituency. . . . Our focus is on equipping family shepherds and holding them accountable for the work to which God has called them."[12] Some pastors go so far as to say, "The sermon is for the men."[13]

Not all male-oriented churches will be as explicit as these examples are. The prioritization of men over women may be more subtle. Comparing what kinds of studies and resources the men and the women are using in a church can be enlightening.

WOMEN AS THROW PILLOWS IN THE CHURCH

If you've ever decorated your bedroom or living room, you're probably familiar with throw pillows. These pillows add elements of color and texture to a room. They're decorative additions that are nice to have—as long as you don't have too many of them—but they are ultimately unnecessary. When churches prioritize men, women are often relegated to the status of throw pillows: pretty but not essential.

As we mentioned earlier, Paul called women co-laborers in the church who were working with him for the gospel. Women aren't supposed to be throw pillows in the life of the church. But that's exactly what ends up happening in male-oriented churches. Many conservative churches

11. JP Jones, "God Is Looking for Men to Change the World," Truth That Changes Lives, OnePlace, accessed June 19, 2018, https://www.oneplace.com/ministries/truth-that-changes-lives/read/articles/god-is-looking-for-men-to-change-the-world-16047.html.

12. Voddie Baucham Jr., *Family Shepherds: Calling and Equipping Men to Lead Their Homes* (Wheaton, IL: Crossway, 2011), introduction, loc. 153–55 of 3015, Kindle.

13. Andrea, "A Church for Men."

have made women increasingly ancillary. Men are the leaders and the doers. They have the calling to work. Women are to submit and respond to male initiative. They are supposed to help men fulfill *their* calling. As a result, women are left to "adorn the gospel" and to stay out of the way of the real work.

Adorning the Gospel

In Titus 2:10, Paul tells believing slaves to show "all good faith so that they will adorn the doctrine of God our Savior in every respect." Adorning the doctrine of God, or the gospel, means that the good work we do brings honor and glory to God. While this passage is directed at slaves, it is certainly true that the actions of all of us, whether good or bad, either give glory to or dishonor God. But some have taken the concept of adorning the gospel and equated it specifically with the purpose of women in the church.

According to some conservative Christians, women serve in the church by upholding appropriately feminine roles. Many consider domesticity and hospitality to be essential to femininity, and they apply this belief to the expectations they have for women in the church. Aside from nursery duty and teaching children in Sunday School and VBS, women are expected to show hospitality by making meals, visiting the sick, throwing baby and bridal showers, and inviting visitors over for dinner. In addition, older women are expected to teach younger women these domestic arts. By doing so, women fulfill their purpose of adorning the gospel—making it beautiful and attractive for others.[14] "Living our lives as Titus 2 women enables us to fulfill the purpose for which we were created," writes Nancy DeMoss Wolgemuth. "It helps our families and churches to flourish and the beauty of the gospel to shine forth in our world."[15]

There's nothing wrong with women practicing hospitality. The problem arises when these are the *only* activities that are considered appropriate for women in the church. Because, as helpful as this work is to the

14. See Mary A. Kassian and Nancy Leigh DeMoss, *True Woman 201: Interior Design; Ten Elements of Biblical Womanhood* (Chicago: Moody Publishers, 2015), p. 285, NOOK.

15. Nancy DeMoss Wolgemuth, *Adorned: Living Out the Beauty of the Gospel Together* (Chicago: Moody Publishers, 2017), 20.

church, the women who are carrying out the work aren't considered to be essential to the gospel and the church's ministry. If women disappeared from the church and these jobs weren't done, it wouldn't be as pleasant and things wouldn't go as smoothly, but the real work of the church could continue.

"You Can't Do That—You're a Woman"

Another thing that undervalues women in the church is the addition of extrabiblical restrictions. To protect the biblical boundaries of qualified male ordination, churches often build hedges to help them stay on the safe side. Those hedges are often reinforced by the belief that men are created to lead and women are created to submit. The Bible might not specifically say that women aren't allowed to do certain activities in the church, but some consider it contrary to a woman's nature to do them.

Lists and guidelines are made for which roles women should and shouldn't have in church. Roles with high authority or influence and public visibility or recognition aren't suitable for women. For example, teaching theology at a Christian college or a Christian conference isn't appropriate, but leading the singing on Sunday or writing about theology may be suitable.[16]

Not everyone agrees about what the guidelines and restrictions should be. Women can teach children in most churches, but often there's an age cutoff. Where that cutoff is will vary, but typically it's somewhere between junior high and college. Women are usually allowed to teach other women, but not always.[17] Not many conservative churches allow women to teach coed groups of adults in any setting. Similarly, women teaching at women's conferences is generally allowed. Women speaking at coed conferences? Not so much. If the conference is held at a church, sometimes a woman will speak from a podium away from the pulpit or with her husband on stage to show that she's covered by his authority.

16. See Wayne Grudem, *Evangelical Feminism & Biblical Truth: An Analysis of More Than 100 Disputed Questions* (Colorado Springs: Multnomah Publishers, 2004), 84–97.
17. See Timothy J. Hammons, "Protecting the Weaker Vessel," *Theology That Matters* (blog), October 30, 2016, https://web.archive.org/web/20170427123603/https:/timothyjhammons.com/2016/10/30/protecting-the-weaker-vessel/.

Some conservative Christians debate whether women should blog and write about theology. Some say that it's fine. Others say it's appropriate only if they are writing, blogging, or podcasting to a female audience. A few say that it's inappropriate, because men shouldn't learn theology from women.[18]

Some are also concerned about women bloggers and writers correcting or addressing false teaching. That kind of confrontation is considered by some to be contrary to a woman's nature as yielding and submissive and to put her in a position to judge or lead men.[19] Women who write or speak publicly about theology, especially if the topic involves false teaching, are likely to get one of two responses. Those who disagree with them will often tell them, "You can't correct a man—especially a pastor/teacher as respected as So-and-So. You're a woman!" The response isn't much better from those who share their concerns. From those people, women may very well be told, "I appreciate the work you're doing. But you shouldn't be doing this, because you're a woman."[20]

In these ways, women in the church are being restricted beyond the boundaries that the Bible sets in place. Instead of being respected for their essential contributions to the ministry and life of the church, women are being treated as unnecessary accessories when they follow the extrabiblical rules and as rebellious troublemakers when they don't.

THE DAMAGE TO THE CHURCH

When the focus in the church is on authority and submission between men and women, it tends to put men between God and women. We saw earlier that teaching that men are priests for their families puts men in the position of being mediators between God and women. Mediator is a role that only Christ Himself can or should hold. Every

---

18. See Emilio Ramos, "Why We Do Not Allow Women Bloggers on RGM," Red Grace Media, May 19, 2014, http://redgracemedia.com/allow-women-bloggers-rgm/.

19. See Tim Bayly, "Rachel Miller and Valerie Hobbs: Where Is the Apostle Paul When We Need Him?" *Baylyblog*, September 4, 2015, http://baylyblog.com/blog/2015/09/rachel-miller-and-valerie-hobbs-where-apostle-paul-when-we-need-him.

20. I've heard this personally.

believer—female and male, young and old—has direct access to God through Christ. Believing women have the Holy Spirit working actively in their lives to sanctify them, just as believing men do. No other mediator or priest is needed.

Women are responsible for their relationship with God and should pursue the ordinary means of grace for themselves. This includes reading the Bible, praying, and listening to the preached Word. Believing women should have a direct relationship with their church leadership that provides them with pastoral care and discipling.

Men should encourage their families to pursue God through the ordinary means of grace. They should model and promote holiness in their lives and in the lives of their families. But while God uses every part of our lives, including our relationships with others, in the process of our sanctification, men aren't capable of doing what only God can do. They shouldn't be asked or expected to. It's an unfair burden to put on anyone.

A focus on masculine authority in the church diminishes qualified male ordination rather than promoting it. If churches consider men to be leaders simply because they are male, it can lead to the ordination of unqualified men or of men who haven't been called to leadership. As we have discussed, the Bible restricts ordination to qualified men, but that doesn't mean that every man is qualified to lead.

Besides the ordination of unqualified men, other types of damage are done when disqualified church officers aren't removed and when unordained men do the work that only ordained leaders should do. Certain aspects of church life should be done by our ordained leaders, such as preaching the Word, administering the sacraments, and performing the disciplinary function of the church. The attitude in our churches shouldn't be "These are roles for the ordained leaders, but any man can do them in a pinch." When just any man, ordained or not, is allowed to carry out these roles in the church, it undermines the importance of ordination and the ministerial work that ordained leaders should be doing. It also contributes to a masculine culture in the church—one in which men are prioritized over women in the church's work.

When churches focus on training men, they often pay little attention to what the women are learning. Some think that it doesn't matter too much—it's only the women. And so false teaching creeps into the church by way of poorly trained and neglected women.[21]

Another problem is the way that women who are interested in theology are treated. If women are prone to deception and will attempt to usurp power, then they can't be trusted in the church. Women who want to learn and help in the work of the church are viewed with suspicion. As a result, women whose gifts could benefit the church are dismissed because they aren't men. There are more spiritual gifts and roles in the church aside from the ones for ordained leaders. The church needs all the gifts God has given—to both men and women.

As it does in marriage, this hyper focus on authority and submission in the church tends to put enmity between women and men. Men can't trust the women around them in the church if they believe that women are their opponents instead of their co-laborers. It's hard for men and women to be acknowledged as equal before God and in Christ when men are taught that women need to be kept in their place.

This isn't a celebration of the beauty of complementarity. It's a perversion of God's design for women and men. It doesn't honor God as the Creator, and it doesn't present a biblical picture of men and women working together for God's glory to fulfill the creation mandate and the Great Commission.

In the next chapter, we'll look at how unity, interdependence, and service can help us to move beyond authority and submission and to focus on being co-laborers in the life of the church.

DISCUSSION QUESTIONS

1. Have you seen examples of "separate spheres" in church?
2. What effect does an emphasis on masculine authority and feminine submission have on churches?
3. What does it mean for women to be "throw pillows" in the church?

21. See Aimee Byrd, *No Little Women: Equipping All Women in the Household of God* (Phillipsburg, NJ: P&R Publishing, 2016), 31.

4. How does a focus on masculine authority undermine qualified male ordination?
5. What happens to women who are interested in theology in masculine-oriented churches?

14

"NOT SECOND-CLASS CITIZENS"

THE BIBLE ON WOMEN AND THE CHURCH

*We should also recognize that women are not second-class citizens in
the church. They have certain God-given authority to govern themselves
in worship. Just like single women, wives have direct relationships
with Christ, not relationships mediated through their husbands.*

RICHARD PRATT[1]

A Sunday school teacher started her lesson by telling the kids in her class
to raise their hands when they figured out what she was describing. The
kids listened intently as she said, "It has a long, bushy tail and lives in the
trees." No one raised a hand. She continued, "It eats nuts and pine cones."
Still no one raised a hand. The teacher was surprised that no one had
guessed yet, so she said, "It has gray fur and little ears. It makes a lot of
chittering noises and likes to eat from bird feeders."

To the teacher's great relief, one little hand finally went up. "Yes,
Beth. Do you know what I'm describing?"

1. Richard L. Pratt Jr., *I & II Corinthians*, Holman New Testament Commentary, ed.
Max Anders (Nashville: Holman Reference, 2000), 190.

Beth answered, "Well, I could have sworn it was a squirrel, but I'm pretty sure it's supposed to be Jesus."

This story is an amusing illustration of how easy it is to get stuck on assumptions. Kids in Sunday school begin to guess that the answer must be Jesus, whatever the question is, because talking about Jesus is what we do at church.

The same thing can happen when we discuss the roles of women and men in the church. We're conditioned to answer in certain ways. Women in the church? The answer must be "They can't be pastors!" or "Biblical womanhood!" Those may be the right answers to particular questions, but they aren't actually the answers to *all* questions about women in the church.[2]

DEFINING THE CHURCH

Before we can discuss the role of women in the church, we need to discuss what we mean when we say "the church." The *universal* or *invisible* church is made up of every believer who has ever lived or will ever live. These believers are united to Christ as His bride.[3] In the new heavens and new earth, they will be together with Jesus.

"The church" can also mean all the people around the world who profess faith in Christ. This is the *visible* church. Many believe that this includes all those who profess faith, as well as their children.[4] Others believe that the visible church is made up of all baptized adult believers. While there should be considerable overlap between the visible and the invisible church, some who profess faith are not actually believers who are united to Christ. Jesus said that the wheat (true believers) and the tares (false believers) will be separated at the judgment (see Matt. 13:24–30). Until then, we may not always know who belongs in which group.

Our local congregations are also known as churches—the word can indicate the particular church congregation and denomination that

---

2. This chapter focuses on women in the church because there are fewer questions and concerns in most conservative churches about what men can and can't do in church.

3. See the Westminster Confession of Faith, chapter 25.1.

4. See the Westminster Confession of Faith, chapter 25.2.

each of us joins as a member. Our churches have officers, pastors, elders, and/or deacons. In order for a church to be a true church, its officers should preach the Word, administer the sacraments, and practice church discipline.[5]

Each of these definitions of the church is useful for our discussion. In the last chapter, we used a fairly broad definition that included the wider visible church. The boundaries that the Bible sets for appropriate behavior in the church is focused mostly on what happens in the local church. This chapter's primary focus will be the local church, but its themes also apply more generally to the greater conservative Christian community.

UNITY IN THE CHURCH

When we talk about women and men in the church, our conversations often get caught up on setting boundaries and deciding who should be leaders. Those are legitimate concerns. As we have seen, the Bible does give clear guidelines about who should and shouldn't be ordained for church leadership. But, like the Sunday school story illustrated, there is so much more to the discussion about women and men in the church.

The ordained leadership of the church represents a small percentage of the whole body. For the rest of us, the question is how lay members of the church, both male and female, can be active in the church's life. By focusing on unity, interdependence, and service, we can move beyond a default preoccupation with male authority and female submission in our discussions.

As believers, we are united in Christ and together form the church—the household of God (see 1 Tim. 3:15). The Bible uses several metaphors from family life to explain the relationships that Christians have with one another and with God. Believers are brothers and sisters in Christ (see 1 Tim. 5:1–2). We're adopted sons and daughters of God (see Eph. 1:5). Together, believers are the church—the bride of Christ

5. See the Belgic Confession, article 29, available online at "The Belgic Confession Circa 1561 A.D.," A Puritan's Mind, accessed June 5, 2019, http://www.reformed.org /documents/BelgicConfession.html.

(see Eph. 5:22–33). We are also the body of Christ (1 Cor. 12:27). These analogies highlight our unity as believers.

Our unity is also seen in the fact that the majority of the Bible, including most of the instructions that are given to New Testament Christians, is written to all believers—both women and men. Short passages address men, women, husbands, fathers, mothers, wives, and other specific groups of people; but, on the whole, the Bible is for everyone.

In 1 Thessalonians 5, Paul tells us to "encourage one another and build up one another" (v. 11), to "live in peace with one another" (v. 13), and to "admonish the unruly, encourage the fainthearted, help the weak, be patient with everyone" (v. 14). In Galatians 6, Paul tells us to "bear one another's burdens" (v. 2) and to "do good to all people, and especially to those who are of the household of the faith" (v. 10). Colossians 3 says that we are to "[teach] and [admonish] one another with psalms and hymns and spiritual songs, singing with thankfulness in your hearts to God" (v. 16).

Peter also encourages us to care for each other.

> Above all, keep fervent in your love for one another, because love covers a multitude of sins. Be hospitable to one another without complaint. As each one has received a special gift, employ it in serving one another as good stewards of the manifold grace of God. (1 Peter 4:8–10).

The writer of Hebrews tells us to "consider how to stir up one another to love and good works" (Heb. 10:24 ESV). As Christians, men and women are to encourage, teach, admonish, help, and serve one another. We're to be equipped for service and built up as the body of Christ (see Eph. 4:12). We are united. We need each other. There are many examples, in both the Old and New Testaments, of women being active in the church in different ways.[6]

---

6. See "Report of the Ad Interim Committee on Women Serving in the Ministry of the Church" (paper presented to the Forty-Fifth General Assembly of the Presbyterian Church in America, Greensboro, NC, June 2017), http://www.pcaac.org/wp-content/uploads/2017/06/Women-Serving-in-Min.-of-Ch.-Study-Committee-Report-with-admended-recommendations.pdf.

Women Singing

Women and men are united in the Bible in singing to worship God. In the Old Testament, Miriam and Deborah led the Israelites to worship God. After God drowned Pharaoh and his men in the sea, Moses led the "sons of Israel" in praising God for saving His people (see Ex. 15:1–18). Miriam then picked up her timbral and led the women in praising God, singing, and dancing in response (see Ex. 15:20–21). In Judges 5, Deborah and Barak sang praise to God after the Israelites defeated Sisera.

Female singers are mentioned in a couple of places in the Old Testament. In 2 Chronicles 35:25, male and female singers lament for Josiah. In Nehemiah 7:67, male and female singers are among those who return from captivity. David and Solomon mention men and women singing (see 2 Sam. 19:35; Eccl. 2:8). Psalm 68:24–25 says that singers, musicians, and women with tambourines were part of a procession into the sanctuary. Scripture includes the songs of praise and thanksgiving that Hannah (see 1 Sam. 2:1–10) and Mary (see Luke 1:46–55) composed and sang.

Women Praying and Prophesying

Women and men are also united in the Bible in praying and prophesying. Not all examples of this in the Bible have a direct correlation to the modern church; but, while I believe that the gift of prophecy does not continue today, these passages are still relevant to our discussion. Several prophetesses are named in Scripture, including Miriam, Deborah, and Isaiah's wife, "the prophetess" (Isa. 8:3). The prophetess Huldah advised King Josiah when the people of Judah recovered the book of the law. She spoke for the Lord, sending a message to the king that condemned the people who had rejected God. She also comforted Josiah because of his tender heart toward God (see 2 Kings 22:14–20).

In the New Testament, the prophetess Anna was one of the first witnesses of the Messiah. She was at the temple, where she served day and night, when Mary and Joseph brought Jesus to be presented. The passage says she gave "thanks to God, and continued to speak of Him to all those who were looking for the redemption of Jerusalem" (Luke 2:38). Philip, one of the men who was chosen to care for the widows in Acts 6, had four prophetess daughters (see Acts 21:9). The New Testament also mentions women praying and prophesying in church (see 1 Cor. 11:5).

Women Sharing Good News

Women and men are also united in the call to share the gospel. Even in the Old Testament, "the women who proclaim the good tidings are a great host" (Ps. 68:11). Just as Anna shared the good news that the Messiah had come, many other women in the Bible shared good news about God's work.

When Jesus told the Samaritan woman at the well that He was the Messiah, she dropped everything and ran back to town. "The woman . . . said to the men, 'Come, see a man who told me all the things that I have done; this is not the Christ, is it?'" (John 4:28–29). The amazing thing is that the men believed her and went to see Jesus for themselves. John writes, "From that city many of the Samaritans believed in Him *because of the word of the woman who testified*, 'He told me all the things that I have done'" (v. 39).

Women were also the first witnesses to the resurrection. Having gone to the tomb to tend to Jesus's body, the women were surprised to find the tomb empty. The angels told them that Jesus was risen and that they should go tell the disciples. Then Jesus Himself met them and told them to go tell the disciples (see Matt. 28:1–10). Sadly, the disciples didn't believe the women until after they saw Jesus themselves (see Luke 24:11, 22–31). John Calvin noted that even though the disciples didn't believe the women at first, "when they afterwards proclaimed the gospel, they must have borrowed from *women* the chief portion of the history."[7]

Lois and Eunice taught Timothy; and Priscilla and her husband, Aquila, taught Apollos. Paul tells the older women of the church to help teach the younger women (see Titus 2:3–5). Women, alongside men, have always played an important part in spreading the gospel. All believers should be equipped to share the gospel with others (see 1 Peter 3:15).

---

7. John Calvin, *Commentary on a Harmony of the Evangelists, Matthew, Mark, and Luke*, vol. 3, in *Harmony of Matthew, Mark, Luke, John 1–11*, trans. William Pringle, Calvin's Commentaries 17 (repr., Grand Rapids: Baker, 2003), 329, emphasis in original,

INTERDEPENDENCE IN THE CHURCH

We don't all have the same gifts or responsibilities in the church. For this reason, we need to remember our interdependence. We need each other, just as we do in marriage and in the home. We each have different gifts, abilities, and perspectives. We should use these to serve one another and glorify God (see 1 Peter 4:10–11), as we will discuss in a moment.

The interdependence of women and men in the church is demonstrated in Paul's letters, when he thanks and commends several people for their work in the church. He includes many women in addition to the men: Phoebe, Mary, Junia, Persis, Julia, Tryphena, Tryphosa, Nereus's sister, and Rufus' mother (see Rom. 16). Paul specifically calls three women, Priscilla (see Rom. 16:3), Euodia, and Syntyche (see Phil. 4:2–3), "co-laborers" in Christ or in the gospel. The words that he uses suggest athletes on the same team or soldiers fighting together on the same side.[8]

John Calvin translates this term of Paul's as meaning "fellow-soldiers in the gospel." He explains that Paul "calls them his companions in war, inasmuch as they had struggled hard with him in the gospel."[9] He writes that Paul showed Priscilla "singular honor" for her work, even naming her before her husband (see Rom. 16:3). Paul didn't dismiss having "a woman as his associate in the work of the Lord; nor was he ashamed to confess this."[10]

Matthew Henry notes that Euodia and Syntyche are examples of women who shared in the work of the gospel with Paul and are models for us today. They weren't preachers or public teachers, but they were active

---

quoted in Aimee Byrd, *No Little Women: Equipping All Women in the Household of God* (Phillipsburg, NJ: P&R Publishing, 2016), 108.

8. See "*sunergos*," Bible Hub, accessed June 18, 2018, http://biblehub.com/greek /4904.htm, Strong's number 4904, and "*sunathleó*," Bible Hub, accessed June 18, 2018, http://biblehub.com/greek/4866.htm, Strong's number 4866.

9. John Calvin, *Commentary on the Epistle to the Philippians*, trans. William Pringle, in *Galatians–Philemon*, Calvin's Commentaries 21 (repr., Grand Rapids: Baker, 1979), 112–13.

10. John Calvin, *Commentaries on the Epistle of Paul to the Romans*, trans. John Owen, in *Acts 14–28 & Romans 1–16*, Calvin's Commentaries 19 (repr., Grand Rapids: Baker, 1979), 544.

in the church, "entertaining the ministers, visiting the sick, instructing the ignorant, convincing the erroneous. Thus women may be helpful to ministers in the work of the gospel."[11]

While Paul doesn't specifically call Phoebe a co-laborer, he commends her for her work in the church (see Rom. 16:1–2). As Calvin explains, "She was evidently a great helper of the Christian cause, as some other women also are mentioned in this chapter, and she had been the helper of many, (verse 2,) and not of one Church, and also of Paul himself."[12]

SERVICE IN THE CHURCH

To be a leader in the church is to serve. Consider what New Testament leaders are called: *shepherds, elders, overseers,* and *stewards.* These titles emphasize the servant nature of church leadership. In the Old Testament, God gave His people priests to act as mediators and to offer sacrifices for His people. Because Christ fulfilled that role forever, we don't need mediators or priests to offer sacrifices for us anymore.

Christ's life, death, and resurrection made it possible for us to pray directly to God. We are a priesthood of believers, male and female. We don't need priests, but we do need elders, overseers, shepherds, and stewards to teach, guide, discipline, and protect us.

As in the home, there is order in the church, but there shouldn't be a hierarchy of all men over all women. Women aren't called to ordained leadership in the church, but that doesn't mean that they are lesser or secondary in the church. "Women are not second-class citizens in the church. They have certain God-given authority to govern themselves in worship," writes theologian and author Richard Pratt. "Just like single women, wives have direct relationships with Christ, not relationships mediated through their husbands. Women also have the freedom to pray and prophesy in church. While Paul taught that women should not hold ordained positions (1 Tim. 2:11–12), he expected them to take active

11. Philippians 4:1–9 in *Matthew Henry Commentary on the Whole Bible (Complete),* available online from Bible Study Tools, accessed June 12, 2019, https://www.bible studytools.com/commentaries/matthew-henry-complete/philippians/4.html.
12. Calvin, *Commentaries on the Epistle of Paul to the Romans,* 542–43.

roles in public worship. He required that they do it in ways that honored their Lord, their husbands, and the church's reputation."[13]

As are husbands, church leaders are called to sacrifice and servanthood. There is authority in the offices of the church, as we discussed in chapter 1. However, the emphasis of these offices isn't on power and privilege but on the responsibilities that the leaders have to protect and care for the congregation, who are their brothers and sisters in Christ. "Church leaders are not to grasp for power but are to be the first to set the example of sacrifice and suffering, to give up the rights of their position for the sake of the whole," Michelle Lee-Barnewall writes.[14]

Church members, both women and men, are also called to service and sacrifice. We serve the church in part by honoring our church leaders and upholding the central ministry of Word and sacrament that they're called to carry out. But we are also called to use our gifts for the benefit of the church and to the glory of God.

Women Serving

The Old Testament tells us that women served "at the doorway of the tent of meeting" (Ex. 38:8). It's unclear who exactly these women were and what they did, but commentators speak of their devotion and piety. "It should seem these women were eminent and exemplary for devotion, attending more frequently and seriously at the place of public worship than others did; and notice is here taken of it to their honour," writes Matthew Henry. "Anna was such a one long afterwards, who departed not from the temple, but served God with fastings and prayers night and day."[15]

In the New Testament, the early church often met in the homes of women, such as Priscilla and Aquila (see Rom. 16:3–5), Nympha (see

---

13. Pratt, *I & II Corinthians*, 190.

14. Michelle Lee-Barnewall, *Neither Complementarian nor Egalitarian: A Kingdom Corrective to the Evangelical Gender Debate* (Grand Rapids: Baker Academic, 2016), p. 218, NOOK.

15. Exodus 38:1–8 in *Matthew Henry Commentary on the Whole Bible (Complete)*, available online from Bible Study Tools, accessed June 12, 2019, https://www.bible studytools.com/commentaries/matthew-henry-complete/exodus/38.html.

Col. 4:15), and likely Lydia (see Acts 16:40). Other women in the early church, such as Dorcas (see Acts 9:36), were commended for acts of kindness and mercy as they cared for the needs of others in the church community.

Women Following Jesus

During Jesus's ministry, women and men served as they followed him. Jesus's twelve male disciples weren't his only followers. Many of His followers were women, including Mary Magdalene, Joanna, Susanna, sisters Mary and Martha, Mary the mother of James, and Salome. These women also funded Jesus's ministry (see Luke 8:3) and ministered to Him (see Matt. 27:55).

Mary and Martha, along with their brother, Lazarus, were Jesus's friends. He stayed with them in Martha's house (see Luke 10:38; John 12:2). Mary sat at Jesus's feet and learned from Him, and Jesus praised her for it (see Luke 10:39–42). Women of the time rarely learned theology. "Mary broke the stereotype by being catechized by Jesus when her sister Martha thought she should be making coffee for the next group."[16]

When Jesus was crucified, most of his followers had deserted Him. Several of the women, however, watched from a distance (see Matt. 27:55–56). These women saw where He was buried so that they could tend to Him after the Sabbath (see Luke 23:55–56). From His mother, Mary, to Mary Magdalene, women cared for and served Jesus throughout his life and ministry.

WOMEN IN THE CHURCH TODAY

While women were never priests in the Old Testament or ordained leaders in the New, it doesn't mean that women weren't active in the church. As we have seen, the Bible gives clear examples of women who participated in the work and life of the church. Women sang, prayed, and prophesied. They served in the church, ministered to and cared for the

16. Michael Horton, "Muscular Christianity," *Modern Reformation* 21, no. 3 (2012), 46–47.

needs of others, and provided their homes and money for the needs of the church. They were Jesus's followers, witnesses to His life, death, and resurrection, sharers of the gospel, and co-laborers in Christ.

Instead of developing a list of things that women can and can't do in church, it would be more helpful for us to consider the boundaries we've already discussed. Only ordained leaders may preach, administer the sacraments, and perform discipline. Outside that, we should reflect on the kinds of activities the Bible shows women performing in the life of the church.

Paul called women in the early church his co-laborers for the gospel. Can we say the same in our churches? If so, great! But if women aren't co-laboring with the men in our churches, if they've been relegated to throw-pillow status, then we need to go back to the Bible and see how to better incorporate women into the life of the church.

Here are some thoughts to ponder.

- Women in the Bible sang and led others in song. Are there ways that women in our churches can do the same?
- Women in the New Testament prayed and prophesied. Even if you believe that prophecy was a gift that ended with the apostolic era, are there ways that women today can participate similarly?[17]
- Women taught and shared the good news—not as pastors or apostles, but as members of the church. How can we encourage women to teach and evangelize today?
- Women followed Jesus and sat at His feet to learn theology. How can we support women in our churches in their desire to learn?
- Women served in the early church and ministered to the needs of others. How can we encourage women to be involved in areas of ministry in our churches?

Look around. Are there areas in our churches where certain people's gifts aren't being put to use? There will likely be differences in how things are applied across different churches. For example, some conservative

17. One suggestion might be for women to pray and read Scripture in group settings.

churches allow women to teach adult Sunday school or Bible study classes. Some also incorporate unordained members, including women, in certain aspects of public worship. Others may allow women to use their gifts in administrative roles in the church, such as office or church staff. If your church has a different approach, how else can women assist elders, deacons, and pastors and use their gifts as lay members of the congregation?

We don't need to push the envelope or see how close we can get to the biblical boundaries without crossing the line. My goal in this chapter is to encourage us to see women in our churches as more than throw pillows. To do so, we need to acknowledge, appreciate, and use the gifts God has given us all so that we can be built up together as co-laborers in the body of Christ and so that God would be glorified in all we do.

In the next chapter, we'll look at some common questions that are raised about male ordination. Specifically, we'll consider what male ordination does and doesn't mean for our churches.

DISCUSSION QUESTIONS

1. How do women and men demonstrate our unity in the church?
2. How do women and men demonstrate our interdependence in church?
3. How do women and men serve others in church?
4. Paul called women in the early church his co-laborers for the gospel. What would that look like in our churches?
5. How can women assist elders, deacons, and pastors and use their gifts as lay members of the congregation?

15

"REDISCOVER THE MINISTRY THAT CHRIST HAS ORDAINED"

WHAT MALE ORDINATION

DOES AND DOESN'T MEAN

We pretend not that Women shou'd teach in the Church,
or usurp Authority where it is not allow'd them; permit us
only to understand our own duty, and not be forc'd to take it
upon trust from others; to be at least so far learned, as to be
able to form in our minds a true Idea of Christianity.

MARY ASTELL[1]

One afternoon, as the story goes, a woman got out a ham to cook for dinner. As she prepped the ham, she cut the end off of it and set it in a pan. Her daughter, watching her mom, asked, "Why do you cut off the end of the ham?"

---

1. Mary Astell, "A Serious Proposal to the Ladies," in *First Feminists: British Women Writers; 1578–1799*, ed. Moira Ferguson (Bloomington, IN: Indiana University Press, 1985), 189.

The woman paused for a moment. "My mother always did it this way. I think it makes the ham cook more evenly." Later that evening, when her parents arrived for dinner, she mentioned the ham to her mom and asked her why she always cut off the end of the ham.

Her mom replied, "It's what your grandmother always did. Seems to make the ham taste better." Just then, the elderly grandmother stepped into the kitchen. The young woman smiled and said, "Look, Grandma, we have a nice ham for dinner, and we've cut off the end, just like you always taught us."

The grandmother returned the smile as she replied, "You know, the only reason I cut off the end is because the ham wouldn't fit in my pan any other way."

Just like "Grandma's ham" and other traditions, sometimes we do things in the church without knowing why. When we don't know for sure why we do what we do, we can easily end up with wrong ideas. It's one thing not to know why we always cut off the end of the ham, but it's quite another not to know why we ordain only men as leaders in the church. Without understanding what the Bible does and doesn't teach about ordination, we can end up making dangerous assumptions.

WHY AREN'T WOMEN ORDAINED FOR CHURCH LEADERSHIP?

When Paul lays out the qualifications for ordination, he references Adam and Eve and the order of creation (see 1 Tim. 2:13–14). Order in God's household, the church, is connected to order in the home. G. K. Beale, professor of New Testament and biblical theology at Westminster Theological Seminary, explains that this connection goes back to the garden of Eden. Adam was placed in the garden and given the command to cultivate and to keep it (see Gen. 2:15). Beale notes that the words *cultivate* and *keep* are often translated as "serve" and "guard," which are priestly duties.[2]

---

2. See G. K. Beale, *The Temple and the Church's Mission: A Biblical Theology of the Dwelling Place of God* (Downers Grove, IL: IVP Academic, 2004), 66–68.

Adam, then, had multiple responsibilities—as a king or vice-regent over creation, as a priest in the first temple (the garden), and as a husband. Leadership in the home, church, and society were united in Adam. When Adam sinned, he didn't guard the garden as he'd been tasked to do. Because of his sin, he was sent out of the garden and removed from his role as priest. Home, church, and society became separate domains and are still separate today.[3]

These roles of priest and king remained separate until Christ, the second Adam, succeeded where Adam had failed.[4] Christ is *the* priest, *the* king, and *the* husband. Since we have Christ as our High Priest, we no longer need priests in the church, but we do need shepherds who guard and defend the sheep. As leaders of the church, pastors and elders have a particular responsibility to teach and protect the church.[5]

Our church leaders aren't more important or more valuable than the rest of the congregation is. Those of us who are in the pews are needed and should be glad to use the gifts that God has given us. Everyone has a necessary role to fill in the church. Women and men should co-labor together in the life of the church, seeking to serve one another and to serve God.

All that we do in church should be done decently and in good order (see 1 Cor. 14:40). Paul wanted women and men in the early church to behave appropriately in corporate worship. He discusses aspects of worship and the dangers of disruptions in several passages (see 1 Cor. 11–14; 1 Tim. 2–5; Titus 1–3) and gives instructions.[6] There shouldn't be disruptions in church. Congregations should avoid false teaching and dissension. Women should dress in a way that doesn't draw inappropriate attention to themselves. Wives shouldn't dishonor their husbands. Women should also learn quietly, respectfully, and with self-restraint.

---

3. See Aimee Byrd, *No Little Women: Equipping All Women in the Household of God* (Phillipsburg, NJ: P&R Publishing, 2016), 70.

4. See Beale, *The Temple and the Church's Mission*, 70.

5. See Carl Trueman, "1 Timothy 2:11–15" (sermon, Cornerstone Presbyterian Church, Ambler, PA, November 11, 2011), available online at https://web.archive.org /web/20160324093349/http://cornerstoneopc.com/media/2011-11-20.mp3.

6. For example, when Paul gave instructions about how to celebrate the Lord's Supper in 1 Corinthians 11, he warned believers not to get drunk or eat separately without everyone taking part.

We don't know exactly what was going on in these early churches. Some commentators believe that since churches were meeting in private homes, there was confusion about appropriate behavior. "Women may have felt more comfortable in a home setting and were more expressive. Certain behaviors permissible at home, however, were out of place in the church,"[7] New Testament scholar David Garland explains.

Paul didn't want behavior in the church to reflect poorly on Christianity. Outsiders might very well be offended by the gospel, but they shouldn't be unnecessarily offended by Christians' behavior. In Paul's culture, respectable married women wore their hair covered in public. A woman with her hair uncovered was considered "available."[8] By telling women to cover their hair in worship regardless of their marital status, Paul provided protection for all women in church and ensured that those outside the church wouldn't get the wrong ideas about what was going on in Christian worship.[9]

When Paul instructed women to "learn quietly" (1 Tim. 2:11 ESV) and "keep silent in the churches" (1 Cor. 14:34), his concern was over disruptive behavior. You may wonder if Paul was telling women not to say anything at all in church, but what Paul was concerned about seems to be disruptions that would arise from women teaching men or asking questions during the discussion of prophecies in corporate worship.[10]

While we notice Paul's emphasis on women learning "quietly" or being "silent," the stunning part of what he says is that women were supposed *to learn*.[11] As we saw with the Greeks and the Romans, women weren't encouraged to learn theology at the time. Even among the Jews it wasn't common for women to be taught theology. As one rabbi said, "The words of the Torah should be burned rather than entrusted to women."[12]

---

7. David E. Garland, *1 Corinthians*, Baker Exegetical Commentary on the New Testament (Grand Rapids: Baker Academic, 2003), 669.

8. Garland, 521.

9. See Cynthia Long Westfall, *Paul and Gender: Reclaiming the Apostle's Vision for Men and Women in Christ* (Grand Rapids: Baker Academic, 2016), 33–34.

10. See Philip H. Towner, *1–2 Timothy & Titus*, The IVP New Testament Commentary Series (Downers Grove, IL: InterVarsity Press, 1994), 69.

11. See Towner, 76–77.

12. Eliezer ben Hyrcanus, *The Jerusalem Talmud, Sotah* 3:4, 19a.

In contrast, Paul wants women to learn—but not by being distracting or unruly.

DON'T HEAR WHAT WE'RE NOT SAYING

Because the Bible teaches that ordained leaders of the church should be qualified men and not women, some conservative Christians think that churches ought to be masculine. As we saw, some believe that pastors are meant to represent a masculine Christ and to exemplify masculinity, and that worship should have a "masculine feel." Some churches prioritize men and expect husbands and fathers, rather than church leaders, to teach their wives and children.

When, in connection with the qualifications he gives for ordination, Paul says that Eve was deceived (see 1 Tim. 2:14), some conservative Christians believe this is why women can't be ordained. They believe that all women are easily deceived and can't be trusted to make sound theological decisions.

These two topics—masculine churches and women being easily deceived—are common misapplications of the biblical boundaries we've discussed. Let's consider how each of these is *not* what the biblical boundaries mean.

Should We Have Masculine Churches?

In many churches, women outnumber men.[13] Some churches attribute that to effeminate worship and leadership.[14] To combat this, some churches want to become more masculine in order to reach men. While men should be encouraged to be active in the life of the church, so should women. The problem comes with the emphasis that some conservative

13. The Pew Research Center found that more Christian women (53 percent) than men (46 percent) attended church on a weekly basis. See "The Gender Gap in Religion Around the World," Pew Research Center, March 22, 2016, http://www.pewforum.org/2016/03/22/the-gender-gap-in-religion-around-the-world/.

14. See David Bayly and Tim Bayly, "Masculine Worship: Pounding Guitars and Lots of D Minor?" *Baylyblog*, August 13, 2001, http://baylyblog.com/blog/2011/08/masculine-worship-pounding-guitars-and-lots-d-minor.

churches are placing on masculinity and on the masculine worship that they think will make men want to come to church.

For example, David Murrow's book *Why Men Hate Going to Church* gives suggestions on how to reach men through masculinity: "Pastors should be masculine, strong, and resolute. Men disrespect other guys who are 'overly verbal, expressive, or sensitive.' Pastors must work to overcome the stereotype of femininity that surrounds the ministry. . . . Men like pastors who have the trappings of manhood."[15] Steve Farrar, founder of Men's Leadership Ministries, takes a similar approach: "The key to an effective men's ministry is to have a masculine pastor: a man who thinks like a man, acts like a man and fulfills his God-given calling to be a man."[16] Some churches say that they are "masculine-oriented"[17] and make teaching men their priority.[18] Others call for an emphasis on "sanctified testosterone"[19] or on "masculine piety"[20] in worship.

The reasoning is that Christ is a man. Christ is our example of perfect masculinity. Pastors represent Christ. Therefore, pastors should be men who exemplify masculinity.[21]

This logic, however, doesn't hold up to Scripture. Churches shouldn't be masculine (or feminine) oriented. The body of Christ is made up of men and women. All believers should be taught the Scripture. As

---

15. David Murrow, *Why Men Hate Going to Church* (Nashville: Thomas Nelson, 2005), summarized in Craig Thompson, "Reaching Men from the Pulpit," *Facts & Trends*, LifeWay Christian Resources, July 7, 2014, https://factsandtrends.net/2014/07/07/reaching-men-from-the-pulpit/.

16. Quoted in JP Jones, "God Is Looking for Men to Change the World," Truth That Changes Lives, OnePlace, accessed June 19, 2018, https://www.oneplace.com/ministries/truth-that-changes-lives/read/articles/god-is-looking-for-men-to-change-the-world-16047.html.

17. JP Jones, "God Is Looking for Men to Change the World."

18. See Voddie Baucham Jr., *Family Shepherds: Calling and Equipping Men to Lead Their Homes* (Wheaton, IL: Crossway, 2011), introduction, loc. 153–55 of 3015, Kindle.

19. Jason Allen, "5 Key Ways to Cultivating Biblical Manhood in Your Church," The Council on Biblical Manhood and Womanhood, April 21, 2016, https://cbmw.org/topics/leadership-2/5-key-ways-to-cultivating-biblical-manhood-in-your-church/.

20. Bayly and Bayly, "Masculine Worship."

21. See Wayne Grudem, *Evangelical Feminism & Biblical Truth: An Analysis of More Than 100 Disputed Questions* (Colorado Springs: Multnomah Publishers, 2004), 167.

believers, we should all be encouraged to look to Christ for our salvation and for our example of perfect *humanity*. We need men to be active in our churches, but not at the expense of educating women, training them, and incorporating them into the life of the church.

As Michael Horton argues, instead of focusing on masculine Christianity, we need "to rediscover the ministry that Christ has ordained for making disciples of all nations, all generations, and both genders. We need less niche marketing and more meat-and-potatoes service to the whole body of Christ."[22]

Is Ordination Only for Men Because Women Are More Easily Deceived?

Some conservative Christians teach that women are more prone to deception than men are. They believe this is why only men should be ordained leaders in the church. As one pastor explains, "Paul is saying that she is not to teach men or exercise authority because of her susceptibility to deception. . . . God has not made her to exercise the kind of hard, judgmental discernment that is necessary in theological and Scriptural issues. By nature, a woman will more likely fall prey to the subtleties of mental and theological error."[23]

The argument is that if women are more vulnerable to being misled, they can't be trusted to be spiritually discerning. For that reason, women aren't suited for exercising authority in the church or for teaching theology in general. "It seems that the church should give broader application to Paul's argument than just to the matter of a woman's not teaching men or exercising authority. If she is more susceptible to deception, then, when she teaches other women and children in the church, she should use materials approved by the elders. . . . When the church uses material written by a woman, it needs to be approved by the elders."[24] I agree that church leadership should review the material that is used in children's and

22. Michael Horton, "Muscular Christianity," *Modern Reformation* 21, no. 3 (2012), 46–47.

23. Joseph Pipa, "Leading in Worship," Greenville Presbyterian Theological Seminary, April 28, 2017, http://josephpipa.com/leading-in-worship/.

24. Pipa, "Leading in Worship."

women's ministries, but not because women are "prone to deception." All materials that are used in a church should be evaluated by church leadership.

A few go further and say that women shouldn't teach anyone—not even other women. As another pastor explains, "The role of women in the church is quite clear to those who will actually look at what Scripture says. There is no call for women to be leading large masses of women in Bible studies, or at conferences, or any other such notion. According to the passage in Titus, and the way God created women, they are to be at home serving their husbands."[25]

The reasoning can be summarized like this:

Eve was deceived.
All women, like Eve, are more easily deceived than men are.
No woman can be trusted on theological matters.

But if that's Paul's point in 1 Timothy 2, men can't be trusted either. After all, if the point is that Adam wasn't deceived, then he sinned willfully. If all women are like Eve, then all men are prone to outright rebellion like Adam. That's not a strong argument for male leadership.

The contrast between Adam and Eve isn't that Adam was never deceived, but that he wasn't deceived first. Eve, having been deceived, led Adam into sin.[26] Eve is an example for all believers, as Paul warns: "I am afraid that, as the serpent deceived Eve by his craftiness, your minds will be led astray from the simplicity and purity of devotion to Christ" (2 Cor. 11:3). Similarly, in 1 Timothy, Paul deals with false teaching that was infecting the church. Like Eve, some women were being deceived by false teachers. Some commentators believe that these women were

25. Timothy J. Hammons, "Protecting the Weaker Vessel," *Theology That Matters* (blog), October 30, 2016, https://web.archive.org/web/20170427123603/https:/timothyjhammons.com/2016/10/30/protecting-the-weaker-vessel/.

26. See 1 Timothy 2:9–15 in *Matthew Henry Commentary on the Whole Bible (Complete)*, available online from Bible Study Tools, accessed June 12, 2019, https://www.biblestudytools.com/commentaries/matthew-henry-complete/1-timothy/2.html.

spreading false teaching, as Eve did to Adam.[27] Paul's concern, then, is that all believers be on their guard against false teaching.

Not being deceived by false teachers is a common theme in many of Paul's letters. It appears in 2 Timothy 3:6, where Paul warns that deceitful men are preying on particularly vulnerable women. His point isn't that all women are weak or easily deceived but that "a particular type of immature woman was being targeted by false teachers looking to manipulate and infect households."[28]

The Bible doesn't teach that women are more easily deceived than men are. It's important that all believers, both male and female, are taught good doctrine so that none of us will be susceptible to deception. We are all encouraged to grow in maturity in the faith so that we won't be "tossed here and there by waves and carried about by every wind of doctrine, by the trickery of men, by craftiness in deceitful scheming" (Eph. 4:14).

WHERE DO WE GO FROM HERE?

There's a legitimate need for us to affirm the biblical qualifications for ordained leaders. But if we aren't careful about how we defend male ordination, we'll end up with false assumptions and bad applications. These will only hurt women, men, and the church. Most women in conservative churches want to be faithful to Scripture. We want a place to serve and use our gifts—not as ordained leaders, but as devoted members of the church that we love.

The fall damaged our relationships. We tend to see one another as people to contend against. But it shouldn't and doesn't have to be that way. Women and men in the church are meant to labor alongside each other—to fight against our common enemies and for the gospel. Too often we find ourselves fighting each other face-to-face instead of fighting side-by-side as we were meant to.

From the beginning, when Eve was made to be a helper for Adam, we were meant to work together for God's glory and for His kingdom.

---

27. See Towner, *1–2 Timothy & Titus*, 75.
28. Byrd, *No Little Women*, 24.

As believing men and women, we have been united together in Christ. Instead of being distracted by what could divide us, we should focus on what unites us. We are the body—the church. Through the work of the Spirit, we are knit together and our true goal has been restored: women and men united and interdependent, serving together as co-laborers, glorifying God and enjoying Him forever.[29]

In the next chapter, we will turn our attention to what's being taught by many conservative Christians about how women and men should work together in society. As we will see, the emphasis is still strongly on male authority and female submission.

DISCUSSION QUESTIONS

1. Why aren't women ordained for church leadership?
2. What are some false assumptions about male ordination?
3. Do churches need to be more "masculine" in order to reach men?
4. Is ordination only for men because women are more easily deceived? Why or why not?
5. How can women and men work as co-laborers in the church?

29. See the Westminster Shorter Catechism, answer 1.

PART 6

WOMEN AND MEN

IN SOCIETY

16

"GOD-ORDAINED SOCIAL ROLES"

PREVALENT TEACHING ON

WOMEN AND MEN IN SOCIETY

A God-honoring society will likewise prefer male leadership in civil and
other spheres. . . . It is not the ordinary and fitting role of women to work
alongside men as their functional equals in public spheres of dominion.
. . . The exceptional circumstance (singleness) ought not redefine the
ordinary, God-ordained social roles of men and women as created.

VISION FORUM MINISTRIES[1]

Greek mythology tells the story of a man named Procrustes. A son of the
god Poseidon, Procrustes would lure unsuspecting travelers into his home.
When he showed them to their room, he would force them to lie down
on an iron bed, then try to make the hapless victims fit. If they were too
short, he'd stretch them on a rack. As painful as that surely would have
been, those who were too tall were in for a worse surprise. Any part of

---

1. "The Tenets of Biblical Patriarchy," Vision Forum Ministries, accessed December
1, 2018, https://homeschoolersanonymous.files.wordpress.com/2014/04/the-tenets
-of-biblical-patriarchy-vision-forum-ministries.pdf.

their bodies that hung off the bed, Procrustes would cut off. No one who lay down on Procrustes's bed survived.[2]

Like Procrustes's bed, the prevalent conservative definitions of masculinity and femininity are often rigid and unforgiving. Men and women either lack the qualities they need in order to fit the mold or else need to have parts of their personalities removed. While we saw evidence of this in our discussions about marriage and the church, the clearest examples of it are found in how definitions of masculinity and femininity are applied to women and men in society. These views about the nature of women and men require men and women to behave in strictly defined ways toward all people in all contexts.

SEPARATE SPHERES

When you believe that all interactions between men and women boil down to an interplay of authority and submission, it's impossible to restrict the application of this to only the home and the church. If it's the *nature* of men to be leaders, providers, and protectors, then that will apply to society as well. Likewise, if it's the *nature* of women to be submissive and responsive to male leadership, then there are appropriate and inappropriate ways for women to behave in society.[3]

The concept of separate spheres is an important aspect of what's being taught about women and men in society. As we noted in chapter 10, some see particular significance in the details of the creation of Adam and Eve. James Jordan, theologian and director of Biblical Horizons ministries, explains that men initiate, after the pattern of Adam, and that women "complete what men begin,"[4] after the pattern of Eve. In marriage, men initiate and provide. Women complete this and bring glory

2. See *Encyclopaedia Britannica*, s.v. "Procrustes," last modified January 4, 2011, https://www.britannica.com/topic/Procrustes.

3. Society, for the purpose of our discussion, applies to everything outside the home and church community.

4. James B. Jordan, "Liturgical Man, Liturgical Women: Part 2," Biblical Horizons, June 2004, https://web.archive.org/web/20060209192735/http://www.biblicalhorizons .com:80/rr/rr087.htm.

through bearing children and decorating the home. In the church, men lead because they were created to initiate, and women "lend glory to worship."[5] And in society, "men tend to be the guardians and protectors of society, a society that is decorated and glorified by women."[6]

Alastair Roberts, a fellow at the Greystone Institute, builds on Jordan's explanation and interprets creation as having a framework that can be applied to the roles of men and women.[7] According to the framework hypothesis, on days 1–3 of creation, God created the form: light, sky, water, and land. On days 4–6 of creation, God filled those forms by creating the sun, moon, stars, animals of the air and sea, land animals, and man.

In Roberts's application, men were created to carry on the forming tasks of the first three days. Women were created to continue the filling tasks of the second three days: "The forming, taming, and naming task—the task associated with the first three days, the task associated with the work of Christ—is particularly given to the man. The man is the one especially given the task of naming, of establishing and guarding the boundaries, and serving and taming the ground. The woman, while she assists the man in his calling, finds her chief calling in being the one who addresses Adam's aloneness, forming communion, establishing the promise of a future, glorifying what Adam starts, and filling what he has formed with life and love."[8]

While conservative Christians often focus on the roles of men and women in the church and the home, there has been discussion from the beginning over how to apply these beliefs to all life. Many believe that men and women have different and distinct "spheres of responsibility" because God created them differently and gave them distinct duties. They believe that men should be the preferred leaders in all aspects of life. The belief is that in *all* relationships between men and women, men are called

5. Jordan, "Liturgical Man, Liturgical Women."

6. Jordan, "Liturgical Man, Liturgical Women."

7. See Alastair Roberts, "Male and Female," *Alastair's Adversaria* (blog), November 27, 2005, https://alastairadversaria.com/2005/11/27/male-and-female/.

8. Alastair Roberts, "A Biblical Gender Essentialism?" *Alastair's Adversaria* (blog), September 1, 2014, https://alastairadversaria.com/2014/09/01/a-biblical-gender -essentialism/.

to exercise leadership. On the flip side, women weren't created to be in authority over men—not in the home, not in the church, and not in the public sphere of government and business.[9]

As the Greeks, Romans, and Victorians did, many believe that men are meant to inhabit and work in the public sphere. Women are meant to focus their energy on the domestic sphere as keepers of the hearth. Because most of society falls into the public sphere, society is properly a man's world. "He charged the man to lead in taking dominion of all things, a call that entailed steady work, creativity, stewardship, entrepreneurship, an aesthetic impulse, and so much more. He gave the woman the truly unbelievable chance to bear a living child in her body and then to nurture the child once born."[10]

MEN INITIATE AND FORM

In conservative Christian thinking, men were created to be protectors as well as leaders. It is contrary to a woman's nature to go to war. Men are called to protect women, not the other way around.[11] Beyond protecting their families and going to war to defend their country, men are also expected to protect women in society and in the workforce. A man should feel a masculine instinct to guard and defend a woman,[12] even if that woman is his boss: "Not only should you honor your boss like a mother, but you should also guard her like a sister. . . . Be supportive and look for ways that you can protect her from enemies, threats, or danger."[13]

9. See Douglas Wilson, "The Creation Order and Sarah," Blog & Mablog, September 10, 2008, http://dougwils.com/books/the-creation-order-and-sarah.html.

10. Owen Strachan and Gavin Peacock, *The Grand Design: Male and Female He Made Them* (Fearn, UK: Christian Focus Publications, 2016), p. 115, NOOK.

11. See Dale Johnson, "Marriage: A Portrait of the Gospel from the Beginning," *The Journal for Biblical Manhood & Womanhood* 21, no. 1 (Spring 2016), http://cbmw.org /topics/marriage-public-square/jbmw-21-1-marriage-a-portrait-of-the-gospel-from -the-beginning/.

12. See John Piper, "A Vision of Biblical Complementarity: Manhood and Womanhood Defined According to the Bible," in *Recovering Biblical Manhood and Womanhood*, ed. John Piper and Wayne Grudem (repr., Wheaton, IL: Crossway Books, 2006), 43–44.

13. Joey Cochran, "When Working for a Woman . . ." The Council on Biblical

Just as men are leaders and protectors, they are called to be providers, in some way, in all their relationships with women.[14]

You may wonder what happens if a woman is the primary provider for her family. In some scenarios, conservative Christians agree that this would be acceptable. For example, if a man is injured or is somehow unable to work, then his wife may have to work as the primary "bread-winner." If a man is going to grad school or seminary and his wife is supporting the family during that time, that is also acceptable, as long as the man doesn't get too dependent on his wife's work. If so, his manhood may be compromised.[15]

But stay-at-home dads? Under no circumstances should a husband decide to send his wife out to work full-time while he stays home. Even if she has the greater earning potential, a man who's a stay-at-home dad is "not fulfilling his manly mandate."[16]

WOMEN COMPLETE AND FILL

The primary way that women help men is through bearing children and taking care of the home. These are the woman's parallels to the man's responsibilities as the provider and protector. Women, through their work as helpers, mothers, and keepers of the home, can sustain their husbands, children, and marriages. They can even do their part in saving society.

As the Victorians did, proponents of complementarianism believe that women are responsible for maintaining refinement in society. "Worthy men adjust their behavior when a woman enters the room. They become better creatures. . . . Husbands and fathers become better, safer, more responsible and productive citizens, unrivaled by their peers in any

Manhood and Womanhood, February 12, 2015, http://cbmw.org/topics/men/when-working-for-a-woman/.

14. See Mary A. Kassian and Nancy Leigh DeMoss, *True Woman 101: Divine Design* (Chicago: Moody Publishers, 2012), pp. 48–49, NOOK.

15. See Piper, "A Vision of Biblical Complementarity," in Piper and Grudem, *Recovering Biblical Manhood and Womanhood*, 42.

16. Strachan and Peacock, *The Grand Design*, 44.

other relational status. . . . Woman is the most powerful living force on the globe. She creates, shapes, and sustains human civilization."[17]

Bearing children and raising them is *the* joy of a woman. It's her part in the creation mandate of filling the earth. Children are a blessing from the Lord, and families that are blessed by God will have many children.[18] As Douglas Wilson explains, "The fruitfulness of childbearing and child-rearing is frequently very hard work. How could it *not* be? Nevertheless, it is God's doing (Gen. 3:16), and it is the wife's duty to submit to the will of God and gladly bear children for her husband."[19]

Women aren't forbidden to work outside the home. In fact, they are often encouraged to work with their husbands or fathers in family businesses.[20] Home-based businesses are also acceptable. So is real estate—although some disagree on that interpretation of Proverbs 31:16.[21] As long as the work supports her father's or husband's calling and vision and doesn't interfere with her domestic duties, a woman is free to work.[22]

While women weren't created to be providers, circumstances in life might require them to either work as the primary breadwinner or supplement the family income. Working to care for the family's needs is honorable. After all, the Proverbs 31 woman did that. But some believe that working for some kind of self-fulfillment or personal gain isn't honorable for women. It's selfish and unbiblical.[23] Unlike men, women weren't created to pursue their own ambitions or glory.[24]

---

17. Glenn T. Stanton, "Why Man and Woman Are Not Equal," First Things, August 26, 2016, https://www.firstthings.com/blogs/firstthoughts/2016/08/why-man-and -woman-are-not-equal.

18. See Voddie Baucham Jr., *What He Must Be: . . . If He Wants to Marry My Daughter* (Wheaton, IL: Crossway, 2009), p. 125, Kindle.

19. Douglas Wilson, *Reforming Marriage* (Moscow, ID: Canon Press, 1995), 48–49, emphasis in original.

20. See Anna Sofia Botkin and Elizabeth Botkin, *So Much More: The Remarkable Influence of Visionary Daughters on the Kingdom of God* (San Antonio: Vision Forum, 2005), 153.

21. See Lori Alexander, "She Plants a Vineyard—Proverbs 31:16," *The Transformed Wife* (blog), September 8, 2017, https://thetransformedwife.com/she-plants-a-vineyard/.

22. See Baucham, *What He Must Be*, 134.

23. See Dorothy Patterson, "The High Calling of Wife and Mother in Biblical Perspective," chap. 22 in Piper and Grudem, *Recovering Biblical Manhood and Womanhood*.

24. See Botkin and Botkin, *So Much More*, 118.

Some believe that working outside the home in an independent career might make a woman less feminine. She might usurp her husband's masculine role as provider. She might work for other men and help them in their careers instead of helping her own husband. Working with other men might also create opportunities for infidelity and undermine marriage: "The grand idea dictates that a man should be able to work with a woman and treat her like any of the other 'guys' at work. If he and another guy could go out for lunch, why not have the same standard for a female co-worker? The answer . . . is that under the clothes, their bodies are *different*, and hers looks like it would be a lot more fun than some male co-worker's body. In other words, one situation is sexually charged and the other one isn't."[25]

Some jobs are believed to require women to behave in ways that stretch their femininity too far. For example, careers that encourage aggression or require great physical strength wouldn't be right.[26] Other jobs, especially those that result in direct oversight of men, aren't deemed appropriately feminine. John Piper believes that a woman's influence on men is probably acceptable as long as it's not personal and that personal influence may be appropriate as long as it's not also direct. According to this model, it's acceptable for a woman to be a city planner, because she's leading men but only indirectly. But a woman police officer or drill sergeant would have to lead men face to face, and that wouldn't be appropriate.

In Piper's view, following these guidelines keeps women from leading men in ways that "offend a man's God-given sense of responsibility and leadership and thus controvert God's created order. . . . The God-given sense of responsibility and leadership in man will not generally allow him to flourish long under personal directives of a female leader. Conversely, if a woman's relation to a man is very personal, then the way she exercises leadership will need to be nondirective."[27]

---

25. See Douglas Wilson, *Fidelity: What It Means to Be a One-Woman Man* (Moscow, ID: Canon Press, 2011), chap. 4, loc. 701–7 of 1956, Kindle (emphasis in original).

26. See John Piper, *What's the Difference? Manhood and Womanhood Defined According to the Bible* (Wheaton, IL: Crossway Books, 1990), 63–64.

27. John Piper, "How Should a Woman Lead?" Desiring God, May 18, 1984, https://www.desiringgod.org/articles/how-should-a-woman-lead.

In this view, women should be educated with all of this in mind. College education isn't necessarily bad, but college debt and career-oriented thinking may hinder women from performing their God-given vocation.[28]

THE DAMAGE TO SOCIETY

Just as it has in marriage and the church, a hyper focus on authority and submission has damaging consequences in society. Women and men are placed on a procrustean bed—expected to conform to arbitrary and unyielding definitions of masculinity and femininity. For example, a man who is gentle and sensitive is told that he isn't fulfilling the masculine role of strong, assertive leadership. A woman who's direct and decisive is told that she isn't feminine. She should instead be deferential and quiet.

In our conservative culture, men who enjoy art, music, clothing, or literature are often called effeminate. Women who like sports, politics, history, and working outside are considered masculine. Such women and men are told that they must be homosexual or, at the very least, unbiblical and somehow lacking because they don't fit extrabiblical definitions of gender. Consider the damage that this does to a person. Maybe you've experienced this yourself. I know I have.

When everything is about authority and submission, women end up being treated as children or objects, and being demeaned and devalued either way. For example, Wilson instructs husbands to give their wives work to do, to make sure they do it well, and to correct them if they don't.[29] This is how we treat small children who don't have enough wisdom and experience to make wise choices. But it's not how we should treat grown women who were created to labor together with men. Many define women by their relationship to men and by how useful they are to men instead of defining them as necessary allies and coheirs. This reduces women to objects—a wife is "a man's vessel" for "sexual possession."[30]

28. See Strachan and Peacock, *The Grand Design*, 62.
29. See Wilson, *Reforming Marriage*, 80.
30. Wilson, 117.

But women made in the image of God have inherent worth regardless of their relationships with others.

As we have seen, in this system of beliefs, the further you move away from the home, the less necessary women become. You can't have marriage, family, or children without women. But how necessary are women in the church, in this system? Not very. And in society? When you believe that women were created to inhabit the domestic sphere, there's not much need for them or their gifts in the public sphere.

ABUSE: THE ELEPHANT IN THE ROOM

With the rise of the #MeToo and #ChurchToo movements, society as a whole is paying increasing attention to abuse[31] and how it is addressed by leaders of institutions and churches. This intensifying focus is appropriate as we consider how much teaching by conservative Christians is to blame in this area. We need to ask whether these beliefs about men and women create an environment for abuse to flourish. Are abusers finding protection and cover for their abusive behavior? Are victims being helped or harmed?

A Dangerous Environment

The hyper focus on authority and submission can create an environment that is emotionally, spiritually, and physically abusive for women and children—especially when a man's authority over his wife and children is almost absolute. In this system, men are the authority that's been put into place by God over families. To reject or resist that authority, even when it's used abusively, is to put oneself at risk of spiritual and physical harm.[32] As a result, women are told to submit to their husbands' authority

---

31. Because of the confusion over what abuse is and isn't, it is helpful to have a summary definition of it. Abuse is "oppression [that] occurs when one [person] seeks to control and dominate the other through a pattern of coercive, controlling, and punishing behaviors." Darby A. Strickland, *Domestic Abuse: Recognize, Respond, Rescue* (Phillipsburg, NJ: P&R Publishing, 2018), 3.

32. See "What Is an 'Umbrella of Protection'?" Institute in Basic Life Principles, accessed June 19, 2018, http://iblp.org/questions/what-umbrella-protection.

even if their husbands are cruel, harsh, or abusive. They are taught to accept however their husbands treat them without complaint. When husbands are abusive and cruel, women are encouraged to suffer in silence as Jesus did, and so to glorify God.[33]

Sometimes flawed teachings on women and men are in themselves spiritually abusive. Teaching that men represent Christ to their families leads to the belief that men are mediators for women and children. This denies women and children direct access to God and contradicts the priesthood of all believers. It's also spiritually abusive to teach that women are more easily deceived than men and are prone to usurping male authority. This view undermines the important role that women have as co-laborers with men, and it creates a climate of suspicion and distrust. Because believing women are indwelt by the Holy Spirit, just as believing men are, they can be trusted counselors for men even in spiritual and theological matters.

Physical and sexual abuse can also flow out of this system. Teaching that sexual intimacy between a husband and a wife is an expression of authority and submission can lead to sexual abuse of women. If a wife has no rights over her own body and no power to deny her husband, then a husband has the authority to compel his wife. This is a system ripe for abuse, and it's contrary to what Paul tells married couples about their duties to each other. Husbands *and* wives have mutual authority over each other (see 1 Cor. 7:4).

A good husband would never abuse his wife and demand what she is unwilling to give freely. But not all men are good. The system provides little protection for women whose husbands would demand or force intimacy.

In addition, these teachings create a system that tolerates abuse by calling on women to endure abuse or "difficult" marriages as a holy burden, by teaching that marriage is primarily about holiness and procreation, and by insisting that divorce isn't a biblical option even in the

---

33. See Debi Pearl, *Created to Be His Help Meet: Discover How God Can Make Your Marriage Glorious* (Pleasantville, TN: No Greater Joy Ministries, 2010), pp. 263–64, Kindle.

case of abuse. If a man is abusing his wife emotionally or verbally but not physically, the advice from many conservative Christians is for the wife to endure the abuse. Some men are more aggressive or prone to anger than others. In those cases, women are advised to examine their own behavior to see how they may be provoking their husbands' anger.[34] If the abuse continues despite women being appropriately submissive, women can address their husbands in a humble and submissive way.[35] A gentle appeal is encouraged, but it has to be done in a way that upholds the husband's authority.[36]

Reactions to Abuse

Most conservative Christians allow for some type of separation and protection for women who are in physically abusive marriages. But these women are often told that they can't divorce.[37] Even in the case of sexual abuse, wives are encouraged to forgive their husbands and to remember that a man still has authority over his family, even when he abuses that authority.[38]

An undercurrent of this advice, which is expressed as a desire for wives to handle things "in-house," dissuades them from going to the civil authorities. If a man is physically abusive and his abuse is at the level of criminal behavior, then a wife may be allowed to talk to her church or the civil authorities about it. Likewise, if a man is sexually abusing his children, then a wife may be advised to seek help from the church and from the civil authorities.

Even physical abuse isn't always considered to be a reason for separation. John Piper advises women who are being verbally abused to "endure . . . for a season" and if "smacked" to endure maybe one night before

34. See Pearl, 79.

35. See Helen Andelin, *Fascinating Womanhood*, updated ed. (New York: Bantam Books, 2013), p. 402, Kindle.

36. See Nancy Wilson, *The Fruit of Her Hands: Respect and the Christian Woman* (Moscow, ID: Canon Press, 2011), chap. 3, loc. 471–74 and 480–81 of 1215, Kindle.

37. See Denny Burk, *What Is the Meaning of Sex?* (Wheaton, IL: Crossway, 2013), 135.

38. See "How Can I Help My Husband Take Spiritual Leadership?" Institute in Basic Life Principles, accessed June 19, 2018, http://iblp.org/questions/how-can-i-help-my -husband-take-spiritual-leadership.

getting the church's help.[39] And there's even less support for or protection against emotional, verbal, and spiritual abuse. "Tough" marriages are just part of life. "I think that word [*abuse*] is greatly misused in our society. . . . Maybe you're in a tough marriage . . . where for 29 years you're experiencing verbal abuse. Maybe your husband is coming and going. There are tough issues. Many times in our society that's viewed as abuse."[40] Wives are encouraged to seek reconciliation with their husbands through the assistance of the church, while living separately from them if the situation is dangerous.[41]

Women in difficult marriages are encouraged to persevere—to see their present sufferings in light of the eternal reward for godly wives. "In the judgment to come she will receive her reward for her submission. And in that final, glorious exaltation, she will reflect Jesus Christ who was exalted for his humble submission."[42]

Despite the numerous examples of women who have shared how these teachings have been used to facilitate domestic abuse,[43] many conservative Christians strongly disagree that these teachings are responsible for creating an environment that tolerates and facilitates abuse. "Have I witnessed some men use the argument of wifely submission to justify abuse?" writes Mary Kassian. "Yes I have. It's deplorable. But I've witnessed them use the cover of egalitarianism too. Abusive men use whatever cover they can to justify their violent sinful behavior."[44]

She's right. Abusive men *will* use whatever they want to justify their

---

39. "John Piper: Does a women submit to abuse?" September 1, 2009, video, 3:57, https://www.youtube.com/watch?v=3OkUPc2NLrM.

40. Holly Elliff, in "Physical Abuse," Revive Our Hearts Radio, July 14, 2006, https://www.reviveourhearts.com/radio/revive-our-hearts/physical-abuse/.

41. See Burk, *What Is the Meaning of Sex?* 135.

42. P. J. Tibayan, "Seeing Jesus on the Stage of Marriage," in John Piper, Francis Chan, et al., *Happily Ever After: Finding Grace in the Messes of Marriage; 30 Devotions for Couples* (Minneapolis: Desiring God, 2017), 8.

43. See, for example, Ruth A. Tucker, *Black and White Bible, Black and Blue Wife: My Story of Finding Hope after Domestic Abuse* (Grand Rapids: Zondervan, 2016).

44. Mary Kassian, "Black and White Bible, Black and Blue Wife," Girls Gone Wise, accessed June 19, 2018, https://girlsgonewise.com/black-and-white-bible-black-and-blue-wife/.

behavior. Abusive men are abusive regardless of their religious or cultural backgrounds. However, beliefs about the natural authority of men and the natural submission of women create and maintain a system that provides cover for a particular kind of abusive man. Ignoring this poisonous fruit isn't helpful. Something rotten is growing, and the practical outworkings of these beliefs about the nature of men and women need to be addressed.

The Damage We Cause

The world is watching how the church treats women, how it responds to abuse, and how it protects the vulnerable—or fails them. When women are belittled, when men in authority dismiss abuse charges and circle the wagons, when churches and institutions fail to protect the weak and vulnerable, the world sees this and judges. And it's not only the individuals and particular churches that are judged. The gospel, Christianity, the universal church, and Christ Himself are judged by our response to abuse. As Paul warned, the gospel is in danger of being reviled because of our actions.

As we move on, we'll consider what the Bible teaches about women and men in society. We'll see how the biblical themes of unity, interdependence, and service help us to move beyond authority and submission and move toward co-laboring together in society.

DISCUSSION QUESTIONS

1. How has the concept of the separate spheres been applied to society?
2. What similarities do you notice between prevalent conservative teachings and the Greek, Roman, and Victorian beliefs about women and men in society?
3. What are considered the dangers of women working in the workforce?
4. How does the hyper focus on authority and submission damage men and women in society?
5. How has abuse been (mis)handled in the church? Why does that matter?

17

"THE DAUGHTERS OF ZELOPHEHAD ARE RIGHT"

THE BIBLE ON WOMEN AND MEN IN SOCIETY

Women did almost every type of work that was done by men, with a few
important exceptions: men did not work as midwives or wet nurses (or
nurses, for that matter), and women were not soldiers or politicians. Women
took care of the family farm, laboring in the fields or watching the herds.
Women bought, sold, rented, and owned property. They ran businesses,
employed staff, and owned slaves. They were artists, artisans, and vendors.

LYNN COHICK[1]

People in many cultures have told tales of perfect or idealized societies
that either existed in the past or still exist hidden away somewhere, such as
Atlantis or Camelot. Why do we have such a fascination with these places?
Inside each of us is a recognition that our world isn't what it should be.

Cults, dictators, and political and religious leaders offer various solu-
tions to this. Most haven't ended well. The more we try to achieve utopia,

---

1. Lynn H. Cohick, *Women in the World of the Earliest Christians: Illuminating Ancient*
Ways of Life (Grand Rapids: Baker Academic, 2009), 240.

the further we seem to get from it. No, our only hope is found in God's promises for the future. God has promised us reconciliation and restoration through Jesus's sacrifice, which paid for our sins. A glorious future awaits all believers—a day when "God Himself will be among them, and He will wipe away every tear from their eyes; and there will . . . no longer be any mourning, or crying, or pain" (Rev. 21:3–4). Because Jesus defeated death and hell, this future is secure.

In this present world, sin has broken our relationships and damaged our societies. Creation bears the scars of the fall and our sin. God tells us that we should expect life to be difficult, but He also promises to be with us through it all (see Matt. 28:20; John 16:33). We can't bring about utopia here on earth, but we can have peace because God is with us.

Should we throw up our hands and say, "Oh well! Nothing we can do about the awful things in the world"? No—we have been given a ministry of reconciliation (see 2 Cor. 5:18). We have a calling to spread the gospel. Though we can't change people, God can. The Spirit works in us to unite us to Christ. He also works in us to make us more and more like Christ. Through the gospel and the Spirit, people are changed. While we will never be perfect this side of heaven, we should see our lives and the lives of others being transformed by the gospel.

We can't expect utopia, but we should expect men and women to learn to work together in society. In fact, we need to all work together. The question is how.

APPLYING BIBLICAL GUIDELINES TO SOCIETY

Before we can answer that question, we also need to ask the question of what we mean by *society*. For our purposes, society is the world outside the home and the church. There are, of course, areas where home, church, and society overlap. Each aspect of our lives influences and affects the others, but there are profound differences between these facets of life. What's necessary in one might be inappropriate in another. For instance, marriage requires a certain intimacy that is wrong in any other circumstance. And church leadership has requirements that don't apply to all types of leadership.

When it comes to applying the Bible to society, we can fall into one of two extremes. One extreme, which we often hear from our secular society, says that the Bible isn't relevant today. The other extreme wants to apply the Bible's boundaries for marriage and the church to all aspects of life. This means that some people believe women should never teach men or have authority over them in any setting. Women who are civil or societal leaders are said to be rebellious—or possibly even a punishment from God.

A slightly softer version of this view sees a significant overlap in the roles of women and men in marriage, church, and society. Those who teach this version don't focus so much on biblical rules for men and women in society. Instead they believe that the nature of men and women determines what behavior is appropriate for them. Since they believe that authority and submission are inherent masculine and feminine traits, respectively, they believe that the work or activities men and women do should fit those differences in their natures.

Neither of these two extremes represents what the Bible teaches about men and women in society. Contrary to what the first extreme claims, the Bible does give us guidance on how to live. The Bible is "the only rule of faith and obedience"[2] and is relevant to any society. Believers should be good employees—honest and hardworking (see Col. 3:22–25). We should be good citizens—responsible and peaceful (see Rom. 13:1–7; 1 Peter 2:13–17). We should love our neighbors and do good to others. As Romans 12:18 says, "If possible, so far as it depends on you, be at peace with all men."

Despite what the second extreme says, the Bible has far fewer gender-specific instructions for society than it does for marriage and the church. After Adam's sin separated the domains of home, church, and society, the household order that applies to the home and the church doesn't have the same application for society. The Bible doesn't restrict women from serving in leadership positions in society, and neither should we. Leadership isn't uniquely masculine, and submission isn't uniquely feminine.

Women and men were created to fill the earth, subdue it, and rule over it together. God has equipped women and men to work in various ways. We all have gifts and abilities that are useful for different jobs and

2. Westminster Larger Catechism, answer 3.

careers. If we're going to be faithful to Scripture, we need to move beyond authority and submission and incorporate the biblical themes of unity, interdependence, and service into our understanding of how women and men co-labor in society.

WORK IS A SHARED CALLING

Conservative Christians often lament the attacks from our society on traditional family values and morality. The definitions of marriage, men, and women are constantly being stretched and changed, as we have seen. There's a strong push for the church to abandon our beliefs about marriage and ordination. It's tempting for us to give in and go along with the changes that our society wants to make. We might be more popular if we did, but it wouldn't be right.

It's important that we take a stand for what the Bible teaches. But as we affirm its truths about men, women, marriage, and the church, we need to be careful not to go beyond Scripture. In our discussions about how women and men should work together in society, we need to separate what the Bible teaches from "the way things have always been." As we have seen, not everything that's traditional is biblical.

We also need to be careful not to let our appropriate discussions on authority and submission in the home and church become the lens through which we see all male-and-female interactions. As we have seen with marriage and the church, we need to move beyond an exclusive focus on authority and submission as being the pattern for how women and men should work together.

The unity of women and men is clear from the calling to work that we all share. The creation mandate to be fruitful, to fill the earth and subdue it, and to rule was given to Adam and Eve (see Gen. 1:28). We were created to work together in families and communities. And all the work that we do, inside and outside the home, should be done to glorify God, who is ultimately the Master we all serve (see Eph. 6:9; Col. 3:23–24).

In the Scriptures, we see examples of women working alongside men. The Proverbs 31 woman is described as being active in business. She makes food and clothing (see vv. 13–15, 19, 22, 24). She sells her goods in the marketplace (see v. 24). She makes business decisions. She "considers a field and buys it; from her earnings she plants a vineyard" (v. 16). Few women could do everything that the Proverbs 31 woman does, but the passage gives us a picture of a woman who works—and not only in her home.

Don't miss the other women who are mentioned in Proverbs 31. Verse 15 says that the woman "gives food to her household and portions to her maidens." These maidens are female servants working for the woman. They are also active in business. Servants, male and female, were a significant portion of the economy of that time. It's easy to overlook, but it's important for us to remember that women who work for others are just as much Proverbs 31 women as the "lady of the house" is.

Midwives Shiphrah and Puah are mentioned in Exodus 1 for their courageous protection of the male Hebrew babies. It's not a stretch to say that they were career women working outside their own homes. Several women in the Old Testament worked as shepherds and cared for their families' flocks and herds. Rachel and Zipporah both took animals to public watering places to get water for them.

Part of business is dealing with inheritance and property rights. Daughters in Israel had the right to inherit. When the Israelites came into Canaan, the land was divided up among the tribes and families. Zelophehad's daughters went to Moses and asked if they could have their father's portion. He had died before the land was divided. God answered their request this way:

> The daughters of Zelophehad are right in their statements. You shall surely give them a hereditary possession among their father's brothers, and you shall transfer the inheritance of their father to them. Further, you shall speak to the sons of Israel, saying, "If a man dies and has no son, then you shall transfer his inheritance to his daughter. If he has no daughter, then you shall give his inheritance to his brothers." (Num. 27:7–9)

The Israelites who returned to Jerusalem after the exile rebuilt the temple and the city walls. One man's daughters worked alongside him (see Neh. 3:12). These women helped to construct Jerusalem's walls— not an easy task.

The New Testament gives us examples of businesswomen. Lydia, a key woman in the early church, sold purple fabric and had her own household (see Acts 16:14–15, 40). Priscilla was a tentmaker, along with her husband, Aquila (see Acts 18:2–3). Phoebe, who Paul commends in Romans 16:1, seems to have been in Rome on some business.[3]

Although some believe that men shouldn't work directly for a woman, the Bible gives examples of women who had men and women working for them. Abigail had male servants who followed her commands (see 1 Sam. 25:19). The Shunammite woman also had servants whom she directed (see 2 Kings 4). Having male and female servants was common in biblical times. These servants were part of the household and were expected to obey the wife, as well as the husband, of the house.

The same was true in the New Testament. Lydia would certainly have had men and women who worked for her. Women, as well as men, were slave owners in the time of the early church. Paul's instructions to masters applied to both men and women who owned slaves. As Cynthia Long Westfall explains, "A wife was expected to run the household for her husband, which involved the management of any household slaves. Women who had their own households owned the slaves in the household. Paul included women slave owners in his instructions to masters (Eph. 6:9; Col. 4:1)."[4]

These examples from Scripture show us women working in the home, working from home, working in family businesses, working with their husbands, working for themselves, and working for others. We see women buying and selling goods and property in the marketplace. We see them inheriting property. We see them working in a variety of industries, from domestic help to construction. Women in the Bible displayed a wide range of interests and abilities as they worked in society along with men.

3. "It appears probable that she was a woman carrying on some business or traffic, and that she went to Rome partly at least on this account." John Calvin, *Commentaries on the Epistle of Paul to the Romans*, trans. John Owen, in *Acts 14–28 & Romans 1–16*, Calvin's Commentaries 19 (repr., Grand Rapids: Baker, 1979), 543.

4. Cynthia Long Westfall, *Paul and Gender: Reclaiming the Apostle's Vision for Men and Women in Christ* (Grand Rapids: Baker Academic, 2016), 264.

THE IMPORTANCE OF EDUCATION FOR EVERYONE

As it is in marriage and the church, the interdependence of men and women is visible in society. We need each other. We need the gifts that each person has been given. We have strengths and weaknesses that make us dependent on one another. Women as well as men should be educated and trained to use their gifts. As we will soon see, men as well as women should be inclined toward the home and thoughtful of how their work and careers affect their families.

In order for us to best use our different gifts, we need education and training. Formal education isn't mentioned often in the Bible, but learning and teaching are. God told the Israelites to teach their children about all He had done for them. He also told parents to teach their children all His commandments, "talking of them when you are sitting in your house, and when you are walking by the way, and when you lie down, and when you rise" (Deut. 11:19 ESV).

In the New Testament, Jesus encourages believers to learn from Him (see Matt. 11:29). In the Great Commission, He tells His disciples to go and make other disciples, baptizing them and teaching them (see Matt. 28:19–20). Paul also encourages women in the early church to learn (see 1 Tim. 2:11). In Titus 2, he tells older women to teach "what is good" and to encourage younger women (see vv. 3–5). Women and men of all ages are to learn and to teach others.

Our culture tends to have a limited view of education. We see it as a means to an end: a lucrative career. While this may be a worthy goal, everything that we do should ultimately be "to glorify God and enjoy Him forever." Our education allows us to study God's Word so we can know Him and how to serve Him better. When we study science, math, history, art, music, and literature, we explore the world that God has created and what God has done. Author Hannah Anderson suggests that education "is less about what you *do* with your knowledge than it is about the person you become in the process . . . less about how to make a living and more about how to live."[5]

5. Hannah Anderson, *Made for More: An Invitation to Live in God's Image* (Chicago: Moody Publishers, 2014), 104, emphasis in original.

There are many ways for us to be well-educated and to learn. Education is valuable for everyone, because we are made in God's image and are worthy of the investment. The Protestant Reformers believed that all men and women should be educated so that they could understand Scripture and the world around them. Protestants were key in establishing schools and universities and in encouraging parents to teach their children. Mark Noll writes that "Protestants were encouraged to labor as scientists so that their scientific work could rise to the praise of God. By so doing, the early Protestants expressed their belief that God had made the natural world to be explored and that the results of such exploration showed forth his glory."[6] And it wasn't just theology or science that Protestants thought students should learn. The arts, both music and visual, flourished during the time of the Reformation.[7]

Wisdom is also a significant theme in Scripture. Proverbs is full of passages on wisdom. Its opening passage explains that Proverbs is a book of instruction for a son. His father and mother want him to "know wisdom and instruction" (Prov. 1:2).

The Proverbs teach us about the origin of wisdom—"The fear of the Lord is the beginning of wisdom" (Prov. 9:10); "the Lord gives wisdom" (Prov. 2:6). They also stress the importance of gaining wisdom and understanding (see Prov. 4:7). Wisdom protects us from evil and wickedness (see Prov. 4:11–15).

Proverbs ends with a description of an impressive woman. She is described as having wisdom and "the teaching of kindness" (Prov. 31:26). And in order for a woman to learn wisdom, she must be taught.

SERVING EACH OTHER

Our Western society believes that we need to look out for ourselves and not depend on anyone. The only way for us to get ahead is by being willing to do whatever it takes, regardless of the cost to others. We need to

6. Mark A. Noll, *The Scandal of the Evangelical Mind* (Grand Rapids: William B. Eerdmans Publishing, 1994), 39.
7. See Noll, 38–39.

push ourselves to gain power, recognition, prosperity, wealth, influence, and awards.

But that's the opposite of what the Bible teaches. Instead of seeking to promote ourselves, we are called to a life of service. This service takes many forms in our lives. We serve in our families as we work to care for the needs of our children, spouses, and extended family members. We serve in our churches as we work to spread the gospel, disciple other believers, and worship the Lord. In our society, we serve our neighbors as we work to protect others, to meet the needs of those around us, and to live peaceful, quiet, godly lives (see 1 Tim. 2:2).

In all aspects of our lives, we should seek ways that we can serve others using the gifts that God has given us. We should use our strengths to serve others. We are called to put others first and not to be selfish or arrogant; for example, men who are strong or powerful may use their strength and power to dominate or harm others—particularly women. Anyone who has authority or power should use his or her strength to serve the needs of others. We desperately need people in our society who are willing to protect the vulnerable and weak. Similarly, women who are more adept at maintaining relationships and picking up on the emotional cues of others may be tempted to use their gifts for personal advantage. Instead, those who are so gifted should provide wisdom, insight, and help to guide others.

However we have been gifted, our society needs us to use our gifts. We need both women and men in government, education, medicine, business, and all aspects of society, because of our different strengths and weaknesses. Together we can do the work God has called us to do. We aren't all the same or interchangeable, but we are all essential.

INCLINED TOWARD THE HOME

When it comes to what the Bible says about women and men in society, another of the prevalent conservative teachings needs to be addressed. Did God create women to be focused on the home while men were created to be focused on the outside world?

Mary Kassian writes, "The Bible teaches that God created woman with a uniquely feminine 'bent' for the home. 'Working at home' is on its top ten list of important things that older women need to teach the younger ones (Titus 2:5). It encourages young women to 'manage their households' (1 Timothy 5:14). It praises her who 'looks well to the ways of her household' . . . (Proverbs 31:27). The Bible casts women whose hearts are inclined away from the home in a negative light (Proverbs 7:11)."[8]

The verses that Kassian uses here are often referred to in discussions about women working outside the home. The first two verses are from Paul's advice for women in the church. In Titus 2:5, Paul says that older women should teach younger women "to be sensible, pure, workers at home, kind, being subject to their own husbands, so that the word of God will not be dishonored." In 1 Timothy 5:14, he says, "I want younger widows to get married, bear children, keep house, and give the enemy no occasion for reproach."

First Timothy 5 gives us the context for these passages. Paul was concerned about how the women were behaving: "They also learn to be idle, as they go around from house to house; and not merely idle, but also gossips and busybodies, talking about things not proper to mention" (v. 13). He encourages women to be busy taking care of their families and homes instead of being idle, gossips, and busybodies. Women have work to do, and they shouldn't be neglecting it in order to make trouble.[9]

As with Paul's concerns over appropriate behavior in church, his point here is that believers should behave in ways that glorify God and don't dishonor the gospel or the church. Paul warns believers, both men and women, to do their work honestly and not to be lazy gossips who meddle in other people's business.

> For even when we were with you, we used to give you this order: if anyone is not willing to work, then he is not to eat, either. For we hear that some among you are leading an undisciplined life, doing no work at all, but acting like busybodies. Now such persons we command and

8. Mary A. Kassian, *Girls Gone Wise in a World Gone Wild* (Chicago: Moody Publishers, 2010), 76.

9. See Titus 2:5 in John Gill, *Exposition of the Entire Bible*, available online from Bible Hub, accessed June 18, 2018, http://biblehub.com/commentaries/gill/titus/2.htm.

exhort in the Lord Jesus Christ to work in quiet fashion and eat their own bread. (2 Thess. 3:10–12)

His point isn't *where* women should be but that everyone has work that they should be busy doing, including caring for the needs of their households.[10] This concern for the affairs or state of the home isn't just for women, either. Consider what the Bible says in its requirements for elders and deacons. First Timothy 3:4 says that an elder must "[manage] his own household well." The same is said for deacons—they must be "good managers of their children and their own households" (1 Tim. 3:12). Likewise, while Proverbs 7:11 says of the adulterous woman, "She is boisterous and rebellious, her feet do not remain at home," the book of Proverbs similarly warns about the dangers of adultery and faithlessness in a verse about men: "Like a bird that wanders from her nest, so is a man who wanders from his home" (Prov. 27:8).

Given the differences between the roles of husbands and wives, and because of the nature of childbearing, managing a household may have different emphases for men and women. But the Scriptures indicate that both women *and* men should be "inclined toward the home." That inclination or concern for the well-being of the home will lead husbands and wives, mothers and fathers to work inside and outside the home in order to meet the needs of their families.

THE IMPORTANCE OF WISDOM

The Bible provides us with guidelines and boundaries for men and women in the home, church, and society. It also gives us examples of the liberty that we have within those boundaries and guidelines. We should examine our beliefs about women and men closely and hold them up to the light of Scripture. Where our beliefs don't conform with the Bible or go beyond it, we should be willing to reform them.

There may be differences of opinion about how to apply the

10. See William D. Mounce, *Pastoral Epistles*, Word Biblical Commentary 46 (Nashville: Thomas Nelson, 2000), 411.

knowledge that the Bible gives us with wisdom. We have liberty as Christians to decide for ourselves and our families how to answer questions about women and men working in society. But, as Christians, we need to be thoughtful and careful about how we address these kinds of questions. The world is watching what we do.

While the relationships between women and men in the home and the church are equally important, the truth is that our unchurched, nonbelieving friends and neighbors aren't going to have much contact with us in those settings. What they're going to see is how we treat each other in society. They are going to see how we live out our faith in the way we interact as women and men in the world outside our homes and churches.

We know that the secular world is going to be offended and even going to hate us because of our faith, our beliefs about marriage and sexuality, and our beliefs about women and men in the church. We shouldn't be afraid to offend when we're standing for the truth, but we should be careful not to give unnecessary offense. We should be ready to give gentle answers with firm conviction about the gospel, about our hope, and about how God calls us to live.

DISCUSSION QUESTIONS

1. How is work a shared calling for women and men?
2. Why are education and wisdom important for everyone?
3. How can we use our gifts and strengths to serve others in our societies?
4. Did God create women to be focused on the home while men were created to be focused on the outside world? Why or why not?
5. What have you learned from this book, and how will you apply it in your life?

CONCLUSION

Prove all things by the Word of God:—all ministers, all teaching, all
preaching, all doctrines, all sermons, all writings, all opinions, all
practices,—prove all by the Word of God. . . . That which can abide
the fire of the Bible, receive, hold, believe, and obey. That which cannot
abide the fire of the Bible, reject, refuse, repudiate, and cast away.

J. C. RYLE[1]

We all inherit something from our families. Maybe you got your sense of
humor from your mom. Maybe your eyes look just like your grandfather's.
Or maybe your grandmother left you her china or her favorite necklace.
Some of what we inherit is great. Some of it, not so much. Few people are
grateful for going prematurely bald or gray. If you've inherited your great-
aunt's velvet Elvis collection, you might not be thrilled.

As believers and as Protestants, we have an inheritance that we can be
thankful for. We sometimes take for granted that when we go to church
on Sundays, we will understand what is being said. We sing hymns in
our own language. We pray in our own language. The pastor preaches in
our own language. We read the Bible in our own language. But it wasn't
always that way.

---

1. J. C. Ryle, *Wheat or Chaff?* (New York, 1857), 133–34.

Imagine going to church and not understanding a single word that was said or sung. Imagine not knowing what was going on in the service. Imagine being a spectator and not a participant. That was the reality for most people by the end of the Middle Ages. The priests performed the mass, the priests sang the hymns, the priests read the Bible, the priests took communion. And all in a language that you couldn't understand. You just had to trust the priests to tell you what you needed to do.

In 1517, when the German monk Martin Luther nailed his 95 Theses to the church door in Wittenberg, his small act helped to start the Reformation. Luther wasn't trying to start a new church. He wanted to reform the church and to return to what the Bible actually teaches. Eventually, however, Luther, John Calvin, Huldrych Zwingli, John Knox, and others formed what would become the Protestant denominations. The reforms that they wanted can be summarized by the five *solas* of the Reformation: *Sola Scriptura* (by Scripture alone), *Sola Fide* (by faith alone), *Sola Gratia* (by grace alone), *Solo Christo* (through Christ alone), and *Soli Deo Gloria* (to God alone be the glory).[2]

Sola Scriptura, in particular, was central for the Reformers and continues to be for us today. By Scripture alone, we know who God is, how we are saved, what we must believe, and how we should live and work and honor God. As believers, we need to read the Bible for ourselves and know what it teaches. While our pastors and elders play an important role in teaching us and preserving sound doctrine, we are responsible for testing what we're taught against the Scriptures.

The Scriptures have been handed down to us over many generations. That's a great inheritance—but we need to consider what's being taught in our churches, as our Protestant ancestors did. We must always be willing to be reformed according to the Word and to return to the Bible in order to make sure that we're staying on the path and not wandering off.

---

2. For a good overview of the history and importance of the five *solas*, see Terry L. Johnson, *The Case for Traditional Protestantism: The Solas of the Reformation* (Carlisle, PA: Banner of Truth, 2004).

BEYOND AUTHORITY AND SUBMISSION

We've inherited a mixture of good and bad beliefs—particularly about women and men. As we consider our cultural inheritance, we need to be willing to get rid of the parts of it that aren't consistent with Scripture. Much of what we believe about women and men is actually inherited from our Greco-Roman and Victorian ancestors. We have ended up with layers of unbiblical and extrabiblical beliefs that obscure and cover up the beauty of what the Bible actually teaches about men and women. Some of these beliefs may have the appearance of wisdom, but at the root they lack the ability to help us to grow in grace, faith, and godliness. Instead they have permeated, weakened, and confused our teachings about women and men.

Specifically, the hyper focus on authority and submission has done considerable damage to relationships between men and women in the home, in the church, and in our societies. Instead of promoting unity, interdependence, and service, this fixation on authority and submission as the crucial distinction between men and women promotes antagonism and disunity.

Authority and submission are important aspects of our relationships, but they shouldn't be the lens through which we view all of life. There is so much more to who we are and how we should relate to each other. By moving beyond an exclusive focus on authority and submission, we can incorporate the biblical themes of unity, interdependence, and service into our teachings on how women and men should live and work together as co-laborers in marriage, church, and society.

What a difference these themes have on our relationships with each other. We were created as women and men to be co-laborers together. If we focus on being co-laborers in marriage, we will build each other up and demonstrate love by serving each other. In the church, a focus on being co-laborers will strengthen us as we encourage and exhort each other and support the leadership of the church as we grow in grace and faith. And our societies will be blessed by an emphasis on laboring together.

Can you imagine the beauty of women and men defending, protecting, caring for, and serving each other as we use the gifts God has given us? Together we can proclaim the hope of the gospel to a world that is full of dying people. If not, we're as useless as salt that has lost its flavor (see Mark 9:50).

WHERE DO WE GO FROM HERE?

So where do we go from here? Following Scripture is always the best answer, but it's not always the easiest. It would be nice to have straightforward lists saying "Do" and "Don't Do." It would be neat and clean. Then we could set up hedges around the rules that we don't want to break. No mess, no struggle, no wrestling with the truth, no danger of getting close to doing the wrong thing.

Hedges and lists would seem easier, but they aren't good for us. As my dad likes to say, "The path of least resistance leads to crooked rivers and crooked men." Doing what's easy isn't always helpful. Instead, it's better for us to struggle and wrestle with what God teaches us in the Bible. Hard-won victories mean more to us. When we study the Scriptures for ourselves, we seek to "examine everything carefully" so that we can "hold fast to that which is good" (1 Thess. 5:21).

God has given us clear boundaries in Scripture when it comes to women and men and particular aspects of marriage, the church, and society. He's also left us with liberty within those boundaries. When we try to make lists and build hedges, we end up with extrabiblical and unbiblical rules to follow.

What we can do is evaluate our beliefs and attitudes about women and men and test everything against Scripture. My goal in this book has been to give you a new or greater awareness of the layers of unbiblical and extrabiblical beliefs that need to be peeled back. You should have the tools now to "renovate the house," as you recognize the origins of what's being taught.

And then you can ask yourself some diagnostic questions. What layers do you need to peel back from your own beliefs about women and men? Consider your relationships in the home, in the church, and in your society. Do your relationships with others tend toward co-laboring or toward antagonism? What changes can you make in your own life to improve how you co-labor with others—especially those of the other sex?

Every generation has to contend for the faith. It doesn't take much for us to get off course. We should seek to be faithful to what the Bible teaches in all things, especially as it applies to women and men and how we can be co-laborers together in marriage, the church, and society. The world needs what only the Bible can offer—the truth about God and humanity and the way of salvation. My hope is that individuals, marriages, churches, and societies will be strengthened and that God will be glorified in all our relationships.

SELECT BIBLIOGRAPHY

Allen, Jason. "5 Key Ways to Cultivating Biblical Manhood in Your Church." The Council on Biblical Manhood and Womanhood. April 21, 2016. https://cbmw.org/topics/leadership-2/5-key-ways-to -cultivating-biblical-manhood-in-your-church/.

Alsup, Wendy. *Is the Bible Good for Women? Seeking Clarity and Confidence Through a Jesus-Centered Understanding of Scripture.* Colorado Springs: Multnomah, 2017.

———. "The Third Way on Gender." Practical Theology for Women. September 22, 2014. https://theologyforwomen.org/2014/09/the -third-way-on-gender.html.

Andelin, Helen. *Fascinating Womanhood.* Updated ed. New York: Bantam Books, 2013. Kindle.

Anderson, Hannah. *Made for More: An Invitation to Live in God's Image.* Chicago: Moody Publishers, 2014.

Andrea. "A Church for Men." *Spirits Reclaimed* (blog). August 14, 2012. https://spiritsreclaimed.wordpress.com/2012/08/14/a-church -for-men/.

Anthony, Susan B. "Social Purity." Lecture given at the Mercantile Library, St. Louis, March 14, 1875. In *The Selected Papers of Elizabeth Cady Stanton & Susan B. Anthony.* Vol. 3, *National Protection for National Citizens: 1873 to 1880,* edited by Ann D. Gordon, 155–74. New Brunswick, NJ: Rutgers University Press, 2003.

Aristotle. *Politics*. Translated by Benjamin Jowett. Reprint, Los Angeles: IndoEuropean Publishing, 2009.

Astell, Mary. "A Serious Proposal to the Ladies." In *First Feminists: British Women Writers; 1578–1799*, edited by Moira Ferguson, 181–89. Bloomington, IN: Indiana University Press, 1985.

Baucham, Voddie, Jr. *Family Shepherds: Calling and Equipping Men to Lead Their Homes.* Wheaton, IL: Crossway, 2011. Kindle.

———. *What He Must Be: . . . If He Wants to Marry My Daughter.* Wheaton, IL: Crossway, 2009. Kindle.

Beale, G. K. *The Temple and the Church's Mission: A Biblical Theology of the Dwelling Place of God.* Downers Grove, IL: IVP Academic, 2004.

Beeke, Joel R. *Friends and Lovers: Cultivating Companionship and Intimacy in Marriage.* Hudson, OH: Cruciform Press, 2012. Kindle.

Blackwell, Elizabeth. *Pioneer Work in Opening the Medical Profession to Women: Autobiographical Sketches.* London, 1895.

Block, Daniel I. *Judges, Ruth.* The New American Commentary 6. Nashville: Broadman & Holman, 1999.

Bordow, Todd. *What Did Jesus Really Say about Divorce? An Alternative Interpretation of Matthew 5:31&32 and Its Implications for Counseling Troubled Marriages in the Church.* Saarbrücken, Germany: Blessed Hope Publishing, 2014.

Botkin, Anna Sofia, and Elizabeth Botkin. *So Much More: The Remarkable Influence of Visionary Daughters on the Kingdom of God.* San Antonio: Vision Forum, 2005.

Browder, Sue Ellen. *Subverted: How I Helped the Sexual Revolution Hijack the Women's Movement.* San Francisco: Ignatius Press, 2015. Kindle.

Burk, Denny. *What Is the Meaning of Sex?* Wheaton, IL: Crossway Books, 2013.

Byrd, Aimee. *No Little Women: Equipping All Women in the Household of God.* Phillipsburg, NJ: P&R Publishing, 2016.

Calvin, John. *Commentaries on the Epistle of Paul to the Romans.* Translated by John Owen. In *Acts 14–28 & Romans 1–16.* Calvin's Commentaries 19. Reprint, Grand Rapids: Baker, 1979.

———. *Commentaries on the First Epistle to Timothy.* Translated by William Pringle. In *Commentaries on the Epistles to Timothy, Titus, and Philemon.* Calvin's Commentaries 21. Reprint, Grand Rapids: Baker, 1979.

———. *Commentary on a Harmony of the Evangelists, Matthew, Mark, and Luke,* vol. 3. In *Harmony of Matthew, Mark, Luke, John 1–11.* Translated by William Pringle. Calvin's Commentaries 17. Reprint, Grand Rapids: Baker, 2003.

———. *Commentary on the Epistle to the Philippians.* Translated by William Pringle. In *Galatians–Philemon.* Calvin's Commentaries 21. Reprint, Grand Rapids: Baker, 1979.

———. *Genesis.* Translated by John King. Calvin's Commentaries 1. Reprint, Grand Rapids: Baker, 1979.

Cochran, Joey. "When Working for a Woman . . ." The Council on Biblical Manhood and Womanhood. February 12, 2015. http://cbmw.org /topics/men/when-working-for-a-woman/.

Cohick, Lynn H. *Women in the World of the Earliest Christians: Illuminating Ancient Ways of Life.* Grand Rapids: Baker Academic, 2009.

The Council on Biblical Manhood and Womanhood. "Mission & Vision." https://cbmw.org/about/mission-vision/.

———. "The Danvers Statement." June 26, 2007. https://cbmw.org /uncategorized/the-danvers-statement/.

Crouch, Andy. *Strong and Weak: Embracing a Life of Love, Risk, and True Flourishing.* Downers Grove, IL: InterVarsity Press, 2016.

Darwin, Charles. *The Descent of Man and Selection in Relation to Sex.* Vol. 2. New York, 1871.

DeMoss, Nancy Leigh. *Lies Women Believe and the Truth that Sets Them Free.* 2001. Reprint, Chicago: Moody Publishers, 2007.

Elliff, Holly. In "Physical Abuse." Revive Our Hearts Radio. July 14, 2006. https://www.reviveourhearts.com/radio/revive-our-hearts /physical-abuse/.

Elliot, Elisabeth. "The Essence of Femininity: A Personal Perspective." In Piper and Grudem, *Recovering Biblical Manhood and Womanhood,* 394–99.

Elmy, Elizabeth Wolstenholme. *Women and the Law.* Congleton, UK, 1896.

Foh, Susan T. "What is the Woman's Desire?" *The Westminster Theological Journal* 37 (1974): 376–83.

Freedman, Estelle B. *No Turning Back: The History of Feminism and the Future of Women.* New York: Ballantine Books, 2002.

Friedan, Betty. *The Feminine Mystique.* New York: W.W. Norton, 1963.

Galen. *Galen on the Usefulness of the Parts of the Body.* Vol. 2. Translated by Margaret Tallmadge May. Ithaca, NY: Cornell University Press, 1968.

Garland, David E. *1 Corinthians.* Baker Exegetical Commentary on the New Testament. Grand Rapids: Baker Academic, 2003.

Gibson, Greg. "Thinking Different about Teenagers and Dating." The Council on Biblical Manhood and Womanhood. February 19, 2015. https://cbmw.org/topics/courtship-dating/thinking-different-about-teenagers-and-dating/.

Gill, John. *John Gill's Exposition of the Bible.* Available online from Bible Study Tools. https://www.biblestudytools.com/commentaries/gills-exposition-of-the-bible/.

Grubbs, Judith Evans. *Women and the Law in the Roman Empire: A Sourcebook on Marriage, Divorce and Widowhood.* New York: Routledge, 2002.

Grudem, Wayne. *Evangelical Feminism & Biblical Truth: An Analysis of More Than 100 Disputed Questions.* Colorado Springs: Multnomah Publishers, 2004.

———. In "Marriage and the Trinity." Revive Our Hearts Radio. May 19, 2005. https://www.reviveourhearts.com/radio/revive-our-hearts/marriage-and-the-trinity/.

Gunter, J. D. "Men as Providers." The Council on Biblical Manhood and Womanhood. November 11, 2013. https://cbmw.org/topics/leadership-2/men-as-providers/.

Hammons, Timothy J. "Protecting the Weaker Vessel." *Theology That Matters* (blog). October 30, 2016. https://web.archive.org/web/20170427123603/https://timothyjhammons.com/2016/10/30/protecting-the-weaker-vessel/.

Hardwick, Julie. "Did Gender Have a Renaissance? Exclusions and Traditions in Early Modern Western Europe." In *A Companion to Gender History,* edited by Teresa A. Meade and Merry E. Wiesner-Hanks, 343–57. Malden, MA: Blackwell Publishing, 2004.

Heimbach, Daniel R. "The Unchangeable Difference: Eternally Fixed Sexual Identity for an Age of Plastic Sexuality." In *Biblical Foundations for Manhood and Womanhood*, edited by Wayne Grudem, 275–89. Wheaton, IL: Crossway Books, 2002.

Henry, Matthew. *Matthew Henry Commentary on the Whole Bible (Complete)*. Available online from Bible Study Tools. https://www.biblestudytools.com/commentaries/matthew-henry-complete/.

Hesiod. *Hesiod: Theogony, Works and Days, Testimonia*. Edited and translated by Glenn W. Most. Cambridge: Harvard University Press, 2006.

Hipponax. Fragment 68. Translated by Martin Litchfield West. Quoted in Lefkowitz and Fant, *Women's Life in Greece & Rome*, 16.

Hoffmann, Isabelle. "The Glory of Hair." Recovering Grace. January 9, 2012. http://www.recoveringgrace.org/2012/01/the-glory-of-hair/.

Horton, Michael. "Muscular Christianity." *Modern Reformation* 21, no. 3 (2012): 46–47.

Hughes, Kathryn. "Gender Roles in the 19th Century." The British Library. May 15, 2014. http://www.bl.uk/romantics-and-victorians/articles/gender-roles-in-the-19th-century.

Institute in Basic Life Principles. "What Is an 'Umbrella of Protection'?" http://iblp.org/questions/what-umbrella-protection.

James, John Angell. *The Family Monitor, or A Help to Domestic Happiness*. Birmingham, 1828.

Jensen, Emily. "Wives, Honor Your Husband's Preferences." The Council on Biblical Manhood and Womanhood. November 13, 2015. http://cbmw.org/topics/marriage-public-square/wives-honor-your-husbands-preferences/.

Jobes, Karen H. *1 Peter*. Baker Exegetical Commentary on the New Testament. Grand Rapids: Baker Academic, 2005.

Johnson, Dale. "Marriage: A Portrait of the Gospel from the Beginning." *The Journal for Biblical Manhood & Womanhood* 21, no. 1 (Spring 2016): 26–31. http://cbmw.org/topics/marriage-public-square/jbmw-21-1-marriage-a-portrait-of-the-gospel-from-the-beginning/.

Johnson, Gregg. "The Biblical Basis for Gender-Specific Behavior." In Piper and Grudem, *Recovering Biblical Manhood and Womanhood*, 280–93.

Jones, JP. "God Is Looking for Men to Change the World." Truth That Changes Lives. OnePlace. https://www.oneplace.com/ministries /truth-that-changes-lives/read/articles/god-is-looking-for-men-to -change-the-world-16047.html.

Jordan, James B. "Liturgical Man, Liturgical Women: Part 2." Biblical Horizons. June 2004. https://web.archive.org/web/2006020919 2735/http://www.biblicalhorizons.com:80/rr/rr087.htm.

Kassian, Mary A., and Nancy Leigh DeMoss. *True Woman 101: Divine Design; An Eight-Week Study on Biblical Womanhood.* Chicago: Moody Publishers, 2012. NOOK.

———. *True Woman 201: Interior Design; Ten Elements of Biblical Womanhood.* Chicago: Moody Publishers, 2015.

Kassian, Mary A. *Girls Gone Wise in a World Gone Wild.* Chicago: Moody Publishers, 2010.

Kassian, Mary. "Black and White Bible, Black and Blue Wife." Girls Gone Wise. https://girlsgonewise.com/black-and-white-bible-black-and -blue-wife/.

———. "Steel Magnolia." *True Woman* (blog). Revive Our Hearts, April 13, 2009. https://www.reviveourhearts.com/true-woman/blog /steel-magnolia/.

Kistemaker, Simon J. *Exposition of the First Epistle to the Corinthians.* New Testament Commentary. Grand Rapids: Baker Academic, 1993.

Knight, George W., III. "The Family and the Church: How Should Biblical Manhood and Womanhood Work Out in Practice?" In Piper and Grudem, *Recovering Biblical Manhood and Womanhood*, 345–57.

Lavender, Catherine J. "Notes on The Cult of Domesticity and True Womanhood." The College of Staten Island. https://csivc.csi.cuny .edu/history/files/lavender/386/truewoman.pdf.

Le Bon, Gustave. "Anatomical and Mathematical Researches into the Laws of the Variations of Brain Volume and their Relation to Intelligence." 1879.

Lee-Barnewall, Michelle. *Neither Complementarian nor Egalitarian: A Kingdom Corrective to the Evangelical Gender Debate.* Grand Rapids: Baker Academic, 2016. NOOK.

Lefkowitz, Mary R., and Maureen B. Fant, eds. *Women's Life in Greece and Rome: A Source Book in Translation*. Baltimore: The Johns Hopkins University Press, 1982.

Lindley, Susan Hill. *"You Have Stept Out of Your Place": A History of Women and Religion in America*. Louisville: Westminster John Knox Press, 1996.

Livy. *Rome and the Mediterranean*. Translated by Henry Bettenson. New York: Penguin, 1976.

Marsh, Jan. "Gender Ideology & Separate Spheres in the 19th Century." Victoria and Albert Museum. http://www.vam.ac.uk/content/articles/g/gender-ideology-and-separate-spheres-19th-century/.

McKinley, John. "Necessary Allies: God as *Ezer*, Woman as *Ezer*." Lecture given at the Hilton Atlanta, November 17, 2015. Mp3 download, 38:35. http://www.wordmp3.com/details.aspx?id=20759.

Mill, Harriet Taylor. "The Enfranchisement of Women." In *The Essential Feminist Reader*, edited by Estelle B. Freedman, 67–72. New York: Modern Library, 2007.

Mill, John Stuart. *The Subjection of Women*. London, 1869.

Moore, Jared. "The Complementarians Win: A Review of *One God in Three Persons*." *All Truth Is God's Truth* (blog). May 18, 2015. http://jaredmoore.exaltchrist.com/christian-truth/the-complementarians-win-a-review-of-one-god-in-three-persons/.

Mounce, William D. *Pastoral Epistles*. Word Biblical Commentary 46. Nashville: Thomas Nelson, 2000.

Noll, Mark A. *The Scandal of the Evangelical Mind*. Grand Rapids: William B. Eerdmans Publishing, 1994.

O'Brien, Brandon. "A Jesus for Real Men." *Christianity Today*. April 18, 2008. http://www.christianitytoday.com/ct/2008/april/27.48.html.

Ortlund, Raymond C., Jr. "Male-Female Equality and Male Headship: Genesis 1–3." In Piper and Grudem, *Recovering Biblical Manhood and Womanhood*, 95–112.

Patmore, Coventry. *The Angel in the House*. London, 1854.

Patterson, Dorothy. "The High Calling of Wife and Mother in Biblical Perspective." In Piper and Grudem, *Recovering Biblical Manhood and Womanhood*, 364–77.

Pearl, Debi. *Created to Be His Help Meet: Discover How God Can Make Your Marriage Glorious*. Pleasantville, TN: No Greater Joy Ministries, 2010. Kindle.

Phintys. Treatise. In *The Pythagorean Texts of the Hellenistic Period*, edited by Holger Thesleff, 151–54. Turku, Finland: *Åbo* Akademi, 1965. Quoted in Lefkowitz and Fant, *Women's Life in Greece & Rome*, 104–5.

Pipa, Joseph. "Leading in Worship." Greenville Presbyterian Theological Seminary. April 28, 2017. http://josephpipa.com/leading-in-worship/.

Piper, John, and Wayne Grudem. "Charity, Clarity, and Hope: The Controversy and the Cause of Christ." In Piper and Grudem, *Recovering Biblical Manhood and Womanhood*, 403–22.

Piper, John, and Wayne Grudem, eds. *Recovering Biblical Manhood and Womanhood: A Response to Evangelical Feminism*. Reprint, Wheaton, IL: Crossway Books, 2006.

Piper, John. "A Vision of Biblical Complementarity: Manhood and Womanhood Defined According to the Bible." In Piper and Grudem, *Recovering Biblical Manhood and Womanhood*, 31–59.

———. "Does the Bible Allow for Divorce in the Case of Adultery?" Desiring God. January 9, 2009. https://www.desiringgod.org/interviews/does-the-bible-allow-for-divorce-in-the-case-of-adultery.

———. "Do You Use Bible Commentaries Written by Women?" Desiring God. March 27, 2013. http://www.desiringgod.org/interviews/do-you-use-bible-commentaries-written-by-women.

———. "How Should a Woman Lead?" Desiring God. May 18, 1984. https://www.desiringgod.org/articles/how-should-a-woman-lead.

———. "John Piper: Does a women submit to abuse?" September 1, 2009. Video, 3:57. https://www.youtube.com/watch?v=3OkUPc2NLrM.

———. "Just Forgive and Forbear?" In John Piper, Francis Chan, et al. *Happily Ever After: Finding Grace in the Messes of Marriage; 30 Devotions for Couples*, 93–95. Minneapolis: Desiring God, 2017.

———. "Lionhearted and Lamblike: What Does It Mean to Lead? Part 2." Desiring God. March 25, 2007. https://www.desiringgod.org

/messages/lionhearted-and-lamblike-the-christian-husband-as
-head-part-2.

———. "To a Spouse Considering Divorce." Desiring God. July 31, 2014.
http://www.desiringgod.org/interviews/to-a-spouse-considering
-divorce.

———. *What Jesus Demands from the World*. Wheaton, IL: Crossway
Books, 2006.

Plato. *Republic*. Book 5, section 455d. Translated by B. Jowett. Quoted in
Lefkowitz and Fant, *Women's Life in Greece & Rome*, 66–67.

Plutarch. "Antony." In *Plutarch's Lives*, translated by Bernadotte Perrin.
Vol. 9, *Demetrius and Antony, Pyrrhus and Caius Marius*, 137–333.
London: William Heinemann, 1920.

———. *Moralia*. Vol. 2. Translated by Harold Cherniss. Cambridge:
Harvard University Press, 1957.

Ponder, Doug. "The Heart of Femininity." Re | Source. http://www
.remnantresource.org/the-heart-of-femininity/.

Pratt, Richard L, Jr. *I & II Corinthians*. Holman New Testament Commentary, edited by Max Anders. Nashville: Holman Reference, 2000.

Pyle, Nate. *Man Enough: How Jesus Redefines Manhood*. Grand Rapids:
Zondervan, 2015.

"Report of the Ad Interim Committee on Divorce and Remarriage." Paper
presented to the Twentieth General Assembly of the Presbyterian
Church in America, Roanoke, VA, June 1992. http://pcahistory
.org/pca/2-203.pdf.

"Report of the Ad Interim Committee on Women Serving in the Ministry
of the Church." Paper presented to the Forty-Fifth General
Assembly of the Presbyterian Church in America, Greensboro, NC,
June 2017. http://www.pcaac.org/wp-content/uploads/2017/06
/Women-Serving-in-Min.-of-Ch.-Study-Committee-Report-with
-admended-recommendations.pdf.

Roberts, Alastair. "A Biblical Gender Essentialism?" *Alastair's Adversaria* (blog). September 1, 2014. https://alastairadversaria.com
/2014/09/01/a-biblical-gender-essentialism/.

———. "Male and Female." *Alastair's Adversaria* (blog). November 27,
2005. https://alastairadversaria.com/2005/11/27/male-and-female/.

Rotundo, E. Anthony. *American Manhood: Transformations in Masculinity from the Revolution to the Modern Era.* New York: HarperCollins Publishers, Inc, 1993.

Ruskin, John. "Of Queen's Gardens." In *Sesame and Lilies: Two Lectures Delivered at Manchester in 1864,* 119–96. London, 1865.

Sayers, Dorothy. *Are Women Human?* Grand Rapids: Eerdmans, 1971.

Schreiner, Thomas R. "The Valuable Ministries of Women in the Context of Male Leadership: A Survey of Old and New Testament Examples and Teaching." In Piper and Grudem, *Recovering Biblical Manhood and Womanhood,* 209–24.

Schrock, David. "Gender Specific Blessings: Bolstering a Biblical Theology of Gender Roles." *The Journal for Biblical Manhood and Womanhood* 21, no. 1 (Spring 2016): 15–18. Available online at http://cbmw.org/topics/complementarianism/jbmw-21-1-gender-specific-blessings-bolstering-a-biblical-theology-of-gender-roles/.

Segal, Marshall. "Dads, Date Your Daughter's Boyfriend." Desiring God. June 12, 2014. http://www.desiringgod.org/articles/dads-date-your-daughter-s-boyfriend.

Semonides of Amorgos. *On Women.* Translated by H. Lloyd-Jones. Quoted in Lefkowitz and Fant, *Women's Life in Greece & Rome,* 14–16.

Shanley, Mary Lyndon. *Feminism, Marriage, and the Law in Victorian England, 1850–1895.* Princeton: Princeton University Press, 1989.

"Slaughter of the Innocents." *Woodhull & Claflin's Weekly,* June 20, 1874.

Sophocles. *Tereus.* Translated by Helene P. Foley. In Elaine Fantham, Helene Peet Foley, Natalie Boymel Kampen, Sarah B. Pomeroy, and H. Alan Shapiro. *Women in the Classical World: Image and Text,* 70. Oxford: Oxford University Press, 1994.

Sowerwine, Charles, with Patricia Grimshaw. "Equality and Difference in the Twentieth-Century West: North America, Western Europe, Australia, and New Zealand." In *A Companion to Gender History,* edited by Teresa A. Meade and Merry E. Wiesner-Hanks, 586–610. Malden, MA: Blackwell Publishing, 2004.

Sproul, R.C., Jr. *Bound for Glory: A Practical Handbook for Raising a Victorious Family.* Dallas, GA: Tolle Lege Press, 2008. Kindle.

Stanton, Elizabeth Cady. "Declaration of Sentiments." In *The Selected Papers of Elizabeth Cady Stanton & Susan B. Anthony*. Vol. 1, *In the School of Anti-Slavery: 1840 to 1866*, edited by Ann D. Gordon, 78–82. New Brunswick, NJ: Rutgers University Press, 1997.

———. "The Solitude of Self." In *The Selected Papers of Elizabeth Cady Stanton & Susan B. Anthony*. Vol. 5, *Their Place Inside the Body-Politic: 1887 to 1895*, edited by Ann D. Gordon, 423–36. New Brunswick, NJ: Rutgers University Press, 2009.

Stanton, Glenn T. "Why Man and Woman Are Not Equal." First Things. August 26, 2016. https://www.firstthings.com/blogs/first thoughts/2016/08/why-man-and-woman-are-not-equal.

Stark, Rodney. "Reconstructing the Rise of Christianity: The Role of Women." *Sociology of Religion* 56, no. 3 (Autumn 1995): 229–44.

Strachan, Owen, and Gavin Peacock. *The Grand Design: Male and Female He Made Them*. Fearn, UK: Christian Focus Publications, 2016. NOOK.

Tallman, Brian. "Bringing Marriage Back to Earth." Ligonier Ministries. December 1, 2012. https://www.ligonier.org/learn/articles/bringing -marriage-back-to-earth/.

Tertullian. "To His Wife." Translated by S. Thelwall. In *Ante-Nicene Fathers*. Vol. 4, *Tertullian, Part Fourth; Minucius Felix; Commodian; Origen, Part First and Second*, edited by A. Cleveland Coxe, Alexander Roberts, and James Donaldson, 39–49. Buffalo, NY, 1885.

Thompson, Craig. "Reaching Men from the Pulpit." *Facts & Trends*. LifeWay Christian Resources. July 7, 2014. https://factsandtrends .net/2014/07/07/reaching-men-from-the-pulpit/.

Tibayan, P. J. "Seeing Jesus on the Stage of Marriage." In John Piper, Francis Chan, et al. *Happily Ever After: Finding Grace in the Messes of Marriage; 30 Devotions for Couples*, 5–8. Minneapolis: Desiring God, 2017.

Towner, Philip H. *1–2 Timothy & Titus*. The IVP New Testament Commentary Series. Downers Grove, IL: InterVarsity Press, 1994.

Tracy, Steven R. "What Does 'Submit in Everything' Really Mean? The Nature and Scope of Marital Submission." *Trinity Journal* 29 (2008): 285–312.

Traniello, Vanessa. "Hysteria and the Wandering Womb." Marquette University History Department. http://academic.mu.edu/meissnerd /hysteria.html.

Trueman, Carl. "1 Timothy 2:11–15." Sermon delivered at Cornerstone Presbyterian Church, Ambler, PA, November 11, 2011. Available online at https://web.archive.org/web/20180306015216/http:// cornerstoneopc.com/audio.php.

Valerius Maximus. *Memorable Deeds and Sayings: One Thousand Tales from Ancient Rome.* Translated by Henry John Walker. Indianapolis: Hackett Publishing Company, 2004.

VanDoodewaard, Rebecca. "In Praise of Clerks." The Christian Pundit. October 24, 2012. https://web.archive.org/web/20150204062814 /http://thechristianpundit.org/2012/10/24/in-praise-of-clerks/.

Vision Forum Ministries. "The Tenets of Biblical Patriarchy." https:// homeschoolersanonymous.files.wordpress.com/2014/04/the -tenets-of-biblical-patriarchy-vision-forum-ministries.pdf.

Walton, Mark David. "Relationships and Roles in the New Creation." *Journal for Biblical Manhood and Womanhood* 11, no. 1 (Spring 2006): 4–19. Available online at http://cbmw.org/wp-content /uploads/2013/05/11-1.pdf.

Ware, Bruce A. *Big Truths for Young Hearts: Teaching and Learning the Greatness of God.* Wheaton, IL: Crossway Books, 2009.

———. *Father, Son, and Holy Spirit: Relationships, Roles, and Relevance.* Wheaton, IL: Crossway Books, 2005.

Weber, Stu. *Tender Warrior: Every Man's Purpose, Every Woman's Dream, Every Child's Hope.* Reprint, Colorado Springs: Multnomah, 2009.

Welter, Barbara. "The Cult of True Womanhood: 1820–1860." *Atlantic Monthly* 18, no. 2 (Summer 1966): 151–74.

Welton, Gary. "My Human Identity Transcends Gender." The Aquila Report. July 30, 2017. https://www.theaquilareport.com/human -identity-transcends-gender/.

Westfall, Cynthia Long. *Paul and Gender: Reclaiming the Apostle's Vision for Men and Women in Christ.* Grand Rapids: Baker Academic, 2016.

Wilson, Douglas. "Courtship and Rape Culture." Blog & Mablog. February 4, 2016. https://dougwils.com/books-and-culture/s7 -engaging-the-culture/110222.html.

———. *Fidelity: What It Means to Be a One-Woman Man.* Moscow, ID: Canon Press, 2011. Kindle.

———. *Her Hand in Marriage: Biblical Courtship in the Modern World.* Moscow, ID: Canon Press, 2010. Kindle.

———. *Mother Kirk: Essays and Forays in Practical Ecclesiology.* Moscow: Canon Press, 2001.

———. *Reforming Marriage.* Moscow, ID: Canon Press, 1995.

———. "The Creation Order and Sarah." Blog & Mablog. September 10, 2008. http://dougwils.com/books/the-creation-order-and-sarah .html.

Wilson, Nancy. *The Fruit of Her Hands: Respect and the Christian Woman.* Moscow, ID: Canon Press, 2011. Kindle.

Wolfson, Evelyn. *Roman Mythology.* Berkeley Heights, NJ: Enslow Publishers, Inc, 2002.

Wolgemuth, Nancy DeMoss. *Adorned: Living Out the Beauty of the Gospel Together.* Chicago: Moody Publishers, 2017.

Wollstonecraft, Mary. *A Vindication of the Rights of Women: with Strictures on Political and Moral Subjects.* 3rd ed. London, 1796.

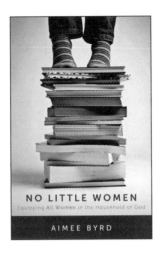

NO LITTLE WOMEN
Equipping All Women in the Household of God

AIMEE BYRD

Why are so many well-intentioned women falling for poor . . . or even *false* . . . theology? Part of the reason is that, in church ministry, women are often left to fend for themselves.

Writing to concerned women and church officers, Aimee Byrd pinpoints the problem, especially the commodification of women's ministry. She answers the hot-button issues—How can women grow in discernment? How should pastors preach to women? What are men's and women's roles within the church?—and points us in the direction of a multifaceted solution.

After all, cultivating resolved, competent women will equip them to fulfill their calling as Christ's disciples and men's essential allies. If we want to strengthen the church, we must strengthen the women in it!

"Women are our most committed resource for doing the work of the kingdom, and they deserve our best thinking and support. . . . Aimee Byrd writes with wit and wisdom, biblical clarity and theological maturity."
  —**Liam Goligher**, Senior Minister, Tenth Presbyterian Church, Philadelphia

Did you find this book helpful?
Consider writing a review online.
The author appreciates your feedback!

Or write to P&R at editorial@prpbooks.com
with your comments. We'd love to hear from you.